## DATE DUE

| | | | |
|---|---|---|---|
| | | | |
| | | | |
| | | | |
| | | | |
| | | | |
| | | | |
| | | | |
| | | | |
| | | | |
| | | | |
| | | | |
| | | | |
| | | | |
| | | | |
| | | | |
| | | | |
| | | | |
| | | | |

# THE WINDSOR BEAUTIES:

## LADIES OF THE COURT

## OF CHARLES II

by

LEWIS MELVILLE

REVISED EDITION

ADDITIONAL FRENCH TRANSLATION
BY COBY FLETCHER

The Windsor Beauties: Ladies of the Court of Charles II, Revised Edition

Second Printing: November 2005

Library of Congress Cataloging-in-Publication Data

Melville, Lewis, 1874-1932.
  The Windsor beauties : ladies of the court of Charles II / by Lewis Melville ; additional French translation by Coby Fletcher.-- Rev. ed., 1st ed.
     p. cm.
  This revised edition has parallel English translations for previously untranslated French sections of the 1928 edition, which includes poems, letters, and epitaphs of St. Evremond.
  Includes bibliographical references and index.
  ISBN-13: 978-1-932690-13-2 (alk. paper)
  ISBN-10: 1-932690-13-1 (alk. paper)
  ISBN-13: 978-1-932690-14-9 (pbk. : alk. paper)
  ISBN-10: 1-932690-14-X (pbk. : alk. paper)
  1. Great Britain--History--Charles II, 1660-1685--Biography. 2. Great Britain--Court and courtiers--Biography. 3. Women--Great Britain--Biography.
I. Title.
  DA447.A3M447 2005
  941.06'6'0922--dc22

                        2005014818

Distributed by: Baker & Taylor, Ingram Book Group

Published by: Victorian Heritage Press, *an Imprint of*
Loving Healing Press,
5145 Pontiac Trail
Ann Arbor, MI 48105   USA

http://www.LovingHealing.com or info@LovingHealing.com
Fax +1 734 663 6861

# Victorian Heritage Press

TO ELIZABETH LUCAS

## ABOUT THE COVER

Front: Barbara Villiers, by Sir Peter Lely

Sir Peter Lely's portrait of Barbara Villiers (later Lady Castle-maine, then Duchess of Cleveland) who was the mistress of Charles II and mother of the First Duke of Grafton. She is portrayed here as the penitent Magdalen. Many of the famous beauties of the day were painted by Lely. This painting is on permanent exhibition at Euston Hall (http://www.eustonhall.co.uk/)

# OTHER WORKS BY LEWIS BENJAMIN

The Life of William Makepeace Thackeray
The Thackeray Country
Some Aspects of Thackeray
Victorian Novelists
The Life and Letters of Laurence Sterne
The Life and Letters of William Beckford of Fonthill
The Life of John Gay
The Life and Letters of Tobias Smollett
The Life and Letters of William Cobbett
The Windham Papers
The Wellesley Papers
The Berry Papers
The Life of Philip, Duke of Wharton
Lady Mary Wortley Montagu: Her Life and Letters
The First George
"Farmer George"
"The First Gentleman of Europe"
An Injured Queen: Caroline of Brunswick
Beau Brummel: His Life and Letters
The Beaux of the Regency
Nell Gwynn: The Story of Her Life
Some Eccentrics and a Woman
Regency Ladies
Maids of Honor
"The Star of Piccadilly" – "Old Q"
The London Scene
Bath Under Beau Nash
Brighton: Its follies, its Fashions, and its History
Royal Tunbridge Wells

# PREFACE

"The Duchess of York wished to have the portraits of the most beautiful women at Court," Anthony Hamilton wrote in the *Memoirs of Count Grammont*. "Lely painted them, and employed all his art in the execution. He could not have had more alluring sitters. Every portrait is a masterpiece."

The original set of "Beauties" painted by Lely were, as we find from James II's catalogue, eleven in number, their names being Barbara, Duchess of Cleveland (*née* Villiers); Frances, Duchess of Richmond and Lennox (*née* Stuart); Mrs. Jane Myddleton (*née* Needham); Elizabeth, Countess of Northumberland (*née* Wriothesley); Elizabeth, Countess of Falmouth (*née* Bagot); Elizabeth, Lady Denham (*née* Brooke); Frances, Lady Whitmore (*née* Brooke); Henrietta, Countess of Rochester (*née* Boyle); Elizabeth, Countess de Grammont (*née* Hamilton); and Madame d'Orleans. Mr. Ernest Law states that all these can now be identified in William III's State Bedroom at Hampton Court Palace, except Lady Falmouth and Madame d'Orleans, one of whom, probably Madame d'Orleans, appears to be missing, altogether; while Lady Falmouth can most likely be recognized in the picture long called "The Countess of Ossory," and more recently "The Duchess of Somerset."

This group of pictures is known as "The Windsor Beauties", because they were hung in the Queen's bedchamber at Windsor Castle. Early in the last century they were removed to Hampton Court.

It will be seen that in this list of "Beauties" Anne Hyde, Duchess of York, does not figure; but since she was responsible for the collection, it would be peculiarly ungracious to omit her from a volume that treats of it. Also, she deserves inclusion for her supreme courage in selecting the sitters—for what must the ladies who were not chosen have said and thought of her?

Nor in the series are Nell Gwyn, Louise de Kéroualle, and the Duchess Mazarin; but no account of the social life of the Court of Charles II can possibly omit mention of them, and therefore something has been said about each of these ladies, although the present author has written a description of the trio in his biography of "Pretty, witty Nell."

Peter Lely, otherwise Pieter van der Faes, was born in 1618, and showing an aptitude for painting he was at the age of nineteen sent to Haarlem to study under Franz Pieter de Grebber. In 1641 he came to England in the train of William, Prince of Orange, who married Mary, daughter of Charles I. He found favour at Court, and soon had a great reputation as a portrait painter. During the Commonwealth he enjoyed considerable private practice. After the Restoration he was again high in the good books of the King and the rest of the Royal Family. It was in 1662 that he was commissioned to paint "The Windsor Beauties." Pepys visited him at his studio while he was at work on that series of portraits. "Thence gone," he wrote on October 20 of that year, "with Commissioner Pett to Mr. Lely, the great painter, who came forth to us; but believing that I come to bespeak a picture, he prevented us by telling us, that he should not be at leisure these three weeks; which methinks is a rare thing. And then to see in what pomp his table was laid for himself to go to dinner; and here, among other pictures, saw the so much desired by me picture of my Lady Castlemaine, which is a most blessed picture; and that that I must have a copy of."

"If Vandyke's portraits are often tame and spiritless, at least they are natural: his laboured draperies flow with ease, and not fold but is placed with propriety," Horace Walpole wrote in his *Anecdotes of Painting*, "Lely supplied the want of taste with clinquant: his nymphs trail fringes and embroidery through meadows and purling streams. Add, that Vandyke's habits are those of the times; Lely's a sort of fantastic night-gowns, fastened with a single pin. The latter was, in truth, the ladies' painter; and whether the age was improved in beauty or in flattery, Lely's women are certainly much handsomer than those of Vandyke's. They please as much more as they evidently meant to please. He caught the reigning character, and

> "...on the animated canvas stole
> The sleepy eye, that spoke the melting soul."

I do not know whether, even in softness of flesh, he did not excel his predecessor. The beauties at Windsor are the Court of Paphos, and ought to be engraved for the memoirs of its charming biographer, Count Hamilton." Also said Walpole, "Lely's nymphs are far too wanton to be taken for anything but Maids of Honour." But since they were Maids of Honour, or otherwise connected with the Court, it seems a little hard on the painter to blame him for that. This, indeed, is one of the principal merits of this series of portraits, which Anthony Trollope described as "female insipidities."

There is every reason to believe that most of these sitters were insipid. So far as the ladies, or at least the majority of them, were concerned, it was the age of insipidity. What could be expected of girls with a minimum of education, many married at the age of sixteen or seventeen, plunged into the atmosphere of a dissolute Court, and there having nothing whatever to do. They read not, neither did they spin. It was simply an age of gallantry — perhaps debauchery is the better word. "Pierce told me," Pepys wrote in November, 1663, "how loose the Court is, nobody looking after business, but every man his lust and gain." Then Grammont: "Lady Myddleton, Lady Denham, the Queen's and Duchess of York's Maids of Honour, and a hundred others, bestow their favours to the right and to the left, and not the least notice is taken of their conduct."

• • • • •

The primary authorities upon which this volume is based are the diaries of Pepys and Evelyn, Hamilton's *Memoirs of Count Grammont*, Burnet's *History of My Own Time*; the autobiographies of Lord Chancellor Clarendon, St. Evremont, and Sir John Reresby; the correspondence of Andrew Marvell, Rachel Lady Russell, and Philip Stanhope, second Earl of Chesterfield; and the *Reports of the Historical Manuscripts Commission*.

Other works that have been consulted are William Harris's *Life of Charles II*, Mrs. Jameson's *Beauties of the Court of Charles II*, Jesse's *Memoirs of the Court of England during the Reign of the Stuarts*; Steinmann's privately printed Life *of the Duchess of Cleveland*, Allan Fey's *Beauties of the Seventeenth Century*, Sergeant's *My Lady Castlemaine*; Forneron's *Louise de Kérouaille, Duchess of Portsmouth*, Noel Williams' *Rival Sultanas: Nell Gwyn and Louise de Kerouaille*, and Dasent's *Nell Gwynne*; Tyke and Davis's *Annals of Windsor*, Horace Walpole's *Anec-*

dotes of *Painting,* Law's *Royal Gallery of Hampton Court,* and Collin Baker's *Lely and the Stuart Portrait Painters.*

My thanks for assistance in the preparation of this work are due to Mrs. E. Constance Monfrino and Mr. Alfred Sydney Lewis, Librarian of the Constitutional Club.

LEWIS MELVILLE

LONDON,
March 1921

# FOREWORD TO THE REVISED EDITION

It has been my great privilege to oversee the restoration of this classic history book by Lewis Melville. The process of book restoration is a long and tedious albeit superficially simple process. From scanning to proofing, quality must be foremost at each turn. Within the context of preserving textual integrity, several modernizations have been made to make the text more accessible to a 21st century audience. First, a glossary of archaic terms used in the text. If you don't know a *bastinado* from a *sack posset*, I suggest browsing the glossary first. Second, footnotes to add more color to historical figures, clarify the value of money, and explain historical events (e.g. The Test Act). Any mistakes in the footnotes are mine alone. Third, a new improved index has been added and a proper bibliography. The rather glib list of books in the preceding preface may be of use to the most erudite scholar, but of little help for the casual reader of this century. Last, I am indebted to Coby Fletcher for translating many previously inaccessible 17th century French language passages, especially the wit of St. Evremond, into contemporary English rhyme.

I hope you will find this revised edition as enjoyable as it is educational.

Victor R. Volkman

ANN ARBOR, MI
May 2005

# CONTENTS

## LIST OF ILLUSTRATIONS

# THE WINDSOR BEAUTIES:
# LADIES OF THE COURT OF CHARLES II

## CHAPTER I

### ANNE, DUCHESS OF YORK (née HYDE) (1)
### 1637-1671

The place of honour — if such there be — in this chronicle of the social life of the Court during the reign of Charles II, belongs by right to the Duchess of York, and that, not because of her rank but because she it was who commissioned her protégé Lely to paint that series of portraits which became known as "The Windsor Beauties" from the fact that they were originally housed at Windsor.

Anne was the eldest daughter of Edward Hyde, afterwards created Earl of Clarendon, by his second wife, Frances, daughter of Sir Thomas Aylesbury, Bart., one of the Masters of the Court of Bequests and Master of the Mint. She was born on March 14, 1637, at Cranbourne Lodge, in Windsor Park, then in the occupation of her maternal grandfather. Hyde came of an old, if not particularly distinguished Cheshire family. He was called to the bar, where he soon acquired a good practice. His rapid progress may, in the first instance, have been due to the influence of his uncle, Chief Justice Sir Nicholas Hyde; but once started, his abilities were more than sufficient to take him along. He was, perhaps, always more interested in politics than in law, and, at the first promising opportunity, he, in 1640, entered Parliament. His first efforts were directed to the improvement of the judicature, and he spoke vigorously against the many perversions of the law that were then rife. At first he joined the popular party, but differing from it on Church matters he soon transferred himself to the King's party, of which he soon became a leader.

Anne, Duchess of York (*née* Hyde)

During the Civil War[1], Hyde was one of the principal advisers of Charles I, and had his suggestions been taken, on many occasions it would probably have been better for the monarch. However, his Majesty was wilful, and the Queen, Henrietta Maria, who cordially

---

[1] The English Civil War that broke out on August 27, 1642 and continued until approximately 1650 is often simply referred to in Britain as the "civil war", sometimes leading to confusion with the American Civil War. It was not, however, the only civil war ever fought in England. There were two other periods of major civil war after the Norman Conquest: "the Anarchy," which occurred during the 12th century reign of King Stephen, and the Wars of the Roses, which lasted for much of the 15th century. (source: Wikipedia)

disliked Hyde, used such influence as she had against him. However, Charles II, immediately after his escape to Paris in November 1651, summoned him to his side to act as Secretary of State. After the death of Cromwell, he it was who laid down the terms on which the King would return. As Dr. Firth put it, Hyde's aim was, as it had been throughout, to restore the Monarchy, not merely to restore the King; and, in the main, he had his way at the time.

Two years before Edward Hyde went to Paris, his wife had taken Anne and the other children to Antwerp. Presently they removed to a residence at Breda, which had been placed at their disposal by the Princess of Orange, the eldest daughter of Charles I and Henrietta Maria. This royal lady took a fancy to Anne, and, when the girl was seventeen, appointed her one of her Maids of Honour, although this appointment was opposed by Henrietta Maria, and was also against the wish of the girl's father, who knowing something of courts, may well have thought that his daughter was too young to be submitted to the temptations that would surround her.

Anne became a general favourite with all she met at The Hague or at the Princess's country residence at Teyling. She was very pretty, most attractive, and, unquestionably, a coquette. She received attentions from many men with equanimity. Her heart, however, was fluttered by the attentions paid her by Henry Jermyn, afterwards first Baron Dover, who was one year her junior, and from his early youth a notorious libertine. He held a position in the Household of the Duke of York, and accompanied his Royal Highness to Holland in 1657. "Jermyn", Anthony Hamilton wrote of him, "supported by his uncle's wealth, found it no difficult matter to make a considerable figure upon his arrival at the court of the Princess of Orange: the poor courtiers of the King, her brother, could not vie with him in point of equipage and magnificence; and these two articles often produce as much success in love as real merit: there is no necessity for any other example than the present; for though Jermyn was brave, and certainly a gentleman, yet he had neither brilliant actions, nor distinguished rank, to set him off; and as for his figure there was nothing advantageous in it. He was little; his head was large, and his legs short; his features were not disagreeable, but he was affected in his carriage and behaviour. All his wit consisted in expressions learnt by rote, which he occasionally employed either in raillery or in love. This was the whole foundation of the merit of a man so formidable in amours. The Princess Royal was the first who was taken with him: Miss Hyde seems to have been following the steps of her mistress: this immediately brought him into credit, and his reputation was established in England before his arrival. Prepossession in the minds of women is sufficient to find access to their hearts: Jermyn found them in dispositions so favourable for him, that he had nothing to do but to speak."

Anne Hyde, however, recovered from her infatuation when in 1657 she met the Duke of York, who had come to Paris to visit his mother, Queen Henrietta Maria. He saw the girl, and paid his court to her according to the manner of Princes of the Blood of that day — that is to say he offered her his bed, but not his hand. No one can say whether Anne fell in love with the man, or whether she was flattered by having the Duke at her feet; all that is known is that they were much together. Their frequent walks and talks gave rise to much scandal, and it was generally assumed that the young lady yielded to the solicitations of her lover. "When his sister, the Princess Royal[2], came to Paris to see the Queen Mother, the Duke of York fell in love with Mrs. Anne Hyde, one of her maids of honour," so runs a passage in the *Memoirs of the Count de Grammont*. "Besides her person, she had all the qualities proper to inflame a heart less apt to take fire than his; which she managed so well as to bring his passion to such an height, that, between the time he first saw her and the winter before the King's restoration, he resolved to marry none but her; and promised her to do it and though, at first, when the Duke asked the King, his brother, for his leave, he refused, and dissuaded him from it, yet at last he opposed it no more, and the Duke married her privately, owned it some time after, and was ever after a true friend to the Chancellor Clarendon for several years."

---

[2] Princess Royal: the eldest daughter of a British sovereign, who has had the title conferred on her for life by the sovereign. Mary Stuart, daughter of Charles I, was the first woman to ever receive this title. After marriage, she was sometimes known as the Princess of Orange.

However, that she withstood him is more likely, for when he saw her again at Breda, he on November 24 contracted an engagement of marriage with her.

Then in May 1660 came the Restoration[3], and the whole situation was altered. There is all the difference between a King in exile and a King on the throne. At this time Charles was a bachelor and the heir-presumptive was the Duke of York, who had married a commoner. The Cophetua business, however romantic, found no favour in the eyes of Charles; it was distasteful to the Court, especially to the ladies, it was violently disagreeable to Henrietta Maria, who opposed it tooth and nail. Even Edward Hyde, who at the Coronation was created Earl of Clarendon, was alarmed, being far-sighted enough to realise that, by jealousy, powerful enmities would be brought into being. He was in a dilemma, confronted with the claims of his daughter and his duty to his Sovereign.

The Duke of York went to see the Chancellor, and told him "that he knew that he had heard of the business between him and his daughter, and of which he confessed he ought to have spoken to him before; but that when he returned from Dover (where he was going with the King to receive the Princess Royal on her arrival from Holland) he would give him full satisfaction: in the meantime he desired him not to be offended with his daughter." To this the Chancellor made no other answer than, "That it is a matter too great for him to speak of."

Clarendon behaved in a manner which now would be regarded as utterly scandalous. Some of the Duke's friends told him that the Chancellor had a great party in Parliament, and that he was resolved within a few days to complain there, and to produce the witnesses who were present at the marriage, to be examined, that their testimony might remain there, which would be a great affront to him."

---

[3] The *Restoration* was an episode in the history of Great Britain beginning in 1660 when the monarchy was restored under King Charles II after the English Civil War. Theatres reopened after having been closed during the protectorship of Oliver Cromwell, Puritanism lost its momentum, and the bawdy 'Restoration comedy' became a recognisable genre. The name Restoration may apply both to the actual event by which the English monarchy was restored, and to the period immediately following the accession of Charles II. (source: Wikipedia)

The Duke was alarmed, and sent for the Chancellor, who has himself described the interview:

"The Duke told him with much warmth, 'what he had been informed of his purpose to complain to the Parliament against him, which he did not value or care for'; however, if he should prosecute any such course, it would be the worse for him; implying some threats, 'what he would do before he would bear such an affront'; adding then, 'that for his daughter, she had behaved so foully (of which he had such evidence as was so convincing as his own eyes, and of which he could make no doubt), that nobody could blame him for his behaviour towards her'; concluding with some other threats, 'that he should repent it, if he pursued his intention of appealing to the Parliament.'"

It would naturally be expected that the Lord High Chancellor of England would stand by his daughter; but not so at all, as he has been at pains to relate:

"As soon as the Duke discontinued his discourse, the Chancellor told him, 'that he hoped he would discover the untruth of other reports which had been made to him by the falsehood of this, which had been raised without the least ground or shadow of truth. That though he did not pretend to much wisdom, yet no man took him to be such a fool as he must be if he intended to do such an act as he was informed. That if his Highness had done anything towards or against him which he ought not to have done, there is One who is as much above him as his Highness was above him and who could both censure and punish it. For his own part, he knew too well whose son he was and whose brother he is, to behave himself towards him with less duty and submission than was due to him, and should always be paid by him.' He said, 'he was not concerned to vindicate his daughter from any of the most improbable scandals and aspersions: she had disobliged and deceived him too much, for him to be overconfident that she might not deceive any other man: and therefore he would leave that likewise to God Almighty, upon whose blessing he would always depend whilst himself remained innocent no longer.'"

Queen Henrietta Maria came over from Paris and, according to Clarendon, expressed her indignation to the King and her younger son, with her natural passion. It was reported, said the same authority, that the Duke had asked his mother's pardon "for having placed his affections so irregularly, of which he was sure there was now an end; that he was not married, and had now much evidence of her unworthiness that he should think no more of her."

The source of these accusations against the honour of Anne Hyde was soon generally known. "It was avowedly said," Clarendon wrote, "that Sir Charles Berkeley (afterwards Lord Falmouth), who was captain of his guard, and in much more credit and favour with the Duke than his uncle (though a young man of dissolute life, and prone to all wickedness in the judgment of all sober men) had informed the Duke, 'that he was bound in conscience to preserve him from taking to wife a woman so wholly unworthy of him; that he himself had lain with her; and that for his sake he would be content to marry her, though he knew well the familiarity the Duke had with her.' This evidence, with so many solemn oaths presented by a person so much loved and trusted by him, made a wonderful impression in the Duke; and now confirmed by the commands of his mother, as he had been before prevailed upon by his sister, he resolved to deny that he was married, and never to see the woman again who had been so false to him."

The story of this disgraceful business is told with more of detail but with some difference in Grammont's memoirs:

"The Duke of York's marriage with the Chancellor's daughter was deficient in none of those circumstances which render contracts of this nature valid in the eye of Heaven: the mutual inclination, the formal ceremony, witnesses, and every essential point of matrimony had been observed.

"Though the bride was no perfect beauty, yet, as there were none at the Court of Holland who eclipsed her, the Duke during the first endearments of matrimony, was so far from repenting of it, that he seemed only to wish for the King's restoration that he might have an opportunity of declaring it with splendour; but when he saw himself enjoying a rank which placed him so near the throne; when the possession of Miss Hyde afforded him no new charms; when England, so abounding in beauties, displayed all that was charming and lovely in the court of the King his brother; and when he considered he was the only prince, who, from such superior elevation, had descended so low, he began to reflect upon it. On the one hand, his marriage appeared to him particularly ill-suited in every respect: he recollected that Jermyn had not engaged him in an intimacy with Miss Hyde, until he had convinced him by several different circumstances, of the facility of succeeding: he looked upon his marriage as an infringement of that duty and obedience he owed to the King; the indignation with which the Court, and even the whole kingdom, would receive the account of his marriage presented itself to his imagination, together with the impossibility of obtaining the King's consent to such an act, which for a thousand reasons he would be obliged to refuse. On the other hand, the tears and despair of poor Miss Hyde presented themselves; and still more than that, he felt a remorse of conscience, the scruples of which began from that time to rise up against him.

"In the midst of this perplexity he opened his heart to Lord Falmouth, and consulted with him what method he ought to pursue. He could not have applied to a better man for his own interests, nor to a worse for Miss Hyde's; for at first, Falmouth maintained not only that he was not married, but that it was even impossible that he could ever have formed such a thought; that any marriage was invalid for him, which was made without the King's consent, even if the party was a suitable match: but it was a mere jest, even to think of the daughter of an insignificant lawyer, whom the favour of his sovereign had lately made a peer of the realm, without any noble blood, and Chancellor, without any capacity; that as for his scruples, he had only to give ear to some gentlemen whom he could introduce, who would thoroughly inform him of Miss Hyde's conduct before he became acquainted with her; and provided he did not tell them that he really was married, he would soon have sufficient grounds to come to a determination.

"The Duke of York consented, and Lord Falmouth, having assembled both his council and his witnesses, conducted them to his Royal Highness's cabinet, after having instructed them how to act: these gentlemen were the Earl of Arran, Jermyn, Talbot, and Killigrew, all men of honour; but who infinitely preferred the Duke of

York's interest to Miss Hyde's reputation, and, who, besides, were greatly dissatisfied, as the whole Court, at the insolent authority of the prime minister.

"The Duke having told them, after a sort of preamble, that although they could not be ignorant of his affection for Miss Hyde, yet they might be unacquainted with the engagements his tenderness for her had induced him to contract; that he thought himself obliged to perform all the promises he had made her; but as the innocence of persons of her age was generally exposed to Court scandal, and as certain reports, whether false or true, had been spread abroad on the subject of her conduct, he conjured them as his friends, and charged them upon their duty, to tell him sincerely everything they knew upon the subject, since he was resolved to make their evidence the rule of his conduct towards her. They all appeared rather reserved at first, and seemed not to dare to give their opinions upon an affair of so serious and delicate a nature; but the Duke of York having renewed his entreaties, each began to relate the particulars of what he knew, and perhaps of more than he knew, of poor Miss Hyde; nor did they omit any circumstance necessary to strengthen the evidence. For instance, the Earl of Arran, who spoke first, deposed that in the gallery at Honslaerdyk, where the Countess of Ossory, his sister-in-law, and Jermyn, were playing at nine-pins, Miss Hyde, pretending to be sick, retired to a chamber at the end of the gallery; that he, the deponent, had followed her, and having cut her lace, to give a greater probability to the pretence of the vapours, he had acquitted himself to the best of his abilities both to assist and to console her.

"Talbot said, that she had made an appointment with him in the Chancellor's cabinet, while he was in Council; and that, not paying so much attention to what was upon the table as to what they were engaged in, they had spilled a bottle full of ink upon a despatch of four pages and that the King's monkey, which was blamed for this accident, had been a long time in disgrace.

"Jermyn mentioned many places where he had received long and favourable audiences: however, all these articles of accusation amounted only to some delicate familiarities, or at most, to what is generally denominated the innocent part of an intrigue; but Killigrew, who wished to surpass these trivial depositions, boldly declared that he had had the honour of being upon the most intimate terms with her: he was of a sprightly and witty humour, and had the art of telling a story in the most entertaining manner, by the graceful and natural turn he could give it: he affirmed that he had found the critical moment in a certain closet built over the water, for a purpose very different from that of giving ease to the pains of love: that three or four swans had been witnesses to his happiness, and might perhaps have been witnesses to the happiness of many others, as the lady frequently repaired to that place, and was particularly delighted with it.

"The Duke of York found this last accusation greatly out of bounds, being convinced he himself had sufficient proofs of the contrary: he therefore returned thanks to these officious informers for their frankness, ordered them to be silent for the future upon what they had been telling him, and immediately passed into the King's apartment.

" As soon as he had entered the cabinet, Lord Falmouth, who had followed him, related what had passed to the Earl of Ossory[4], whom he met in the presence chamber: they strongly suspected what was the subject of the conversation of the two brothers, as it was long, and the Duke of York appeared to be in such agitation when he came out, that they no longer doubted the result had been unfavourable for poor Miss Hyde. Lord Falmouth began to be affected for her disgrace, and to relent that he had been concerned in it, when the Duke of York told him and the Earl of Ossory to meet him in about an hour's time at the chancellor's.

"They were rather surprised that he should have the cruelty himself to announce such a melancholy piece of news; they found his Royal Highness at the appointed hour in Miss Hyde's chamber: a few

---

[4] Thomas Butler, Earl of Ossory (1634-1680): eldest son of James Butler (1st Duke of Ormonde) was born at Kilkenny. Having come to London in 1652 he was rightly suspected of sympathizing with the exiled royalists, and in 1655 was put into prison by Cromwell; after his release about ayear later he went to Holland and married a Dutch lady of good family, accompanying Charles II to England in 1660. 1662 was made an Irish peer as 1st Earl of Ossory. He was an excellent naval strategist and widely known as 'Gallant Ossory'.

tears trickled down her cheeks, which she endeavoured to restrain. The Chancellor, leaning against the wall, appeared to them to be puffed up with something, which they did not doubt was rage and despair. The Duke of York said to them with that serene and pleasant countenance with which men generally announce good news: 'As you are the two men of the Court whom I most esteem, I am desirous you should first have the honour of paying your compliments to the Duchess of York: there she is.'

"Surprise was of no use, and astonishment was unseasonable on the present occasion: they were, however, so greatly possessed with both surprise and astonishment, that in order to conceal it, they immediately fell on their knees to kiss her hand, which she gave them with as much majesty as if she had been used to it all her life."

The next day the news was made public, and the whole Court was eager to pay her that respect, from a sense of duty, which in the end became very sincere.

It had been thought that the accusations of Sir Charles Berkeley would have brought to an end the question of the Duke's marriage, but as Grammont shows it was, in fact, only the beginning.

Public opinion at Court was aroused. "Men of the greatest name and reputation spoke of the foulness of the proceeding with great freedom, and with all the detestation imaginable against Sir Charles Berkeley, whose testimony nobody believed." Clarendon added: "Not without some censure of the Chancellor, for not enough appearing and prosecuting the indignity; but he was not to be moved by any instances, which he never afterwards repented." About this time the Princess Royal died of smallpox, and in her last agonies expressed a dislike of the proceedings in the affair, to which she had contributed so much.

This protest preyed upon the mind of the Duke, who grew more and more melancholy. This, in turn, affected Sir Charles Berkeley, who now came forward and branded himself as a liar. He declared to the Duke, "that the general discourse of men, of what inconvenience and mischief, if not absolute ruin, such a marriage would be to his Royal Highness, had prevailed with him to use all the power he had to dissuade him from it, and when he found he could not prevail with him, he had formed that accusation which he presumed could not but produce the effect he wished; which he now confessed to be false; and without the least ground, and that he was very confident of her virtue"; and he went on to beseech his Royal Highness "to pardon a fault that was committed out of pure devotion to him; and. that he would not suffer him to be ruined by the power of those whom he had so unworthily provoked; and of which he had so much shame, that he had not confidence to look upon them."

The Duke evidently thought that no gentleman could have spoken fairer, and promised Sir Charles "that he should not suffer in the least degree in his own affection, for what had proceeded so absolutely from his good will to him; and that he would take so much care of him, that in the compounding that affair, he should be so comprehended, that he should receive no disadvantage."

The Duke was, in fact, in a forgiving mood, for Berkeley's statement greatly relieved him. He was still in love with Anne, and though he was at all times loose in his amours, he had felt very unhappy at breaking his word. He was now determined that the marriage should take place at once — in fact, if there was to be another marriage it was vital that there should be no delay, for the girl was many months advanced in pregnancy.

The Duke told his brother of Berkeley's confession, and expressed to him his delight that the charges were fabrications, and announced his marriage, which took place privately at Worcester House, the residence of Sir Edward Hyde in the Strand, London, on September 3, 1660, between eleven o'clock at night and two o'clock in the morning, Lord Ossory giving away the bride. During the next month the Duchess was delivered of a son, Charles, who was created Duke of Cambridge, but survived only seven months. In all, there were eight children; but only Mary and Anne lived more than a year beyond infancy.

Of course, the secret was soon out, and the town was agog with excitement.

"To my Lord's; he all dinner-time talking French to me, and tell-ing me the story how the Duke of York hath got my Lord Chancellor's daughter with child, and that she do lay it with him, and that for certain he did promise her marriage, and had signed it with his blood, but that he by stealth had got the paper out of her cabinet. And that the King would have him to marry her, but that he will not. So that the thing is very bad for the Duke and them all." Thus Pepys wrote on October 7; and on the same day there is an en-try in Evelyn's diary[5]:

"There dined with me a French Count, with Sir George Tuke, who came to take leave of me, being sent over to the Queen-Mother to break the news of the marriage of the Duke [of York] with the daugh-ter of Chancellor Hyde. The Queen would fain have undone it, but it seems matters were reconciled on great offers of the Chancellor to befriend the Queen, who was much in debt, and was now to have the settlement of her affairs go through his hands. Henrietta Maria was vastly displeased with the change in the resolution of the Duke, and made strong representations to the King, without, however, obtain-ing any real satisfaction. She was always very angry at the King's coldness, which had been so far from that aversion which she had expected that he found excuses for the Duke, and endeavoured to di-vert her passions: and now pressed the discovery of the truth by Sir Charles Berkeley's confession."

To add to the annoyance of her Majesty, those about her were less strongly opposed to the marriage of the Duke — an attitude which angered her so much that in a passion she declared that whenever "that woman should be brought into Whitehall by one door, she would go out of the palace by another, and never enter it again." In any case, she threatened to leave the country for a lengthy sojourn in France.

---

[5] Evelyn's diaries are largely contemporaneous with those of the other noted diarist of the time, Samuel Pepys, and cast considerable light on the art, culture and politics of the time (he witnessed the deaths of Charles I and Oliver Cromwell, the last Great Plague in London, and the Great Fire of London in 1666.). Evelyn and Pepys corre-sponded frequently and much of this correspondence has been preserved. (Source: Wikipedia)

Then suddenly, quite suddenly, Henrietta Maria told the Duke "that the business that had offended her so much, she perceived so far, that no remedy could be applied to it; and that therefore she would trouble herself no further in it, but pray to God to bless him, and that he might be happy." This change of face aroused much speculation, until the cause of it was declared by Abbot Montagu, who, in the first instance, told Clarendon, "that this change in the Queen had preceded from a letter she had newly received from the Cardinal, in which he had plainly told her, that she would not receive a good welcome in France, if she left her sons in her displeasure, and professed animosity against those ministers who were most trusted by the King. He extolled the services done by the Chancellor, and advised her to comply with what could not be avoided, and to be perfectly reconciled to her children, and to those who were nearly related to the throne, and were entrusted by them."

The next move was that the Duke brought Sir Charles Berkeley to the Duchess, who cast himself at her feet, expressed penitence for his conduct, and begged for forgiveness. Sir Charles proceeded to the Chancellor, and made humble submission, the which we are told he "was obliged to receive civilly. "The Duchess of York," as the *Memoirs of Grammont* relate, "being fully informed of all that was said in the cabinet concerning her, instead of showing the least resentment, studied to distinguish, by all manner of kindness and good offices, those who had attacked her in so sensible a part; nor did she ever mention it to them, but in order to praise their zeal, and to tell them: that nothing was a greater proof of the attachment of a man of honour, than his being more solicitous for the interest of his friend or master than for his own reputation: a remarkable example of prudence and moderation, not only in the fair sex, I but even for those who value themselves upon their philosophy among the men." The marriage of the Duke of York with Anne Hyde was publicly announced by December, 1660. "The marriage of the Chancellor's daughter being now newly owned," Evelyn wrote on the following day, "I went to see her, she being Sir Richard Browne's[6] intimate ac-

---

[6] Sir Richard Browne (1605-1683) was elected Lord Mayor on 3rd October 1660. During his mayoralty, Venner's insurrection took place and the vigour he showed in

quaintance when she waited on the Princess of Orange; she was now at her father's at Worcester House in the Strand. We all kissed her hand, as did also my Lord Chamberlain [Manchester] and the Countess of Northumberland. This was a strange evening — can it succeed well?"

Then came the final scene in the drama, graphically described by Clarendon. "The Duke of York had before presented his wife to his mother, who received her without the least show of regret, or rather with the same grace as if she had liked it from the beginning, and made her sit down by her. When the Chancellor came in, the Queen rose from her chair, and received him with a countenance very serene. The ladies, and others who were near, withdrawing, her Majesty told him, that he could not wonder, much less take it ill, that she had been much offended with the Duke, and had no inclination to give her consent to his marriage; and if she had, in the passion that could not be condemned in her, spake anything of him that he had taken ill, he ought to impute it to the provocation she had received, though not from him. She was now informed by the King, and well assured, that he had no hand in contriving that friendship, but was offended with that passion that really was worthy of him. That she could not but confess, that his fidelity to the King, her husband, was very eminent, and that he had served the King, her son, with equal fidelity and extraordinary success. And therefore as she had received his daughter as her daughter, and heartily forgave the Duke and her, and was resolved ever after to live with all the affection of a mother towards them; so she resolved to make a friendship with him, and hereafter all the offices from him which her kindness should deserve."

---

suppressing it gained him fresh advancement. The City rewarded him with a pension of £500 a year (7th August 1662) and the King created him a baronet.

# CHAPTER II

## ANNE, DUCHESS OF YORK (*née* HYDE) (2)
1637-1671

The married life of the Duchess of York was not all roses. Her consort was a pleasant enough fellow, though not so genial nor so dignified as his brother, the King, and he was certainly as selfish as any of the Stuarts. Anthony Hamilton in his *Memoirs of Grammont* presents a good and fairly reliable penportrait of the Heir-Presumptive. "He was very brave in his youth," he says, "and so much magnified by Monsieur Turenne, that till his marriage lessened him, he really clouded the King, and passed for the superior genius. He was naturally candid and sincere, and a firm friend, till affairs and his religion wore out all his first principles and inclinations. He had a great desire to understand affairs: and in order to do that he kept a constant journal of all that passed, of which he showed me a great deal.

"The Duke of Buckingham gave me once a short but severe character of the two brothers. It was the more severe, because it was true: the King (he said), could see things if he would: and the Duke would see things if he could. He had no true judgment, and was soon determined by those whom he trusted: but he was obstinate against all other advices. He was bred with high notions of kingly authority, and laid it down for a maxim, that all who opposed the King were rebels in their hearts. He was perpetually in one amour or another, without being very nice in his choice: upon which the King once said, he believed his brother had his mistress given him by his priests for penance. He was naturally eager and revengeful: and was against the taking off any, that set up in opposition to the measures of the Court. He was for rougher methods. He continued many years dissembling his religion, and seemed zealous for the Church of England, but it was chiefly on design to hinder all propositions, that tended to unite us among ourselves. He was a frugal prince, and brought his court into method and magnificence, for he had £100,000 a-year allowed him. He was made High Admiral, and he came to understand all the concerns of the sea very particularly."

It was not to be expected that a lady not of royal blood who, married the Heir-Presumptive to the throne would at once become popular with the ladies of the Court or with society generally. In fact, jealousy was, not unnaturally, rampant. Nor did her relations by marriage accept her with equanimity. The Duke of Gloucester said that his sister-in-law smelt of her father's green-bag, and that in a parvenue the pride habitually imputed to her was naturally resented. However, after a time, she contrived to live down her unpopularity. Anthony Hamilton wrote of her: "The Duchess of York's want of birth was made up by endowments, and her carriage afterwards became her acquired dignity. She had a majestic air, a pretty good shape, not much beauty, a good deal of wit, and so just a discernment of merit, that, whoever of either sex were possessed of it, were sure to be distinguished by her: an air of grandeur in all her actions made her to be considered as if born to support the rank which placed her so near the throne."

Of her, Pepys wrote in 1667, "The Duchess is not only the proudest woman in the world, but the most expenceful." Anyhow, whether the fault lay with her or her husband, the fact remains that the cost of their household was £20,000 a year in excess of their revenue, and that about the time that Pepys reflected on the matter Commissioners were appointed to control the Duke's revenue. The Duchess of York was, in fact, a woman of sense, and contrived, by the exercise of her tact, to keep her husband within reasonable bounds—a task that was none too easy. "The Duke of York," says Pepys, "in all things but his amours, was led by the nose of his wife." His Royal Highness's amorous propensities she could not, indeed, check. He flitted after every fresh face, and even made love to one at least of his brother's mistresses—to the undisguised annoyance of that monarch, who, for his part, it must in justice be said, never hesitated to poach upon the preserves of others: His Majesty took up the regal attitude that what is sauce for the King, is not necessarily sauce for his younger brother.

It was about this time that the Duchess's father offered his resignation, and expressed his desire to go abroad.

"May it please your Majesty.

"I am so broken under the daily insupportable instances of your Majesty's terrible displeasure, that I know not what to do, hardly what to wish. The crimes which are objected against me, how passionately soever pursued, and with circumstances very unusual, do not in the least degree fright me. God knows I am innocent in every particular as I ought to be; and I hope your Majesty knows enough of me to believe that I had never a violent appetite for money, that could corrupt me. But, alas! your Majesty's declared anger and indignation deprives me of comfort and support even of my own innocence, and exposes me to the rage and fury of those who have some excuse for being my enemies; whom I have sometimes displeased, when (and only then) your Majesty believed them not to be your friends. I hope they may be changed; I am sure I am not, but have the same duty, passion, and affection for you, that I had when you thought it most unquestionable, and which was and is as great as ever man had for any mortal creature. I should die in peace (and truly I do heartily wish that God Almighty would free you from further trouble, by taking me to himself), if I could know or guess at the ground of your displeasure, which I am sure must proceed from your believing, that I have said or done somewhat I have neither said [nor] done. If it be for any thing my Lord Berkeley hath reported, which I know he hath said to many, though being charged with it by me he did as positively disclaim it; I am as innocent in that whole affair, and gave no more advice or counselor countenance in it, than that, which your Majesty seemed once to believe, when I took notice to you of the report, and when you considered how totally I was a stranger to the persons mentioned, to either of whom I never spake word, or received message from either in my life. And this I protest to your Majesty is true, as I have hope in heaven: and that I have never wilfully offended your Majesty in my life, and do upon my knees beg your pardon for any over-bold or saucy expressions I have ever used to you; which, being a natural disease in old servants who have received too much countenance, I am sure hath always proceeded from the zeal and warmth of the most sincere affection and duty.

"I hope your Majesty believes, that the sharp chastisement I have received from the best-natured and most bountiful master in the world, and whose kindness alone made my condition these many years supportable, hath enough mortified me as to this world, and that I have not the presumption or the madness to imagine or desire ever to be admitted to any employment or trust again. But I do most humbly beseech your Majesty, by the memory of your father, who recommended me to you with some testimony, and by your own gracious reflection upon some one service I may have performed in my life, that hath been acceptable to you; that you will by your royal power and interposition put a stop to this severe prosecution against me, and that my concernment may give no longer interruption to the great affairs of the kingdom; but that I may spend the small remainder of my life, which cannot hold long, in some parts beyond the seas, never to return, where I will pray for your Majesty, and never suffer the least diminution in the duty and obedience of,

"May it please your Majesty,
    "Your Majesty's
        "Most humble and most
            "Obedient subject and servant,
                "CLARENDON.
"From my house
this 16th of November."

Gallantry was the fashion of the day, anyhow at Court and in fashionable circles generally. "In fine," Pepys wrote on New Year's Day, 1663, being in moralising mood, probably after thinking of his own peccadilloes as it is right and proper at the beginning of a year, "I find there is nothing almost but bawdry at Court from top to bottom, as, if it were fit, I could instance, but it is not necessary only they say my Lord Chesterfield, Groom of the Stole to the Queen, is either gone or put away from the Court upon the score of his lady's having smitten the Duke of York, so as that he is watched by the Duchess of York, and his lady is retired into the country upon it. How much of this is true, God knows, but it is common talk."

There was, however, no breach between the royal pair at this time. On January 4 Pepys saw them at the theatre, when Tom Killigrew's play *Clarasilla* was being performed: "Neither the King nor Queen were there, but only the Duke and Duchess, who did show some impertinent and, methought, unnatural dalliance there, before the whole world, such a kissing and leaning upon one another." In May of the same year, the diarist makes an entry, "The Duke of York, whose lady, I am told, is very troublesome to him by her jealousy."

The Duchess had cause enough for jealousy. "Pierce tells me also," to quote Pepys, November 2, 1662, "how the Duke of York is smitten in love with my Lady Chesterfield (a virtuous lady, daughter to my Lord of Ormonde), and so much, that the Duchess of York hath complained to the King and her father about it, and my Lady Chesterfield has gone into the country for it. At all which I am sorry; but it is the effect of idleness, and having nothing else to employ their great spirits upon." This was Lady Elizabeth Butler, daughter of James Butler, first Duke of Ormonde, second wife of Philip Stanhope, second Earl of Chesterfield.

The Earl of Chesterfield, who at the time of his marriage in 1668 was only twenty-seven, had acquired an unenviable reputation for drinking and gaming, for wildness and gallantry, and duelling. He had, Anthony Hamilton has said, "a fair head of hair, an indifferent shape, and a coarse air; he was not, however, deficient in wit: a long residence in Italy had made him ceremonious with men, and jealous in his connections with women; he had been much hated by the King, because he had been much beloved of Lady Castlemaine: it was reported that he had been in her good graces prior to her marriage; and as neither of them denied it, it was the more generally believed." As regards the Earl's marriage, Hamilton continued: "He had paid his devoirs to the eldest daughter of the Duke of Ormonde, while his heart was still taken up with his former passion. The King's love for Lady Castlemaine, and the advancement he expected from such an alliance, made him press the match with as much ardour as if he had been passionately in love. He had, therefore, married Lady Chesterfield without loving her, and had lived some time with her in such coolness as to leave her no room to doubt of his indifference. As she was endowed with great sensibility and delicacy, she suffered at this contempt: she was at first much affected with his behaviour, and afterwards enraged at it; and when he began to give her proofs of his affection, she had the pleasure of convincing him of her indifference." If Lord Chesterfield did not love his wife, at least she could make him jealous. He was so angry at the attentions paid her by the Duke of York that he sent her to his country seat. While he had his affair with Lady Castlemaine and made love to Lady Elizabeth Howard (who subsequently married Dryden) she had a devoted admirer in her cousin James Hamilton. "She had greater opportunities," he wrote, "of making advances to him than to any other. She lived at the Duke of Ormonde's at Whitehead, where Hamilton had free admittance at all hours. Her extreme coldness, or rather the disgust she showed for her husband's returning affection, wakened his natural inclination to jealousy. He suspected that she could not so very suddenly pass from anxiety to indifference for him, without some secret object of a new attachment, and, according to the maxim of all jealous husbands, he immediately put into practice all his experience and industry in order to make a discovery, which was to destroy his own happiness. Hamilton, who knew his disposition, was, on the other hand, upon his guard, and the more he advanced in his intrigue, the more attentive was he to remove every degree of suspicion from the Earl's mind. He pretended to make him his confidant, in the most unguarded and open manner of his passion for Lady Castlemaine; he complained of her caprice; and most earnestly desired his advice how to succeed with a person whose affections he alone had entirely possessed. Chesterfield, who was flattered with this discourse, promised him his protection with greater sincerity than it had been demanded. Hamilton was, therefore, no further embarrassed than to preserve Lady Chesterfield's reputation, who, in his opinion, declared herself rather too openly in his favour, but whilst he was diligently employed in regulating, within the rules of discretion, the partiality she expressed for him, and in conjuring her to restrain her glances within bounds, she was receiving those of the Duke of York, and, what is more, made them favourable return." Lady Chesterfield remained in the seclusion of the country until her death in 1665.

Another love adventure of the Duke of York was with Lady Denham, the story of which will be told later — it is only mentioned here, because there was set abroad a rumour that the Duchess, anxious to rid herself of a rival, had poisoned the lady.

A third affair was with Arabella Churchill, the eldest daughter of Sir Winston Churchill, of Wootton Bassett, in Wiltshire, who was the father of John, first Duke of Marlborough. As some slight return for the loyalty of Sir Winston, Arabella, who was born in 1645, was appointed a Maid of Honour to the Duchess of York, and her brother John served as a page to the Duke. When Arabella was about seventeen or eighteen, the Duke cast a favourable eye on her, and she became his mistress. She bore him four I children. There was James Fitzjames, better known as the Duke of Berwick, and Henry Fitzjames, who was created Duke of Albemarle by his father after the Revolution; and two girls, Henrietta, who married Sir Henry Waldegrave of Churton, ancestor of the present Earls of Waldegrave; and Arabella, who became a nun.

When Arabella Churchill's connection with James II ceased, she was granted a pension on the very convenient Irish Establishment. Not long after she married Colonel Charles Godfrey, who by the influence of his wife's brother, the Duke of Marlborough, was given the sinecure offices in the Household of William III and Anne of Clerk Comptroller of the Green Cloth and Master of the Jewel Office. , There is mention of him in the *Journal to Stella* in 1711. On September 20, Jonathan Swift wrote: "To-day I was invited to the Green Cloth by Colonel Godfrey, who married the Duke of Marlborough's sister, mother to the Duke of Berwick by King James: I must tell you those things that happened before you were born. But I made my excuses." On the next day, however, "Colonel Godfrey sent to me again; so I dined at the Green Cloth, and we had but eleven at dinner, the Court always being thin of company till Saturday night." Mrs. Godfrey gave her husband two children: Charlotte, who was appointed a Maid of Honour to Queen Anne, and married Hugh Boscawen, first Earl of Falmouth; and Elizabeth, who became the wife of Edmund Dunch. As Professor Shuckburgh put it: "Surviving to the age of eighty-three (1730), she lived to see her royal lover die an exile at the Court of the French monarch against whom her brother was commanding, while her no less famous son, the Duke of Berwick, was serving the same monarch in Spain."

Anthony Hamilton certainly had no admiration for Arabella Churchill, anyhow as regards her appearance. "A tall creature, pale-faced, and nothing but skin and bone, named Churchill, whom the Duchess of York had taken for a maid of honour, became the object of her jealousy, because she was then the object of the Duke's affection. The Court was not able to comprehend how, after having been in love with Lady Chesterfield, Miss Hamilton, and Miss Jennings, he could have any inclination for such a creature; but they soon perceived that something more than unaccountable variety had a great share in effecting this conquest." There is another reference to the lady in the *Memoirs of Grammont*, on an occasion when the Duke and Duchess were staying in the country: "The Duke attended Miss Churchill, not for the sake of besieging her with soft, flattering tales of love, but, on the contrary, to chide her for sitting so ill on horse-back. She was one of the most indolent creatures in the world; and although the Maids of Honour are generally the worst mounted of the whole Court, yet, in order to distinguish her, on account of the favour she enjoyed, they had given her a very pretty, though rather a high-spirited horse; a distinction she would very willingly have excused them. The embarrassment and fear she was under had added to her natural paleness. In this situation, her countenance had almost completed the Duke's disgust, when her horse, desirous of keeping pace with the others, set off in a gallop, notwithstanding her greatest efforts to prevent it; and her endeavours to hold him, firing his mettle, he at length set off at full speed, as if he was running a race against the Duke's horse. Miss Churchill lost her seat, screamed out, and fell from her horse. A fall in so quick a pace must have been violent, and yet it proved favourable to her in every respect, for, without receiving any hurt, she gave the lie to all the unfavourable suppositions that had been formed of her person, in judging from her face. The Duke alighted, in order to help her. She was so greatly stunned, that her thoughts were otherwise employed than about decency on the present occasion; and those who first crowded round her found her rather in a negligent posture: they could hardly believe that limbs of such exquisite beauty could belong to Miss Churchill's face. After this accident, it was remarked that the Duke's tenderness and affection for her increased every day; and towards the end of the winter it appeared that she had not tyrannised over his passion, nor made him languish with impatience."

On the other hand, the morals of the Duchess of York — not to put too fine a point on it — were probably those of the time, and no better and no worse than those of most of the ladies of the Court. However, the terrible charges against her, voiced by Andrew Marvell in lines that cannot possibly be printed here, may safely be rejected. As an excuse for her — or, anyhow, an explanation — may be edict her consort's outrageous conduct which aroused her jealousy.

From contemporary memoirs it would certainly seem that she had her lovers. Of course, appearances may have been against her; but, on the other hand, that was not the age of harmless philandering. According to Evelyn, she was suspected in 1665 of a *liaison* with Sir Spenser Compton. Anyhow, Charles II said to his intimate friend, Sir Henry Bennet, afterwards Earl of Arlington: "I will try whether Sir Spenser Compton be so much in love as you say, for I will name Mrs. Hyde before him by chance, that except he be very much smitten it shall not at all move him."

Among the Duchess's reported lovers was Henry Sidney. Sidney, the fourth and youngest son of Robert, second Earl of Leicester, was born in 1641, and was four years the junior of the royal lady. He created a favourable impression at Court. He was known as "Handsome Sidney," in fact, although Anthony Hamilton qualified this by saying that he had too little vivacity "pour soutenir le fracas donc menaçoit sa figure." [to sustain for long the turbulence threatened by his appearance.] Vivacity is no necessity, however, and he quickly became a terror to husbands. In 1665 he was appointed a Groom of the Bedchamber to the Duke of York, and soon after was given the office of Master of the Horse to the Duchess.

Scandal soon became rife. Sir John Berkeley wrote:

"His Royal Highness the Duke of York and his Duchess came down to York, where it was observed that Mr. Sidney, the handsomest youth of his time, and of the Duke's Bedchamber, was greatly in love with the Duchess, and indeed he might well be excused, for the

Duchess, daughter to Chancellor Hyde, was a very handsome personage, and a woman of fine wit. The Duchess, on her part, seemed kind to him, but very innocently; but he had the misfortune to be banished the Court afterwards, for another reason, so was reported." Pepys was not so charitable. "As an infinite secret," he wrote on November 17, 1665, "my Lord Orrery tells me, the factions are high between the King and the Duke of York, and all the Court are in an uproar with their loose amours; the Duke of York being in love desperately with Mrs. Stuart. Nay, that the Duchess herself is fallen in love with the new Master of the Horse[1], Harry Sidney, and another, Harry Savill. So that God knows what will be the end of it." In October of the following year, Pepys referred to the matter again: "Thence Sir H. Cholmley and I together to Westminster Hall, on our way talking of matters and passages of State, the viciousness of the Court, the contempt the King brings himself into thereby; his minding nothing, but doing all those things just as his people about him will have it, the Duke of York becoming a slave to this whore Denham, and wholly minds her; that there really was amours between the Duchess and Sidney."

"The Duchess of York," Anthony Hamilton remarked in the *Memoirs of Grammont*, "beheld with indignation a choice [the Duke's preference for Arabella Churchill] which seemed to debase her own merit in a much greater degree than any of the former; at the very instant that indignation and jealousy began to provoke her spleen, perfidious Cupid threw in the way of her passions and resentments the amiable, handsome Sidney; and, whilst he kept her eyes fixed upon his personal perfections, diverted her attention from perceiving the deficiency of his mental accomplishments. She was wounded before she was aware of her danger; but the good opinion Sidney had of his own merit did not suffer him long to be ignorant of such a glorious conquest; and in order more effectually to secure it, his eyes rashly answered everything which those of her Royal Highness had

---

[1] The Master of the Horse in England is an important official of the sovereign's household. The master of the horse is the third dignitary of the court, and is always a member of the ministry (before 1782 the office was of cabinet rank), a peer and a privy councilor. (source: Wikipedia)

the kindness to tell him, while his personal accomplishments were heightened by all the advantages of dress and show.

"The Duchess, foreseeing the consequences of such an engagement, strongly combatted the inclination that hurried her away; but Miss Hobart (one of the Maids of Honour), siding with that inclination, argued the matter with her scruples, and, in the end, really vanquished them. This girl had insinuated into her Royal Highness's confidence with a fund of news with which she was provided the whole year round: the Court and the City supplied her; nor was it very material to her whether her stories were true or false, her chief care being that they should prove palatable to her mistress; she knew likewise, how to gratify her palate, and constantly provided a variety of those dishes and liquors which she liked best. These qualifications had rendered her necessary; but, desirous of being still more so, and having perceived both the airs Sidney gave himself, and what was passing in the heart of her mistress, the cunning Hobart took the liberty of telling her Royal Highness that this unfortunate youth was pining away solely on her account; that it was a thousand pities thatt a man of his figure should lose the respect for her which was most certainly her due, merely because she had reduced him to such a state that he could no longer preserve it; that he was gradually dying away on her account, in the sight of the whole Court; that his situation would soon be generally remarked, except she made use of the proper means to prevent it; that, in her opinion, her Royal Highness ought to pity the miserable situation into which her charms had reduced him, and to endeavour to alleviate the pain in some way or other.

"The Duchess asked what she meant by 'endeavouring to alleviate his pain in some way or other.' 'I mean, Madam,' answered Miss Hobart, 'that, if either his person be disagreeable, or his passion troublesome, you will give him his discharge; or, if you choose to retain him in your service, as all the princesses in the world would do in your place, you will permit me to give him directions from you for his future conduct, mixed with a few grains of hope, to prevent him entirely losing his senses, until you find a proper occasion to acquaint him with your wishes.' , 'What?' said the Duchess, 'would you advise me, Hobart—you, who really love me—to engage in an affair of this nature at the expense of my honour, and the hazard of a thousand inconveniences! If such frailties are sometimes excusable, they certainly are not so in the high station in which I am placed; and it would be an ill-requital on my part for his goodness who raised me to the rank I now fill, to—'

"'All this is very fine,' interrupted Miss Hobart; 'but is it not very well known that he only married you because he was importuned to do so? Since that I refer to yourself whether he has ever restrained his inclinations for a single moment, giving you the convincing proofs of the change that has taken place in his heart, by a thousand provoking infidelities? Is it still your intention to persevere in a state of indolence and humility, while the Duke, after having received the favours, or suffered the repulses,' of all the coquettes in England, pays his addresses' to the Maids of Honour, one after the other, and at present his whole ambition and desires in the conquest of that ugly skeleton, Churchill. What, Madam, must then your prime of life be spent in a sort of widowhood, in deploring your misfortunes, without even being permitted to make use of any remedy that may offer? A woman must be endowed with insufferable patience, or with an inexhaustible degree of resignation, to bear this. Can a husband, who disregards you both night and day, really suppose, because his wife eats and drinks heartily, as, God be thanked, your Royal Highness does, that she wants nothing else than to sleep well, too? Faith, such conduct is too bad. I therefore once more repeat that there is not a princess in the universe who would refuse the homage of a man like Sidney, when a husband pays his addresses elsewhere.'

"These reasons were not morally good; but had they been still worse, the Duchess would have yielded to them, so much did her heart act in concert with Miss Hobart, to overthrow her discretion and prudence."

Presently the Duke of York took active objection to the attentions that Sidney showed to his Consort. There was a rumpus in January, 1666, and the young Master of the Horse was summarily dismissed from his post. It might have been thought that this was the end of his career; on the contrary, the beginning of it. Charles II bore him no ill-will—his cynical sense of humour may have been tickled by the situation. He gave him in the following year a captaincy in the "Holland"regiment. Later, he was sent as Envoy-extraordinary on a congratulatory mission to Louis XIV, and in 1677 he was appointed Master of the Robes. It is unnecessary further to follow his life, save to say, that he entered the House of Commons in 1679; was Warden of the Cinque Ports from 1691 to 1702; Lord Lieutenant of Ireland from 1692 to 1695; Master of the Ordnance from 1693, which office he resigned two years before his death, which took place in 1704. He had in 1694 been raised to the peerage by William, to whose cause at the time of the Revolution he had rendered yeoman's service. The Duke of York does not seem to have taken umbrage at the temporary devotion of Henry Sidney's intimate friend, Henry Savill, to the Duchess. He, too, was appointed in 1665, when he was twenty-three, as Gentleman of the Bedchamber to his Royal Highness. He was an attractive, harum-scarum youth, and the Earl of Clarendon, agreeing that he had wit, was irritated by his "incredible confidence and presumption." He certainly lacked reverence, alike for his elders as for his contemporaries. He numbered among his intimates Dorset and Killigrew and other rake-helly associates, and in the *Hatton Correspondence* it is mentioned that he declared, "no man should keep company with him without drinking, except Ned Walker." His royal master strongly resented his drunken frolics; but the King, less austere than his brother, was rather amused by them than not, and forgave him his offences on the score of his youth. In 1669, however, he fell into disgrace for carrying a challenge from his uncle, Sir John Coventry, to the Duke of Buckingham. He was later restored to favour, and eight years later was appointed Groom of the Chamber to the King, at which time he was returned to Parliament as member for Newark. He held various offices under Charles II; and James II, who had in the meantime forgiven him, made him Vice-Chamberlain, which office he held until his death at the early age of forty-five.

The life of the Duchess was, of course, not entirely devoted to love affairs. In some ways, since amours are personal, and, as a rule, only of family interest, it would have been better had she done so; but she embarked whole-heartedly in politics. Her father, the Earl of Clarendon, had fallen from power in August, 1667, and then the

Duke and Duchess of York allied themselves with Lady Castlemaine, and proceeded to make war on Buckingham and Arlington.

Upon this Pepys remarked on January 16, 1669: "Povy tells me that Sir W. Coventry is with the King alone, an hour this day, and that my Lady Castlemaine is now in a higher command over the King than ever — not as a mistress, for she scorns him, but as a tyrant, to command him; and says that the Duchess and the Duke of York are mighty great with her, which is a great interest to my Lord Chancellor's family, and that they do agree to hinder all they can the proceedings of the Duke of Buckingham and Arlington; and so 'we are in the old mad condition, or rather worse than any; no man knowing what the French intend to do next summer."

Politics were bad enough, and the incursion therein of the consort of the Heir-Presumptive to the throne was not generally approved. The Duchess became much more unpopular, however, when it was suspected that she had left the Church of England and gone over to Rome. It was thought that she took this step, less from strong religious conviction than from a desire to regain her influence over the Duke, who was to all intents and purposes already a convert. Whatever the reason, she was in August, 1670, formally received into the Roman Catholic Church. Of this, though many were convinced, yet few actually knew. "It was observed," Burnet[2] wrote upon the death of the Duchess, "that for fifteen months before that time she had not received the Sacrament, and that upon all occasions she was excusing the errors that the Church of Rome was charged with, and was giving them the best colours they were capable of. An unmarried clergy was also a common topic with her. Morley had been her father confessor: for, he told me she practised secret confession to him from the time that she was twelve years old: and, when he was sent away from the Court, he put her in the hands of Blandford, who died Bishop of Worcester. He also told me, that upon the reports that were brought him of her slackness in receiving the Sacrament, she having been for many years punctual to once a month, he had spoke plainly to her

---

[2] Gilbert Burnet (1643-1715): English bishop and historian, was born in Edinburgh on the 18th of September 1643, of an ancient and distinguished Scottish house. He was the youngest son of Robert Burnet (1592-1661), who at the Restoration became a lord of session with the title of Lord Crimond.

about it, and told her what inferences were made upon it. She pretended ill-health and business; but protested to him she had no scruples with relation to her religion, and was still of the Church of England; and assured him that no Popish priest had ever taken the confidence to speak to her of those matters. He took a solemn engagement of her, that if scruples should arise in her mind she would let him know them, and hear what he should offer to her upon all of them. And he protested to me, that to her death, she never owned to him that she had any scruples, though she was for some days entertaining him at Farnham, after the date of the paper which was afterwards published in her name. All this passed between him and me, upon the Duke's showing me that paper all writ in her own hand, which was afterwards published by Maimburg. He would not let me take a copy of it, but he gave me leave to read it twice; and I went immediately to Morley and gave him an account of it, from whom I had all the particulars already mentioned. And upon that he concluded, that that unhappy Princess had been prevailed on to set lies under her hand, and to pretend that these were the grounds of her conversion. A long decay of health came at last to a quicker crisis than had been apprehended. All of the sudden she fell into the agony of death. Blandford was sent for to prepare her for it, and to offer her the Sacrament. Before he could come, the Queen came in and sat by her. He was modest and humble even to a fault; so he had not presence of mind enough to begin prayers, which probably would have driven the Queen out of the room; but that not being done she, pretending kindness, would not leave her. The Bishop spoke but little, and fearfully. He happened to say he hoped she continued still in the truth: upon which she asked, 'What is truth': and then, her agony increasing, she repeated the word, '*Truth,*' '*Truth,*' very often, and died in a few minutes, very little beloved or lamented. Her haughtiness had raised her many enemies. She was indeed a firm and kind friend: but the change of her religion made her friends reckon her death rather a blessing than a loss at that time to them all. Her father, when he heard of her shaking in her religion, was more troubled at it than at all his misfortunes. He writ her a very good and long letter upon it, inclosed in one to the Duke; but she was dead before it came into England."

The conversion of the Duchess was not made known until after her death, though a few months before the Duke told the King of her intention. Apropos, there is a story in Spence's *Anecdotes*. "'How could the Duke of York make my Mother a Papist,' said the Princess Mary to Dr. Burnet. 'The Duke caught a man in bed with her,' said the Doctor and then had power to make her do anything.' The Prince, who sat by the fire, said, 'Pray, Madam, ask the Doctor a few more questions.'"

Towards the end the Duchess had been suffering from cancer in the breast, and from this disease she died on March 31, 1671, having very lately celebrated her forty-fourth birthday. Before she passed away, she received the viaticum of the Church of Rome. Her remains were interred in the vault of Mary Queen of Scots in Henry Eighth's Chapel at Westminster Abbey.

# CHAPTER III

## BARBARA, DUCHESS OF CLEVELAND (née VILLIERS) (1)
### 1641-1709

BARBARA VILLIERS, afterwards by marriage Lady Castlemaine, and subsequently created by Charles II Duchess of Cleveland, was one of the most notorious women of the day and known far and wide for her licentiousness.

This lady came of a good stock. Born in 1641, she was the daughter of William Villiers, second Viscount Grandison, who was descended from the elder branch of the family — the younger becoming Duke of Buckingham. During the Civil Wars, he fought for the King, and at the siege of Bristol in 1643 he was mortally wounded. Of him Clarendon wrote: "Lord Grandison was a young man of so virtuous a habit of mind, that no temptation or provocation could corrupt him; so great a lover of justice and integrity, that no example, necessity, nor even the barbarities of this war, could make him swerve from the most precise rules of it; and of that rare piety and devotión, that the Court, or camp, could not show a more faultless person, or to whose example young men might more reasonably conform themselves. His personal valour and courage of all kinds (for he had sometimes indulged so much to the corrupt opinion of honour as to venture himself in duels) were very eminent, insomuch as he was accused of being too prodigal of his person; his affection, zeal, and obedience to the King, was such as do become a branch of that family."

Lord Grandison had married Mary, third daughter of Paul, Viscount Bayning, and Barbara was the only child of the union. The story told in the *Secret History of Charles II*, published in 1690, that this lady was the daughter of Queen Henrietta Maria by the Earl of St. Albans, though at one time believed by some, is, in fact, entirely without foundation. Five years after the death of her first husband, Lady Grandison married Charles Villiers, second Earl of Anglesey, who survived only until 1661.

Barbara, Duchess of Cleveland (née Villiers)

Barbara Villiers was very precocious, and while still a very young girl embarked upon a series of amours. Amongst these, as has been said, was Philip Stanhope, second Earl of Chesterfield. "It is evident from the letters in the present publication," says the editor of the *Letters of Philip, second Earl of Chesterfield,* "that the Earl of Chesterfield had received the ultimate favours in the power of a female to bestow, before her union with Mr. Palmer, to whom she adverts with marked aversion and contempt in a future letter in this collection. At all events, the manuscript from which these papers were collected furnishes intelligible proof of their voluptuous intimacy, and in terms adapted to the glowing fervour of the subject." The correspondence fully bears out the contention of the editor.

*Philip, second Earl of Chesterfield, to Barbara Villiers*
"1656.

"MADAM,

"Cruelty and absence have ever been thought the most infallible remedies for such a distemper as mine, and yet I find both of them so ineffectual that they make me but the more incurable, Madam, you ought at least to afford some compassion to one in so desperate a condition, for by only wishing me more fortunate you will make me so. Is it not a strange magic in love, which gives so powerful a charm to the least of your cruel words, that they endanger to kill a man at a hundred miles distance; but why do I complain of so pleasant a death, or repine at those sufferings which I would not change for a diadem? No, Madam, the idea I have of your perfections is too glorious to be shadowed either by absence or time; and if I should never more see the sun, yet I should not cease from admiring his light; therefore do not seek to darken my weakness by endeavouring to make me adore you less:

"'For if you decree that I must die,
Falling is nobler, than retiring,
And in the glory of aspiring
It is brave to tumble from the sky.'"

*Barbara Villiers to Philip, second Earl of Chesterfield*
"1657.

"My LORD,

"I would fain have had the happiness to have seen you at church this day, but I was not suffered to go. I am never so well pleased as when I am with you, though I find you are better when you are with other ladies, for you were yesterday all the afternoon with the person I am most jealous of, and I know I have so little merit that I am suspicious you love all women better than myself. I sent you yesterday a letter that I think might convince you that I loved nothing besides yourself, nor will I ever, though you should hate me; but if you should, I would never give you the trouble of telling' you how much I loved you, but keep it to myself till it had broken my heart. I will importune no longer than to say, that I am, and will ever be, your constant and faithful humble servant."


*Barbara Villiers to Philip, second Earl of Chesterfield*
"1657.

"My LORD,
    "It is ever my ill fortune to be disappointed of what I most desire, for this afternoon I did promise to myself the satisfaction of your company; but I fear I am disappointed, which I assure you is no small affliction to me; but I hope the fates may yet be so kind as to let me see you about five o'clock; if you will be at your private lodgings in Lincoln's Inn Fields, I will endeavour to come, and assure you of my being,

"My Lord,
    "Yours, etc."


*Barbara Villiers to Philip, second Earl of Chesterfield*
"1657.

"My LORD,
    "I do highly regret my own misfortune of being out of town, since it made me incapable of the honour you intended me. I assure you nothing is likelier to make me set too high rate of myself, than the esteem you are pleased to say you have for me. You cannot bestow your favours and obligations on any that has a more passionate desire of them, nor can they ever of any receive a more sincere reception than from,

"My Lord,
    "Yours, etc."

*Barbara Villiers to Philip, second Earl of Chesterfield*

"1657.

"My LORD,

"The joy I had of being with you the last night, has made me do nothing but dream of you, and my life is never pleasant to me but when I am with you or talking of you; yet the discourses of the world must make me a little more circumspect; therefore I desire you not to come to-morrow, but to stay till the party be come to town. I will not fail to meet you on Saturday morning, till when I remain your humble servant."

*Philip, second Earl of Chesterfield, to Barbara Villiers*

"1657.

"MADAM,

"I need not tell your Ladyship how unfortunate I was in missing the opportunity of waiting on you when you were last in town; since you have reason to believe, that the paying you my respects, and your acceptance of my service, are both the ambition and pleasure of my life. I hope this letter will be so fortunate as to kiss your hands, and yet I envy it a happiness that I want myself; but however my ill fate hath divided me from that place which is made happy by your presence, I beseech you to believe that though my joys may languish, yet my passion shall last in its primitive vigour, and preserve me ever,

"Madam,
"Yours, etc."

*From Barbara Villiers to Philip, second Earl of Chesterfield when she was very ill of the smallpox*

"1659.

"My DEAR LIFE,

"I have been this day extremely ill, and the not hearing from you hath made me much worse than otherwise I should have been. The doctor doth believe me in a desperate condition, and I must confess,

that the unwillingness I have to leave you, makes me not entertain
the thoughts of death so willingly as otherwise I should; for there is
nothing besides yourself that could make me desire to live a day;
and, if I am never so happy as to see you more, yet the last words I
will say shall be a prayer for your happiness, and so I will live and
die loving you above all other things, who am,

> "My Lord,
> 　　"Yours, etc."

How long the liaison between Barbara Villiers and Lord Chesterfield lasted cannot be stated with any precision; but judging by the
two letters written by the Earl in 1661, it would seem that the breach
came that year.

"MADAM,
　"After so many years' service, fidelity, and respect, to be banished
for the first offence is very hard, especially after my asking so many
pardons. If heaven with you should be as rigorous as you are with
me, I doubt you never would see it, but in your glass: therefore, use
me as you do your domestics, that is, blame me for the first fault, and
if I do not mend, turn away your very humble servant,

> 　　"C."

"MADAM,
　"Let me not live, if I did believe that all the women on earth could
have given me so great an affliction as I have suffered by your displeasure. It is true, I ever loved you as one should do heaven, that is,
more than the world, but I never thought you would have sent me
there before my time; I confess I have always found you so just, and
so apt to excuse the faults of your friends, that I had rather be condemned to lose the light than your kindness; but therefore do not
suffer one to perish who desires only to live upon your account. Besides, naturally I hate dying, and it is one of the last things I would
willingly do to show my passion; yet, if you will neither answer my
letters, nor speak to me before. I go out of town, it is more than an

even lay that I shall never come into it again; and then above three parts of all the love that mankind has for you, will be lost in

"Your obedient servant,

"C."

Though probably they were never again lovers, the pair became reconciled, and, as the following letter shows, they were on good terms in 1670:

"MADAM,

"Since the greatest pleasure of my thoughts is in thinking how to serve your Ladyship, I hope that some of my actions have been so fortunate as to remove all doubts of my obedience to the least of your commands. Madam, as soon as I came to town, I bespoke a figure for your Ladyship's fountain, which is a Cupid kneeling on a rock and shooting from his bow a stream of water up towards heaven. This may be interpreted by some, that tears are the best arms with which that place is to be assaulted; but my meaning in it is, that your Ladyship, not being content with the conquest of one world, doth now by your devotions attack the other. I hope this style hath too much gravity to appear gallant; since many years ago your Ladyship gave me occasion to repeat these two lines.

"'Vous m'ôtes tout espoir pour vous, belle inhumaine,
Et pour tout autre que vous, vous m'ôtes tout désir.'"

["'You deprive me of all hope for you, O inhuman beauty,
And for any other than you, you deprive me of all desire.'"]

While Barbara Villiers and Lord Chesterfield were still lovers, the lady had married — on April 14, 1659 — Roger Palmer, the son of Sir James Palmer, of Hayes, Middlesex, and Dorney Court, Buckinghamshire, by his second wife, Catherine, daughter of Sir William Herbert (afterwards Lord Powis) and widow of Sir Robert Vaughan, of

Llydearth, Montgomeryshire. Marriage, however, did not interfere with the prosecution of her amours. Not long after she became Mrs. Palmer, she attracted the attention of Charles II, whose acquaintance she made, probably in Holland, where she accompanied her husband in 1659, when he, an ardent loyalist, carried to the King a considerable sum of money from his Majesty's adherents in Britain to aid him in his restoration. When the intimacy began it is not possible to say, but it cannot have been later — and in all probability was much earlier — than May 28, 1660, the day of Charles's return to London, for on that evening, instead of sleeping at Whitehall, he slipped away secretly to the house of Sir Samuel Morland at Vauxhall, where he had an assignation with his mistress. February 25, 1660, Mrs. Palmer was delivered of a child, Anne. "This," said Lord Dartmouth, "was the late Countess of Sussex, whom the King adopted for his daughter, though Lord Castlemaine always looked upon her as his, and left her his estate when he died; but she was generally understood to belong to another, the old Earl of Chesterfield, whom she resembled very much in face and figure." Anyhow, the child was, by a royal warrant dated 1673, acknowledged by the King.

There are several mentions of this amour in the diary of Pepys.

July 13, 1660. "Late writing letters; and great doings of music at the next house, which was Whally's; the King and Dukes there with Mrs. Palmer, a pretty woman that they have a fancy to, to make her husband a cuckold."

October 14, 1660. "To White Hall Chappell... Here I also observed how the Duke of York and Mrs. Palmer did talk to one another very wantonly through the hangings that parts the King's Closet and the Closet where the ladies sit."

April 20, 1661. "Saw 'The Humorous Lieutenant' by [Beaumont and Fletcher] acted before the King, but not very well done. But my pleasure was great to see the manner of it, and so many great beauties, but above all, Mrs. Palmer, with whom the King do discover a great deal of familiarity."

July 23, 1661. "I went to the theatre and saw 'Brennovalt' by [Sir John Suckling], I never saw before. It seemed a good play, but ill acted; only I sat before Mrs. Palmer, the King's mistress, and filled my eyes with her, which much pleased me."

September 7, 1661. "My wife and I took them to the theatre, where we seated ourselves close by the King and Duke of York, and Madame Palmer, which was great content, and, indeed, I can never enough admire her beauty."

December 7, 1661. "So back to Whitehall ... and then to the Privy Seal ... and, among other things that passed, there was a patent for Roger Palmer (Madam Palmer's husband) to be Earl of Castlemaine and Baron of Limerick in Ireland; but the honour is tied up to the males got of the body of his wife, the Lady Barbara: the reason which everybody knows."

Palmer, who sat in the House of Commons as member for New Windsor, was far from pleased at the honour thrust upon him, and would probably have declined it had it been offered to him before it was bestowed. He showed his resentment by not taking his seat in the Irish House of Lords. The "reason whereof everyone knows" was the King's desire to propitiate his mistress, who was much upset by the announcement of the engagement between his Majesty and Catherine of Braganza, to which event she very naturally was opposed. This elevation to the peerage further made Mrs. Palmer eligible for the post of a Lady of the Bedchamber to the new Queen.

Again to quote from Pepys:

January 22, 1662. "There are factions (private ones at Court) about Palmer; but what it is about I know not. But it is something about the King's favour to her now that the Queen is coming."

April 21, 1662. "Sir Thomas Crewe tells me how my Lady Duchess of Richmond and Castlemaine had a falling out the other day; and she calls the latter Jane Shore, and did hope to see her come to the same end that she did."

May 9, 1662. "My Lady told me how my Lady Castlemaine. do speak of going to lie in at Hampton Court, which she and all our ladies are troubled at, because of the King's forced to show her countenance in the sight of the Queen when she comes."

But this was going too far, and the King, though with difficulty, over-ruled this proposal.

"One of the race of Villiers, then married to Palmer, a Papist, soon after made Earl of Castlemaine, who afterwards, being separated from him, was advanced to be Duchess of Cleveland, "wrote Burnet, "was his first and longest mistress, by whom he had five children. She was a woman of great beauty, but most enormously vicious and ravenous, foolish but imperious, ever uneasy to the King, and always carrying on intrigues with other men, while yet she pretended she was jealous of him. His passion for her, and her strange behaviour towards him, did SQ disorder him, that often he was not master of himself, nor capable of minding business, which, in so critical a time, required great application: but he did so entirely trust the Earl of Clarendon that he left all to his care, and submitted to his advisers as to so many oracles."

Further, of Lady Castlemaine's influence, Burnet said so early as August, 1660: "In the disposal of offices and places, as it was not possible to gratify all, so there was little regard had to men's merits or services. The King was determined to most of them by the cabal that met at Mistress Palmer's lodgings. And though the Earl of Clarendon did often prevail with the King to alter the resolutions taken there, yet he was forced to let a great deal go that he did not like. He would never make application to Mistress Palmer, nor let anything pass the Seal in which she was named, as the Earl of Southampton would never suffer her name to be in the Treasury books. These virtuous ministers thought it became them to let the world see that they did not comply with the King in his vices; but whether the Earl of Clarendon spoke so freely to the King about his course of life as was given out, I cannot tell."

Catherine of Braganza arrived in England on May 13, 1662, and received but a cold welcome from her Consort, who was still infatuated with his mistress. "The King dined at my Lady Castlemaine's," Pepys noted on May 21, "and the night that the bonfires were made for joy of the Queen's arrival, the King was there; but that there was no fire at her door, though at all the rest of the doors almost in the street, which was much observed: and that the King and she did send for a pair of scales and weighed one another: and she being with child was said to be the heaviest. But she is a most disconsolate creature, and comes not out of doors, since the King's going." Society watched with interest the struggle for supremacy, not the less fierce because it was silent, between the Queen and the favourite. "The Queen was brought to bed a few days since at Hampton Court," Pepys mentions on May 31, "and all people say of her to be a very fine and handsome lady, and very discreet; and that the King is pleased enough with her: which I fear will put Lady Castlemaine's nose out of joint."

The marriage was a brilliant one, even for a King of Britain. She had been chosen from all other eligible women, because of her immense dowry. Her portion was half a million; Bombay, with full trading privileges in the Indies; the fortress of Tangiers on the coast of Africa (of value as a protection in the Mediterranean for the merchant trade of England); and a share in the trade with Brazil. As a matter of fact, only half of the first item of the dowry was paid, and that not in specie, but in kind.

Catherine was a devout Roman Catholic, and when fetched by Lord Sandwich to come to England, declined to be married by proxy by a Protestant. "The King guided by his mother, had early resolved not to marry a Protestant," Carte says in his *Life of Ormonde*. "When the matter was debated by the Privy Council, and some of his best friends strongly advised him to unite himself with a Protestant Princess, he asked petulantly, where there was a Protestant for him to marry? Some of the German Princesses were mentioned. 'Odds-fish!' says the King impatiently, they are all foggy; I cannot take anyone of them for a wife!'"

Catherine was scarcely the woman to hold Charles to his marital allegiance. It is to be feared that she was dull — the last thing he could tolerate. She, who was now twenty-six years of age, had been accustomed in her childhood to the strict rules, rigid discipline, and narrow intercourse of a convent; and she could not easily accommodate herself to the rakish gaieties of Whitehall.

Lord Clarendon says: "The Queen had beauty and wit enough to make herself agreeable to him (the King); and it is very certain that, at their first meeting, and for some time after, the King had very good satisfaction in her.... Though she was of years enough to have had more experience of the world, and of as much wit as could be desired, and of a humour very agreeable at some seasons, yet, she had been bred, according to the mode and discipline of her country, in a monastery, where she had only seen the women who attended her, and conversed with the religious who resided there, and, without doubt, in her inclinations, was enough disposed to have been one of that number: and from this restraint she was called out to be a great queen, and to a free conversation in a Court that was to be upon the matter now formed, and reduced from the manners of a licentious age to the old rules and limits which had been observed in better times; to which regular and decent conformity the present disposition of men or women was not enough inclined to submit, nor the King enough disposed to exact."

An immediate source of trouble was the large Portuguese suite which had come over with the Queen, the members of which, insistent on their dignity, were at once unpopular at Court.

"The new Queen," Anthony Hamilton wrote, "gave but little additional brilliancy to the Court, either in her person or her retinue, which was then composed of the Countess de Panétra, who came over with her in the quality of a lady of the bedchamber; six frights who called themselves maids of honour, and a duenna, another monster, who took the title of governess to these extraordinary beauties. Among the men were Francis de Melo, brother to the Countess de Panétra; one Taurauvégez, who called himself Don Pedro Francisco Correo de Silva, extremely handsome, but a greater fool than all the Portuguese put together. He was more vain of his names than of his person; but the Duke of Buckingham, a still greater fool than he, though more addicted to raillery, gave him the nickname of Peter of the Wood. Poor Pedro was so enraged at this, that after many fruitless complaints and ineffectual menaces, he was obliged at last to quit England, leaving to the happy Buckingham the possession of a Portuguese nymph, still more hideous than any of the Queen's maids of honour, whom he had taken from him, as well as two of his names.

Besides these, there were six chaplains, four bakers, and a Jew perfumer, and a certain officer, apparently without employment, who called himself her Highness's barber."

A more intimate account is to be found in a letter to a Mr. Bates, written soon after Catherine's arrival, by Lord Chesterfield, who had been appointed Chamberlain to her Majesty. "Since I cannot be a partaker of your country enjoyments," he wrote, "my next satisfaction is to hear from those are there; and yet, all my good nature cannot hinder my wishing you as weary of so much quiet, as I am here of the contrary. You may judge how hard it is to please the Portuguese ladies, by their refusing to lie in any bed wherein any man has ever lain before; and yesterday they complained that they cannot stir abroad without seeing...; and for this and some other reasons, they are speedily to be sent back into their own country.

"Now, as for the Queen, of whom I know you desire the description, you may credit her being a very extraordinary woman; that is extremely devout, extremely discreet, very fond of her husband, and the owner of a good understanding. As to her person, she is exactly shaped, and has lovely hands, excellent eyes, a good countenance, a pleasing voice, fine hair, and, in a word, is what an understanding man would wish a wife. Yet, I fear all this will hardly make things run in the right channel; but, if it should, I suppose our Court will require a new modelling, and then the profession of an honest man's friendship will signify more than it does at present from your very humble servant."

Clarendon summed up this domestic squabble in his autobiography: "There was a numerous family of men and women, that were sent from Portugal, the most improper to promote that conformity in the Queen that was necessary for her condition and future happiness that could be chosen; the women, for the most part, old and ugly, and proud, incapable of any conversation with persons of quality and a liberal education; and they desired and indeed conspired so far to possess the Queen themselves, that she should neither learn the English language, nor use their habit, nor depart from the manners and fashions of her own country in any particular: which resolution, they told, would be for the dignity of Portugal, and would quickly induce the English ladies to conform to her Majesty's practice. And this imagination had made that impression, that the tailor who had been sent into Portugal to make her clothes could never be admitted to see her, or receive any employment. Nor, when she came to Portsmouth, and found there several ladies of honour and prime quality to attend her in the places to which they were assigned by the King, did she receive any of them till the King himself came; nor then with any grace, or the liberty that belonged to their places and offices. She could not be persuaded to be dressed out of the wardrobe that the King had sent to her, but would wear the clothes that she had brought, until she found that the King was displeased, and would be obeyed f whereupon she conformed, against the advice of her women, who continued their open entreaty, without anyone of them receding from their own mode, which exposed them the more to re-proach."

Descriptions of the person of Catherine are not too pleasing. "She was a very little woman, with a pretty, tolerable face; she, neither in person or manners, had anyone article to stand in competition with the charms of the Countess of Castlemaine, since Duchess of Cleve-land, the finest woman of her age." Thus Sir John Beverly; while Lord Dartmouth wrote of her: "She was very short and broad, of a swarthy complexion; one of her fore-teeth stood out, which held up the upper lip; had some very nasty distemper, besides exceedingly proud and illfavoured."

The person principally concerned was, of course, the King, and he put down his early impressions of his Consort in a letter to my Lord Chancellor, written by him on May 21 at Portsmouth, whither he had proceeded to meet her on her arrival:

"I arrived here yesterday, about two in the afternoon, and as soon as l had shifted myself, I went to my wife's chamber.... Her face is not so exact as to be called a beauty, though her eyes are excellent good, and not anything in her face in the least degree can shock one. On the contrary, she has as much agreeableness in her looks, alto-gether, as ever I saw; and if I have any skill in physiognomy, which I think I have, she must be as good a woman as ever was born. Her conversation, as much as I can perceive, is very good; for she has wit enough, and a most agreeable voice. You would much wonder to see how well we are acquainted already. In a word, I think myself very happy, but I am confident our two humours will agree very well together. I have not time to say any more. My Lord-Lieutenant will give you an account of the rest."

There was no doubt as to the line the King took. He was all for the mistress as against his Consort. He had not the slightest desire to be unkind to his bride; but at this time he was under the impression that he could not live happily, or even contentedly, without Lady Castlemaine. There was open trouble between the royal pair when he appointed his mistress one of her Majesty's Ladies of the Bedchamber. It was an outrage—though such outrages were not rare in the days of the Stuart and Hanoverian monarchs—and Catherine protested vigorously. "I hear," Pepys wrote, "that the Queen did prick her out of the list presented to her by the King; desiring that she might have that favour done her, or that he would send her from whence she come: and that the King was angry and the Queen discontented a whole day and night upon it; but that the King hath promised to have nothing to do with her [Lady Castlemaine] hereafter. But I cannot believe that the King can fling her off so, he loving her too well."

Nor was Catherine the only one to protest against Lady Castlemaine's appointments as the following emphatic note to Lord Clarendon shows. Charles, however, was determined not to be thwarted; the appointment was probably a condition laid down by Lady Castlemaine for the continuance of her relations with the King.

"HAMPTON COURT,
"Thursday Morning.
"FOR THE CHANCELLOR,

"I forgot when you were here last to desire you to give Broderick good counsel not to meddle any more with what concerns my Lady Castlemaine, and to let him have a care how he is the author of any scandalous reports, for if I find him guilty of any such thing, I will make him repent it to the last moment of his life.

"And now I am entered on this matter, I think it very necessary to give you a little good counsel, lest you may think that by making a farther stir in the business you may divert me from my resolution, which all the world shall never do, and I wish I may be unhappy in this world and in the world to come, if I fail in the least degree of what I resolved, which is of making my Lady Castlemaine of my wife's Bedchamber, and whosoever I find endeavouring to hinder this resolution of mine, except it be only to myself, I will be his enemy to the last moment of my life. You know how much a friend I have been to you: if you will oblige me eternally, make this business as easy to me as you can of what opinion you are of; for I am resolved to go through with this matter, let what will come of it, which again I solemnly swear before Almighty God; wherefore if you desire to have the continuance of my friendship, meddle no more with this business, except it be to beat down all false and scandalous reports, and to facilitate what I am sure my honour is so much concerned in: and whomsoever I find to be my Lady Castlemaine's enemy in the matter, I do promise upon my word to be his enemy as long as I live. You may show this letter to my Lord-Lieutenant, and if you have both a mind to oblige me, carry yourselves like friends in this matter.

"CHARLES R."

The fight went on. Lord Clarendon, under fear of incurring the King's displeasure, twice urged her Majesty — if only in the interests of peace — to accept Lady Castlemaine as a member of her Household. The Queen held out, however. "The day at length arrived when Lady Castlemaine was to be formally admitted a Lady of the Bedchamber," so runs a passage in Steinman's privately printed *Memoirs of Lady Castlemaine.* "The Royal Warrant, addressed to the Lord Chamberlain, bears date June 1, 1663, and includes with that of her Ladyship, the names of the Duchess of Buckingham, the Countesses of Chesterfield and Bath, and the Countess Mareshall. A separate Warrant of the same day directs his Lordship to admit the Countess of Suffolk [Lady Castlemaine's aunt] as Groom of the Stole and first Lady of the Bedchamber, to which undividable offices she had, with the additional ones of Mistress of the Robes and Keeper of the Privy Purse, been nominated by a Warrant dated April 2, 1662, wherein the reception of her oath is expressly deferred until the Queen's Household shall be established. We here are furnished with the evidence that Charles would not sign the Warrants for the five until Catherine had withdrawn her objection to his favourite one."

Of course, in the end the King had his way. Catherine had all the time, been fighting a losing battle, and when common-sense had forced her to yield, she found it possible to live with her Consort on very easy terms. Charles was always most goodnatured — when he had his own way.

# CHAPTER IV

## BARBARA, DUCHESS OF CLEVELAND (née VILLIERS) (2)
### 1641-1709

SHORTLY after the royal marriage had taken place, Lady Castle-maine — early in June 1662 had given birth to a child, Charles Fitzroy, her first son by Charles II. It may in this place be mentioned that he was created Duke of Southampton in 1675, and on the death of his mother in 1709 succeeded to her dukedom of Cleveland. His birth was followed by an upheaval in the Castlemaine family. His Lord-ship, who apparently was indifferent as to the paternity of the infant, was particular as to the religion into which he should be inducted. He said nothing to his wife, but had Charles Fitzroy baptized by a priest of his own faith. Lady Castlemaine was more than angry, and appealed to the King, with the result that the baby was baptised again, this time at St. Margaret's, Westminster. The immediate result of this rumpus was that the indignant wife left her husband, and, tak-ing her children with her, went to stay with her uncle, Colonel Edmund Villiers, who lived at Richmond Palace. Pepys, on July 16, had, almost as a matter of course, something to say of this occur-rence: "This day, I was told that my Lady Castlemaine (being quite fallen out with her husband) did go away from him, with all her plate, jewels, and other best things; and is gone to Richmond to a brother of hers; which, I am apt to think, was a design to get out of town, that the King might come at her better. But strange it is how for her beauty I am willing to construe all this to the best and to pity her wherein it is to her hurt, though I know well enough she is a whore." The diarist returned to the subject ten days later: "Mrs. Sarah told me how the falling out between Lady Castlemaine and her Lord was about christening of the child lately, which he would have, and had done by a priest: and some days after, she had it again christened by a minister; the King and Lord of Oxford and Duchess of Suffolk being witnesses. Since that she left her Lord, carrying away everything in the house, so much as every desk, and cloth, and servant but the por-ter. He is gone discontented into France, they say, to enter a monastery; and now she is coming back to her house in King Street." As a matter of fact, Lord Castlemaine did go abroad after this quarrel. He travelled not only in France, but also in Italy, and he

presently cruised in the Levant in the Venetian squadron commanded by Cornaro. While away, he wrote "An Account of the
Present War between the Venetians and the Turks; with the State of
Candia" in a letter to the King (Charles II) from Venice, which was
published in London in 1666, and was paid the compliment of translation into Dutch and German. He also served in the Duke of York's
fleet during the Dutch war of 1665 to 1667, on which he wrote in
French a memoir, that was translated into English by Thomas Price
under the title of "A Short and True Account of the Material Passages
in the late war between the English and Dutch," [1671] which
achieved the distinction of running into a second edition. Lord Castlemaine formally separated from his wife in 1668, and his
subsequent career is beyond the scope of this volume.

The story may be carried on by extracts from Pepys's diary:

October 24, 1662. "This noon came to see me and sat with me a little after dinner Mr. Pierce the Chyrugeon, who tells me how ill things
go at Court: that the King do show no countenance to any that belong
to the Queen; nor, above all, to such English as she brought over with
her, or hath here since, for fear they should tell her how he carries
himself to Mrs. Palmer; insomuch that though he has a promise and
is sure of being made her [Majesty's] chyrugeon, he is at a loss what
to do in it, whether to take it or no, since the King's mind is so altered
in favour to all her dependants, whom she is fain to let go back into
Portugal (though she brought them from their friends against their
wills with promise of preferment), without doing anything for them.
But he tells me that her own physician did tell him within these three
days that the Queen do know how the King orders things, and how
he carries himself to my Lady Castlemaine and others, as well as any
body; but though she has spirit enough, yet seeing that she can do no
good by taking notice of it, for the present she forbears it in policy; of
which I am very glad."

November 3, 1662. "I met with Pierce the chyrugeon, who tells me
that my Lady Castlemaine is with child; but though it be the King's,
yet her Lord being still in town, and sometimes seeing of her; though
never to eat or lie together, it will be laid to him."

December 15, 1662. "Sir Charles Berkeley's greatness is only his being pimp to the King and to my Lady Castlemaine."

December 31, 1662. "The King is bringing, as is said, his family, and Navy, and all other his charges, to a less expense. In the meantime, himself following his pleasures more than with good advice he would do; at least, to be seen to all the world to do so. His dalliance with my Lady Castlemaine becoming public, every day, to his great reproach; and his favours of none at Court as much as those that are the confidants of his pleasure, as Sir H. Bennet and Sir Charles Berkeley...

"The Duke of Monmouth is in so great splendour at Court, and so dandled by the King, that some doubt, if the King should have no child by the Queen (which there is yet no appearance of), whether he would not be acknowledged for a lawful son; and that there will be a difference follow on it between the Duke of York and him; which God prevent."

When Lady Castlemaine had recovered from her confinement the King brought her to Court—on August 23 (1663)—to the great delight of Pepys, who would appear to have been somewhat in love with the lady himself. "What pleased me best," he wrote about this occasion, "was that my Lady Castlemaine stood over against us upon a piece of White Hall, when I glutted myself with looking on her. But methinks it was strange to see her Lord and her upon the same place walking up and down without taking notice one of another, only at first entry he took off his hat, and she made him a very civil salute, but afterwards took no notice one of another; but both of them now and then would take their child, which the nurse took in her arms, and dandled it. One thing more: there happened a scaffold below to fall, and we feared some hurt, but there was none, but she of all the great ladies only run down among the common rabble to see what hurt was done, and did take care of a child that received some little hurt, which methought was so noble. Anon there came one there booted and spurred that she talked long with. And, by and by, she being in her hair, she put on his hat, which was but an ordinary one, to keep the wind off. But methinks it became her mightily, as every thing else do. The show being over, I went away, not weary with looking on her."

Catherine was furious when Lady Castlemaine came to Court — this was before she had given her consent. "The Queen," says Clarendon, "was no longer sate in her chair, but her colour changed, and tears gushed out of her eyes, and her nose bled, and she fainted, so that she was forthwith removed to another room, and all the company retired out of that where she was before." However, her Majesty was utterly helpless in this matter, though she endeavoured to make conditions. "All things are bad with reference to Lady Castlemaine," Clarendon wrote on September 9, 1662, "but I think not quite so bad as you hear. Everybody takes her to be of the Bedchamber, for she is always there and goes abroad in the coach. But the Queen tells me that the King 'promised, her, on condition she would use her as she hath others, 'that she should never live in Court'; yet lodgings I think she hath; I hear of no back stairs. The worst is, the King is as discomposed as ever, and looks as little after business, which breaks my heart. He seeks satisfaction in other company; who do not love him as well as you and I do."

However, in the end, the Queen yielded; and in September — only a few months after she had been married — Pepys recorded: "At Somerset House I also saw Madam Castlemaine, and, which pleased me most, Mr. Crofts, the King's bastard, a most pretty spark of about fifteen years old, who, I perceive do hang much upon my Lady Castlemaine, and is always with her; and, I hear, the Queen, both of them, are mighty kind to him.... They stayed till it was dark, and then went away, the King and his Queen, and my Lady Castlemaine and young Crofts, in one coach, and the rest in other coach."

"Young Crofts" was James, son of Charles II by Lucy Walter, daughter of William Walter, of Booh Castle, co. Pembroke. He was born in April 1649, and was brought to England after the Restoration by the Queen-Mother, at which time he bore the surname of Crofts (afterwards Lord Crofts), which was that of his Governor. The young man made such violent love to the royal mistress, that Charles hurried on his son's marriage to the Countess of Buccleugh, which happy event took place in April 1663. Some weeks before, "Mr.

Crofts" had been raised to the peerage as Duke of Monmouth, with precedence over all Dukes not of royal blood.

There is another version of the affair, given by Anthony Hamilton. "The Duchess of Cleveland," he wrote in the *Memoirs of Grammont*, "was out of humour with the King, because the children she had by his Majesty were like so many puppets, compared to this new Adonis. She was the more particularly hurt, as she might have boasted of being the Queen of Love, in comparison with the Duke's mother. The King, however, laughed at her reproaches, as, for some time, she had certainly no right to make any; and, as this piece of jealousy appeared to be the more ill-founded than any she had formerly affected, no person approved of her ridiculous resentment. Not succeeding in this, she formed another scheme to give the King uneasiness. Instead of opposing his extreme tenderness for his son, she pretended to adopt him in her affection by a thousand commendations and caresses, which she was daily and continually increasing. As these endearments were public, she imagined they could not be suspected; but she was too well known for her real design to be mistaken. The King was no longer jealous of her; but as the Duke of Monmouth was of an age not to be insensible to the attractions of a woman possessing so many charms, he thought it proper to withdraw him from this pretended mother-in-law, to preserve his innocence, or at least his fame, uncontaminated: it was for this reason that, therefore, the King married him so young." As a matter of fact, the lady was at this time (1663) twenty-two years of age, and the lad was but fourteen. In the year that the Duke of Monmouth married, Catherine had an illness that nearly proved fatal. "The Queen," Anthony Hamilton wrote, "was given over by her physicians, the few Portuguese women who had not been sent back to their own country filled the Court with doleful cries; and the good nature of the King was much affected with the situation in which he saw a princess whom, though he did not love her, yet he greatly esteemed. She loved him tenderly, and thinking that it was the last time she should ever speak to him she told him that 'the concern he showed for her death was enough to make her quit life with regret, but that, not possessing charms sufficient to merit his tenderness, she had at least the consolation in dying to give place to a consort who might be more worthy of it, and to whom Heaven perhaps might grant a blessing that had been refused to her.' At these words she bathed his hands with some tears, which he thought would be her last; he mingled his own with hers, and, without supposing she would take him at his word, he conjured her to live for his sake. "It was at the time of this illness that the French Ambassador in London. wrote to his Monarch: "I am just come from Whitehall, where I left the Queen in a state in which, according to the doctors, there is little room for hope. She received extreme unction this morning…. The King seems to me deeply affected. He supped, nevertheless, yesterday evening at Madame de Castlemaine's, and had his usual conversations with Mademoiselle Stuart, of whom he is very fond. Everyone gives him a second wife according to his inclination, and there are some who do not look for her out of England." As will presently be mentioned in more detail, the general opinion was that the King, had his Consort died, would have sought in marriage Frances Stuart. Lady Castlemaine, who was far from a stupid woman, did not seek to intervene. In fact, it would appear that she was prepared to bring the King and Miss Stuart together, if by so doing she could keep her influence over his Majesty.

Pepys continued to record all he saw or heard about Lady Castlemaine, indeed, nothing about her was too trivial to insert in his Diary.

February 1, 1663. "This day Creed and I walking in Whitehall Garden did see the King coming privately from my Lady Castlemaine's; which is a poor thing for a Prince to do, and I expressed my sense of it to Creed in terms which I should not have done, but that I believe he is trusty in that point."

February 8, 1663. "Another story was how my Lady Castlemaine, a few days since, had Mrs. Stuart to an entertainment, and at night began a frolic that they two must be married, and married they were, with ring and all other ceremonies of Church Service, and ribbands and a sack posset in bed, and flinging the stocking; but in the close, it is said that my Lady Castlemaine, who was the bridegroom, rose, and the King came and took her place with Mrs. Stuart. This is said to be very true."

February 23, 1663. "This day I was told that my Lady Castlemaine hath all the King's Christmas presents, made him by the peers, given to her, which is a most abominable thing, and that at the great ball she was much richer in jewels than the Queen and the Duchess [of York] put both together."

March 7, 1663. "Creed told me how some words of my Lady Gerard's, against my Lady Castlemaine, to the Queen, the King did the other day affront her in going out to dance with her at a ball, when she desired it as the ladies do, and is since forbid attending the Queen by the King; which is much talked of, my Lord her husband being a great favourite."

April 25, 1663. "Lastly I did hear that the Queen is much grieved of late at the King's neglecting her, he having not supped with her this quarter of a year, and almost every night with my Lady Castlemaine; who has been with him this St. George's feast at Windsor, and came home with him last night; and, which is more, they say is removed as to her bed from her own home to a chamber in Whitehall, next to the King's own, which I am sorry to hear, though I love her much."

June 13, 1663. "In our way we saw my Lady Castlemaine, who, I fear, is not so handsome as I have taken her for, and now she begins to decay something. This is my wife's opinion; for which I am sorry."

July 3, 1663. "Mr. Moore tells me great news that Lady Castlemaine is fallen from Court, and is this day retired. He gives me no account of the reason of it, but that it is so: for which I am sorry: and yet if the King do it to leave off not only her but all other mistresses, I should be heartily glad of it, that he may fall to look after business."

In July Pepys hears from Pierce that "for certain the King is grown colder to my Lady Castlemaine than ordinary, and that he believes he begins to love the Queen, do make much of her, more than he used to do." Charles, however, if in love with anybody, was in love with Frances Stuart, which accounted for his temporary neglect of his mistress: "Here also my Lady Castlemaine rode among the rest of the ladies; but the King took, methought, no notice of her, nor when they 'light did anybody press (as she seemed to express and staid for it) to take her down, but was taken down by her own gentleman. She looked mighty out of humour, and had a yellow plume in her hat (which all took notice of), and yet is very handsome, but very melancholy: nor did any body speak. to her, or she so much as smile or speak to body." Lady Castlemaine was not a woman to put up with any nonsense of this kind, and, knowing her power over the King, took a line that in a short time brought him back to his allegiance. "Captain Ferrers tells me that my Lady Castlemaine is now as great again at Court as ever she was," Pepys noted on July 22, "and that her going away was only a fit of her own upon some slighting words of the King, so that she called for her coach at a quarter of an hour's warning, and went to Richmond; and the King the next morning, under pretext of going hunting, went to see her and make friends, and never was a-hunting at all. After which she came "back to Court, and commands the King as much as ever, and hath and doth what she will. No longer ago than last night, there was a private entertainment made for the King and Queen at the Duke of Buckingham's, and she was not invited: but being at my Lady Suffolk's, her aunt's (where my Lady Jemimah and Lord Sandwich dined) she was heard to say, 'Well, much good may it do them, and for all that I will be as merry as they': and so she went home and caused a great supper to be prepared. And after the King had been with the Queen at Wallingford House [the London residence of the Duke of Buckingham], he came to my Lady Castlemaine's, and was there all night, and my Lord Sandwich with him, which was the reason, my Lord lay in town all night, which he has not done a great while before. He tells me he believes that, as soon as the King can get a husband for Mrs. Stuart, however, my Lady Castlemaine's nose will be out of joint: for that she comes to be in great esteem, and is more handsome than she."

In October of the same year, Lady Castlemaine was in as great favour as ever. On the very first evening after Charles returned to London after a visit to Bath he supped with her, and visited her two other nights in the week.

About this time the Queen was ill, and Charles was much distressed, and sat by her bedside every day, but his anxiety did not prevent his supping every evening with Lady Castlemaine. He was especially distressed that Catherine had not given him a child. More than once there had been hope that she was with child, but these hopes were always disappointed. There was, naturally, much anxiety about the succession to the throne, and the matter was the subject of much thought. Some advocated a divorce, or, at least, a dissolution of the marriage. "This morning," Pepys wrote on September 7, 1667, "I was told by Sir W. Batten that he do hear from Mr. Grey, who hath good intelligence, that our Queen is to go into a nunnery, there to spend her days; and that my Lady Castlemaine is going into France, and is to have a pension of £4000 a year. This latter I do believe more than the other, it being very wise in her to do it, and save all she hath, besides easing the King and kingdom of a burden and reproach." As a matter of fact, neither of these things came to pass.

The relations between Charles and Lady Castlemaine continued, and towards the end of the year she had by him another son, George Fitzroy. It was about this time that the scandal spread among the lower classes, and the following lampoons written after the destruction of the brothels by the London apprentices in March 1665 give an idea of the estimation in which the lady was held.

"The Poor W — es' Petition to the most Splendid, Illustrious, Serene, and Eminent Lady of Pleasure, the Countess of Castlemaine, etc.

"Humbly sheweth,

"That your Petitioners having for a long time conniv'd at, and countenanced in the practice of our... pleasure (a trade wherein your Ladyship has great experience, and for your diligence therein, have arrived to a high and eminent advancement for these late years), but now, we through the rage and malice of a company of London apprentices and other malicious and very bad persons, being mechanic, rude and ill-bred boys, have sustained the loss of our habitations, trades and employments .... Will your Eminence therefore be pleased to consider how highly it concerns you to restore us to our former practice with honour, freedom and safety; for which we shall oblige ourselves by as many Oaths as you please, to contribute to your Ladyship (as our sisters do at Rome and Venice to his Holiness the

Pope) that we may have your protection in the exercise of all our ...
pleasures. And we shall endeavour, as our bounded duty, the pro-
moting of your great name and the preservation of your honour,
safety and interest, with the hazard of our lives, fortunes and hon-
esty.

"Signed by us, Madam Cresswell and Damaris Page, in the behalf
of our sisters and fellow sufferers (in this day of our calamity) in Dog
and Bitch Yard, Lukeners Lane, Saffron Hill, Moor-fields, Chiswell
Street, Rosemary Lane, Nightingale Lane, Ratcliffe Highway, Well
Close, Church Lane, East Smithfield, etc., this present 25th day of
March, 1668."

"The Gracious Answer of the most Illustrious *Lady of Pleasure*, the
*Countess of Castlemaine*...


"*To the Poor-Whores' Petition.*

"Right Trusty and Well-beloved Madam Cresswell and Damaris
Page, with the rest of the suffering Sisterhood in *Dog and Bitch Yard,
Lukeners Lane, Saffron-Hill, Moor-fields, Ratcliffe-Highway*, etc. We greet
you well, in giving you to understand our Noble Mind, by returning
our thanks which you are worthy of, in sending us our Titles of Honour, which are but our Due. For on Shrove-Tuesday last, splendidly
did we appear upon the theatre at W. H., being to amazement wonderfully deck'd with Jewels and Diamonds, which the (abhorred and
to be undone) Subjects of this Kingdom have payed for. We have
been also Serene and illustrious ever since the Day that *Mars* was so
instrumental to restore our Goddess Venus to her Temple and Worship; where by special grant, we quickly became a famous Lady: And
as a Reward of our Devotion, soon created the Right Honourable, the
Countess of Castlemain. And as further addition to our illustrious
Serenity, according to the ancient Rules and laudable Customs of our
Order, we have cum privilegio alwayes (without our Husband) satisfied our self with the Delights of Venus, and in our Husbands
absence have had a numerous off-spring (who are Bountifully and
Nobly provided for), which practice hath Episcopal Allowance also,
according to the Principles of Seer Shelden, etc. *If Women hath not*

*children by their own Husbands, they are bound (to prevent their Damna-tion) to try by using the means'with other men*: which wholesome and pleasing Doctrine did for some time hold me fast to his Religion. But since this Seer hath shewn more Cowardize, than Principles of Policy, in fearing to declare the Church of *Rome* to be the True, Ancient, Uni-form, Universall and most Holy Mother Church; therefore we tell you (with all the Sisterhood) that we are now no longer of the Church of *England*, which is but like a Brazen Bison tied to a Barber's wooden Pole, (viz.) Protestant Doctrine and Order tied by Parliamentary Power to Roman Catholick Foundations, Constitutions, and Rights, etc. And are become a Convert to, and a professed Member of the Church of Rome; where the worthy Fathers and Confessors, as Du-randus, Gentianus, with multitudes of others, (who were not; neither are, of the Protestant, Puritanical, and Fanatical, Conventicling Opin-ion) do declare *That Venereal Pleasures, accompanied with Looseness, Debauchery, and Prophaneness, are not such heynous crimes* and crying Sins, but rather (as the old woman of *Loren* said) *they do mortifie the Flesh.* And the general Opinion of Holy Mother Church is, *That Ven-erial Pleasures, in the strictest sence, are but Venial Sins, which Confessor of the meanest Order can forgive.* So that the adoring of Venus, is by the Allowance of Great Authority, Desirable, Honourable and Profitable.

"But when we understood, in your Address, the Barbarity of those Rude Apprentices, and the cruel Sufferings that the Sisterhood was exposed unto, especially those which were in a hopeful way of Recovery and others that were disabled from giving Accommodation to their Right Honourable Devotaries, with the danger which you convinced us our own Person was in, together with the remembrance of our two new Corivals with *Little Miss*: We were for many Hours swallowed up with Sorrow, and almost drowned in. Tears and could not all be comforted until the sweet sound of the Report came to our Ears, *That the L. C. J. K. and his Brethren, with our Counsel learned in the Law, had Commission and Instruction given to frame a Bill of Indictment against the trayterous and Rebellious Boys, and to select a Jury of Gentle-men that should shew* them no favour: At which our Noble Spirit revived, and presently we consulted how we might express our Grace and Compassion towards you, and also seasonably provide for the future safety of your practice and exercise our Revenge upon those that so grossly abused you, and therein offered such an insufferable Affront to our Eminency, that we cannot bear without great indignation.

"*Item.* To any other then here directed, give no Entertainment without Ready Money, lest you suffer Loss. For had we not been careful in that particular, we had neither gained Honour nor Rewards, which are now (as you know) both conferred upon Us.

"*Given at our Closet in King Street, Westminster, Die Veneris, April 24, 1668.*

"CASTLEM...."

In spite of his waning affection for Lady Castlemaine, Charles continued to shower gifts upon her. While he philandered with other frail beauties, she avenged herself with an affair with Sir Henry Jermyn which particularly infuriated the King, who declared that he would not admit his paternity of her next child. To this she replied with spirited audacity, that if he continued in his threat, she would bring the child to Whitehall and dash out its brains there. Of course the easy-going monarch gave way on this point, and even went so far as to placate the lady by a gift of five or six ounces of plate from the royal jewel-house.

Anthony Hamilton, in the *Memoirs of Grammont*, has something to say of this and the lady's other affairs:

"It was above a year since Jermyn had triumphed over the weakness of Lady Castlemaine, and above two since the King had been weary of his triumphs: his uncle being one of the first who perceived the King's disgust, obliged him to absent himself from Court, at the very time that orders were going to be issued for that purpose; for though the King's affections for Lady Castlemaine were now greatly diminished, yet he did not think it consistent with his dignity that a mistress, whom he had honoured with public distinction, and who still received a considerable support from him, should appear chained to the car of the most ridiculous conqueror that ever existed. His Majesty had frequently expostulated with the Countess upon this subject: but his expostulations were never attended to; it was in one of these differences that he, advising her rather to bestow her favours upon Jacob Hall, the rope-dancer, who was able to return them, than lavish away her money upon Jermyn to no purpose, since it would be more honourable for her to pass for the mistress 6f the first, than for the very humble servant of the other, she was not. proof against his raillery. The impetuosity of her temper broke forth like lightning: she told him 'that it very ill became him to throw out such reproaches against one, who, of all the women in England, deserved them the least: that he had never ceased quarrelling thus unjustly with her, ever since he had betrayed his Own mean low inclinations; that to gratify such a depraved taste as his, he wanted only such silly things as Stuart, Wells, and that pitiful strolling actress [Nell Gwyn], whom he had lately introduced into their society.' Floods of tears, from rage, generally attended these storms; after which resuming the part of Medea, the scene closed with menaces of tearing her children in pieces, and setting his palace on fire. What course could he pursue with such an outrageous fury, who, beautiful as she was, resembled Medea less than her dragons, when she was thus enraged!

"The indulgent Monarch loved peace; and as he seldom contended for it on these occasions without paying something to obtain it, he was obliged to be at great expense, in order to reconcile this last rupture: as they could not agree of themselves, and both parties complained, the Chevalier de Grammont was chosen, by mutual consent, mediator of the treaty. The grievances and pl"etensions on each side were communicated to him, and what is very extraordinary, he managed so as to please them both. Here follow the articles of peace, which they agreed to:

"'That Lady Castlemaine should for ever abandon Jermyn; that as a proof of her sincerity, and the reality of his disgrace, she should consent to his being sent, for some time into the country; that she should not rail any more against Miss Wells, nor storm against Miss Stuart; and this without restraint on the King's behaviour towards her: that in consideration of these condescensions, his Majesty should immediately give her the title of duchess with all the honours and privileges thereunto belonging, and an addition to her pension, in order to enable her to support the dignity.'

"As soon as this peace was proclaimed, the political critics, who in all_ nations, never fail to censure all state proceedings, pretended that the mediator of this treaty, being every day at play with Lady Castlemaine and never losing, had for his own sake, insisted a little too strongly upon this last article."

When Charles presently became the lover of Moll Davis, and Nell Gwyn, his *maîtresse en titre* [mistress in title] bestowed her favours on Charles Hart. There were violent quarrels, but the victory was almost invariably with Lady Castlemaine. About this time, in 1668, Charles gave her Berkshire House, St. James's, which, being always financially embarrassed owing to her extravagance, she sold as building land, reserving only a portion of the gardens on which, at enormous expense, she erected Cleveland House, which considerable mansion was, almost as a matter of course, furnished at the royal expense. It proves her influence that in the following year she received a grant of nearly £5000 a year chargeable upon the revenues of the Post Office; and in 1670 was created Baroness Nonsuch of Nonsuch Park, Surrey, Countess of Southampton, and Duchess of Cleveland, with remainder to her first and third natural sons, Charles and George. It is interesting as throwing a sidelight on the period that these titles, according to the patent, were bestowed on her in consideration of "her personal virtue." It would be tedious to give in detail the grants that were conferred upon her. "Lord St. John, Sir R. Howard, Sir John Bennet, and Sir W. Bicknell, the brewer," Andrew Marvell wrote, "have farmed the Customs; they have signed and sealed ten thousand a year more to the Duchess of Cleveland, who has likewise near ten thousand a year out of the new favour of the County Excise of beer and ale; £5000 a year out of the PostOffice, and, they say, the revenues of all places in the Custom-House, the Green Wax, and, indeed, what not, all promotions spiritual and temporal, pass under her cognisance."

In spite of a vast income, so heavy were the expenses of the Duchess that soon she was compelled to remove from Cleveland House to a more humble residence, and to sell the contents of Nonsuch House, which the King had settled upon her. Her lovers cost her a small fortune, and added considerably to her pension list.

These lovers were of all classes. The most respectable of these was John Ellis, a man two years her junior, who at one time engaged in diplomacy, and became an Under-Secretary. The intrigue was, of course, the talk of Society.' In a poem called "The Town Life," he was perhaps a little unfairly, in connection with this affair, described as "that epitome of lewdness, Ellys"; and Pope had something to say about him in "Sober Advice from Horace." Ellis did not reign solitary in the Duchess's affections. There was, as a contrast to him, one Jacob Hall, a rope-dancer, whom, it is said, her Grace discovered in a booth at Bartholomew Fair, and to whom she granted her utmost favours. As a rope-dancer he was excellent, and he must have had qualities as a lover, for the Duchess fell "mightily in love" with him, and gave him a pension. "He seems," says Pepys, "a mighty strong man." Her Grace, further, took unto herself as a lover John Churchill, afterwards famous as the first Duke of Marlborough, who, rightly or wrongly, was believed to be the father of the Duchess's third daughter, Barbara, who was born in the summer of 1672.

"The Duchess of Cleveland," says Anthony Hamilton, "had been brought to bed while the Court was at Bristol, and never before had she recovered from her lying-in with such a profusion of charm. This made her believe that she was in a proper state to retrieve her ancient rights over the King's heart, if she had an opportunity of appearing before him with his increased splendour. Her friends being of the same opinion, her equipage was prepared for this expedition, but the very evening before the day she had fixed on to set out, she saw young Churchill, and was at once seized with a disease, which had more than once opposed her projects, and which she could never completely get the better of."

There is a story that the King paid an unexpected visit to the Duchess, at the mischievous instigation of Buckingham. Churchill leapt out of the window, but Charles recognised him, and called after him in his delightful cynical manner, "I forgive you, for you do it for your bread." But what he said to the lady has not transpired. Perhaps his Majesty's remark had much of truth in it, for shortly after the young soldier, who was notoriously impoverished, received £5000, with which he purchased an annuity from George Savile, Marquis of

Halifax, which, since he lived till 1722, proved to be an excellent investment.

Then came William Wycherley. The story of the intrigue between him and the Duchess has been told by George Steinman. "In 1672, William Wycherley brought on the stage the first play. The Duchess of Cleveland was so well pleased with the compliment paid to natural children in a song introduced into *Love in a Wood*, as to honour the performance of it with her presence on two consecutive nights. Meeting the author — young (he was only thirty-two), handsome, manly, and brawny — when riding in her chariot in Pall Mall, she leaned half her body out of it, and laughing aloud, in this manner addressed him, but her salutation and the dialogue which followed shall be given in the words of Dennis: 'You, Wycherley,' said she, 'you are the son of a whore.' The saluted passed on in his chariot, and having recovered from his surprise, ordered the coachman to turn back and overtake the Duchess. When this was accomplished, 'Madam,' said he, 'you have been pleased to bestow a title on me which generally belongs to the Fortunate. Will your Ladyship be at the Play tonight? 'Well,' she replied, 'what if I am there?' 'Why, then I shall be there to wait on your Ladyship, tho' I disappoint a very fine woman who has made me an assignation!' 'So,' said she, 'you are sure to disappoint a woman, who has favour'd you for me who has not!' 'Yes,' he reply'd, 'if she who has not favour'd me is the finer woman of the two. But he who will be constant to your Ladyship till he can find a finer woman is sure to die your captive.' The lady is said to have blushed at this speech. The captive and the captor met the same night at Drury Lane Theatre, she sitting in the front row of the King's box, he in the pit, whence he entertained her during the whole play. The intimacy between the couple endangered Wycherley's hopes of preferment at Court. The Duke of Buckingham had for some time engaged spies to watch the Duchess, and had it not been for the intercession of the Earl of Rochester and Sir Charles Sedley, his tongue would have aroused Charles's anger against him. As it came to pass, the favours of the mistress were followed by the favours of the King."

After the passing of the Test Act [1] in 1673, the Duchess, who had become a Roman Catholic ten years earlier, was removed from her post as Lady of the Bedchamber to the Queen. She had little more to hope for from the bounty of the King, and she, in 1677, paid a visit to Paris. "This morning," Pepys wrote in September 1677, "was told that my Lady Castlemaine is going into France, and is to have a pension of £4000 a year." At Paris the Duchess had an intrigue with the English Ambassador there, Ralph Montagu (afterwards Duke of Montagu). Montagu had been Chamberlain to the Queen, who asked the King (having never had an admirer before nor after) what people meant by squeezing one by the hand; the King told her, love; "then," said she, "Mr. Montagu loves me mightily." Upon which he was turned out. Pepys mentions that, "they say the King himself once asked Montagu how his mistress did." The Ambassador is mentioned by Burnet: "Montagu, that was a man of pleasure, was in a lewd intrigue with the Duchess of Cleveland, who was quite cast off by the King, and was then in 1678 in Paris. The King had ordered him to find an astrologer, of whom, no wonder, he had a good opinion, for he had long before his restoration foretold he should enter London on the 29th of May, 1660. He was yet alive, and Montagu found him, and saw him a man capable of being corrupted. So he prompted him to send the King such hints as should serve his own ends, and he was so bewitched with Cleveland, that he trusted her with this secret.

But she, growing jealous of a new amour, took all the ways she could think of to ruin him, reserving this of the astrologer for her last shift: and by it she compassed her ends, for the King looked on this as such a piece of treachery and folly, that Mr. Montagu was entirely lost upon it, and was recalled, Sunderland being sent over Ambassador in his room." As a matter of fact, it was the Duchess who

---

[1] The several Test Acts were a series of English penal laws that imposed various civil disabilities on Roman Catholics and nonconformists. The principle that none but persons professing the established religion were eligible for public employment was adopted by the legislatures of both England and Scotland soon after the Reformation. In England the Acts of Supremacy and Uniformity and the severe penalties denounced against recusants, whether Roman Catholic or Nonconformist, were affirmations of this principle. The Act of James I provided that all such as were naturalized or restored in blood should receive the sacrament of the Lord's Supper.

revealed to Charles his Ambassador's opinion of him. This was her revenge for Montagu having transferred his affection from her to her eldest daughter, Lady Sussex. Montagu went to London to defend himself, but met with a cold reception at Court. The treachery of the Duchess did her no service with the King, as the following correspondence shows.

> "WHITEHALL,
> "Feb. 28, 1678.

"I have already given you my reasons at large, why I think it fit that you should absent yourself for some time beyond sea: as I am truly sorry for the occasion, so you may be sure I shall desire it no longer than it will be absolutely necessary both for your good and. my service. In the meantime I think it proper to give you notice under my hand that I expect this compliance from you, and desire that you may believe with what trouble I write this to you, there being nothing I am more sensible of, than the constant kindness you have ever had for me; and I hope you are so just as to think nothing can ever change me from being

> "Truly and kindly
> "Yours,
> "CHAS. REX."

> "PARIS,
> "Tuesday, 28, 1678.

"I was never so surprised in my whole life time as I was, at my coming hither, to find my Lady Sussex gone from my house and monastery where I left her, and this letter from her, which I here send you the copy of. I never saw in my whole life time such government of herself as she has had, since I went into England. She has never been in the monastery two days together, but every day gone out with the Ambassador; and has often lain four days together at my house, and sent for her meat to the Ambassador, he being always with her till five o'clock in the morning, they two shut up together alone, and would not let any maître d'hôtel wait, nor any of my servants, only the Ambassador's. This made so great a noise at Paris, that she is now the whole discourse. I am so much afflicted, that I can hardly write this for crying, to see a child that I doted on as I did on her, should make so ill return, and join with the worst of men to ruin me. For sure never malice was like the Ambassador's, that only because I would not answer to his love, and the importunities he made to me, was resolved to ruin me. I hope your Majesty will yet have that justice and consideration for me, that though I have done a foolish action, you will not let me be ruined by this most abominable man. I do confess to you that I did write a foolish letter to the Chevalier de Châtillon, which letter I sent enclosed to Madame de Pallas, and sent hers in a packet I sent to Lady Sussex by Sir Henry Tichborn; which letter she has either given to the Ambassador, or else he had it by his man, to whom Sir Henry Tichbom gave it, not finding my Lady Sussex. But as yet I do not know which of the ways he had it, but I shall know as soon as I have spoken with Sir Henry Tichborn. But the letter he has, and I doubt not but he has or will send it to you. Now all I have to say for myself is, that you know as to love, one is not mistress of one's self, and that you ought not be offended with me, since all things of this nature is at an end with you and me, so that I could do you no prejudice. Nor will you, I hope, follow the advice of this ill man, who in his heart I know hates you, and were it not for his interest would ruin you if he could. For he has neither conscience nor honour, and has several times told me, that in his heart he despised you and your brother; and that for his part, he wished with all his heart that the Parliament would send you both to travel, for you were a dull governable fool, and the Duke a wilful fool. So that it were yet better to have you than him, but that you always chose a greater beast than yourself to govern you. And when I was to come over, he brought me two letters to bring to you, which he read both to me before he sealed them. The one was a man's, that he said you had great faith in; for that he had at several times foretold things to you that were of consequence, and that you believed him in all things, like a changeling as you were. And that now he had written you word, that in a few months the King of France and his son were threatened with death, or at least with a great fit of sickness, in which they would be in great danger, if they did not die; and that therefore he counselled you to defer any resolutions either of war or peace till some months were past, for that if this happened, it would make a great change in France. The Ambassador, after he had read this to me, said, 'Now the good of this is,' said he, that I can do what I will with this man; for he is poor, and a good sum of money will make him write whatever I will.' So he proposed to me that he and I should join together in the ruin of my Lord Treasurer and the Duchess of Portsmouth, which might be done thus: The man, though he was infirm and ill, should go into England, and there, after having been a little time, to solicit you for money; for that you were so base, that although you employed him, you let him starve; so that he was obliged to give him £50, and that the man had written several times to you for money. And, says he, when he is in England, he shall tell the King things that he foresees will infallibly ruin him; and so wish those to be removed, as having an ill-star, that would be unfortunate to you if they were not removed: but if that were done, he was confident you would have the most glorious reign that ever was. This, says he, I am sure I can order so as to bring to good effect, if you will. And in the meantime I will try to get Secretary Coventry's place, which he has a mind to part with, but not to Sir William Temple, because he is the Treasurer's creature, and he hates the Treasurer; and I have already employed my sister to talk with Mr. Cook, and to mind to engage Mr. Coventry not to part with it as yet, and he has assured my Lady Harvey he will not. And my Lord Treasurer's lady and Mr. Bertie are both of them desirous I should have it. And when I have it, I will be damned if I do not quickly get to be Lord Treasurer; and then you and your children shall find such a friend as never was. And for the King, I will find a way to furnish him so easily with money, for his pocket and wenches, that we will quickly out Bab [Baptist May]. Nay, and lead the King by the nose. So when I had heard him out, I told him I thanked him, but that I would not meddle with any such thing: and that, for my part, I had no malice to my Lady Portsmouth, or to the Treasurer, and therefore would never be in any plot to destroy them. But that I found the character which the world gave him was true: which was, that the Devil was not more designing than he was, and that I wondered at it; for sure all these things working in his brain made him very uneasy, and would at last make him mad. It is possible you may think I say this out of malice. It is true he has urged me beyond all patience: but what I tell you here is most true; and I will take the sacrament on it whenever you please. It is certain I would not have been so base as to have informed against him for what he had said before me, had he not provoked to it in this violent way that he has. There is no ill thing which he has not done me, and that without any provocation of mine, but that I would not love him. Now, as to what relates to my daughter Sussex, and her behaviour to me, I must confess that afflicts me beyond expression, and will do much more, if what he has done be by your orders. For though I have an entire submission to your will, and will not complain whatever you inflict upon me, yet I cannot think you would have brought things to this extremity with me, and not have it in your nature ever to do cruel things to any thing living. I hope you will not therefore begin with me: and if the Ambassador has not received his orders from you, that you will severely reprehend him for the inhuman proceeding. Besides, he has done what you ought to be very angry with him for. For he has been with the King of France, and told him that he had intercepted letters of mine by your order; by which he had been informed that there was a kindness between me and the Chevalier de Châtillon; and therefore you bade him take a course in it, and stop my letters; which accordingly he has done. And that upon this you ordered him to take my children from me, and to remove my Lady Sussex to another monastery, and that you were resolved to stop all my pensions; and never to have any regard to me in any thing. And that if he would oblige your Majesty, he should forbid the Chevalier de Châtillon ever seeing me, upon the displeasure of losing his place, and being forbidden the Court, for he was sure you expected this from him. Upon which the King told him, that he could not do any thing of this nature: for that this was a private matter, and not for him to take notice of. And that he could not imagine that you ought to be so angry, or indeed be at all concerned; for that all the world knew, that now all things of gallantry were at an end with you and me. And that being so, and so public, he did not see why you should be offended at my loving anybody. That it was a thing so common now-a-days to have a gallantry, that he did not wonder at any thing of this nature. And when he saw the King take the thing thus, he told him if he would not be severe with the Chevalier de Châtillon upon your account, he supposed he would be so upon his own: for that in the letters he had discovered, he had found that the Chevalier had proposed to me the engaging of you in the marriage of the Dauphin and Mademoiselle: and that was my greatest business in England. That before I went over, I had spoken to him of the thing and would have engaged him in it; but that he refused it: for that he knew very well the indifference you had whether it was so or no, and how little you cared how Mademoiselle was married: that since I went into England it was possible I might engage somebody or other in this matter to press it to you; but that he knew very well, that in your heart you cared not whether it was so or no: that this business was set on foot by the Chevalier. Upon which the King told him, that if he would show him any letters of the Chevalier de Châtillon to that purpose, he should then know what he had to say to him, but till he saw those letters he would not punish him without a proof of what he did. Upon which the Ambassador showed a letter, which he pretended one part of it was *double entendre*. The King said he could not see that there was anything relating to it, and so left him, and said to a person there, 'Sure the Ambassador was the worst man that ever was; for because my Lady Cleveland will not love him, he strives to ruin her the basest in the world, and would have me sacrifice the Chevalier de Châtillon to his revenge; which I shall not do, till I see better proofs of his having meddled in the marriage of the Dauphin and Mademoiselle than any yet the Ambassador has shown me.' This methinks is what you cannot be offended at, and I hope you will be offended with him for his whole proceeding to me, and let the world see you will never countenance the action of so base and ill a man. I had forgot to tell you that he told the King of France, that many people had reported that he had made love to me; but there was nothing of it, for that he had too much respect for you to think of any such thing. As for my Lady Sussex, I hope you will think fit to send for her over, for she is now mightily discoursed of for the Ambassador. If you will not believe me in this make inquiry into the thing, and you will find it to be true. I have desired Mr. Kemble to give you this letter, and to discourse with you at large upon this matter, to know your resolution, and whether I may expect that justice and goodness from you which all the world does. I promise you that for my conduct, it shall be such, as that you nor nobody shall have occasion to blame me. And I hope you will be just to what you said to me, which was at my house, when you told me you had letters of mine; you said, 'Madam, all that I ask of you for your own sake is, live so for the future as to make the least noise you can, and I care not who you love.' Oh 1 this noise that is had never been, had it not been for the Ambassador's malice. I cannot forbear once again saying, I hope you will not gratify his malice in my ruin."

*Ralph Montagu to his Cousin*

"PARIS,
"March 29, 1678. O.S.

"SIR,

"I am out of countenance at all the troubles you are pleased to give yourself in my concerns. I have heard something of what you tell me of the Queen's engagement to my Lady Arlington; but so many things come between the cup and the lip, ·especially at Court, that till things are done, one must never despair, no more than I do of being Secretary of State, if my Lord continues his favour to me, and can work off Sir William Temple. I know for certain that there is a great cabal to bring in Mr. Savile, who wrote a letter last post to my Lady Cleveland, that his fortune depended upon her coming over, for that he had engaged his uncle, Secretary Coventry, for his place, but could not compass money to buy it, except she got him the King's leave to sell his Bedchamber place, and some additional money to help. You may let my Lord Treasurer know this, but it must be kept very secret, for else it would hinder me knowing many things that may be for his service. It is not very well in Mr. Savile, who has those obligations to my Lord Treasurer, to manage such an affair under-hand. For my part I care for not the place, except I come in with his favour and kindness. I have tried no other ways to compass it, neither will I. Pray put my Lord Treasurer in mind of me, with the assurance that he has no servant truer to him than myself, nor more entirely,

"Dear Cousin,
"Your most faithful humble servant, "
"R. MONTAGU."

The Earl of Castlemaine died in July, 1705, and the Duchess of Cleveland, being then a widow, married a few months later Major-General Robert Fielding, who was ten years her junior, and had been thrice married. He was known to his contemporaries as "Handsome Fielding" and "Beau Fielding." He was a thoroughly bad, mercenary character, and had behaved shockingly to his wives. Less than a year after his marriage to the Duchess he was committed to Newgate for threatening and maltreating her. It then became known that one of his earlier wives was alive, and the Duchess in 1707 obtained a decree of nullity, while Fielding was prosecuted for bigamy.

The Duchess of Cleveland spent her last years in comparative retirement at Chiswick, where she died in 1709. Though, as has been said, she was of respectable descent, she was neither more nor less than a rapacious courtesan.

# CHAPTER V

## ELIZABETH, COUNTESS DE GRAMMONT (*née* HAMILTON)
### 1641-1708

ELIZABETH HAMILTON was one of the ornaments of the Court of Charles II. Born in 1641, she was the eldest daughter of Sir George Hamilton, fourth son of James, first Earl of Abercorn, by Mary, third daughter of Walter, Viscount Thurles, eldest son of Walter, eleventh Earl of Ormonde. Sir George Hamilton greatly distinguished himself during the Civil Wars, retiring to France on the death of Charles I. At the Restoration he and his family returned to England, and at once Elizabeth, though no heiress, had all the gallants, including practically all the eligible bachelors, at her feet, attracted by her beauty and her tall, rather full figure.

Miss Hamilton had the choice of all the best matches in England; but she was in no hurry to marry, and refused proposal after proposal. The Duke of Richmond was one of the first to come forward. He was a gambler and a sot; but he was well and truly enamoured — yet not so devoted that he was not disturbed by the lady's want of fortune. For this hesitancy, Elizabeth never forgave him. The King took a hand in the game, and begged her to accept the Duke; he even went so far as to offer to dower her handsomely, in consideration of the services of her father to his House, and his own relationship to his Grace. She would have none of him.

Miss Hamilton could, and did, resist the advances of the almost irresistible Henry Jermyn, famous for his conquests. She refused Henry Howard, Earl of Arundel, who in 1667 succeeded to the dukedom of Norfolk. Not himself, nor the prospective dukedom, nor his thirty thousand a year, tempted her. She, it has been put, disdained to be the first peeress of England at the expense of marrying a fool. Berkeley, afterwards Earl of Falmouth, wealthy and attractive in person, though dissipated, a boon companion of the King, and the Duke of York, she would have nothing to do with. Berkeley was deeply in love, and told St. Evremond that "the possession of Miss Hamilton was alone wanting to crown all his desires; but that he had too much pride to own her hand to the inter ference of her parents, and dared not hazard the refusal he anticipated from herself."

Elizabeth, Countess de Grammont (née Hamilton)

Then, about the end of 1663, Philibert, Count de Grammont, came upon the scene. Grammont, who was born in 1621, and so was twenty years older than Elizabeth, was a scion of a noble French house. In his youth he was very much a man about town at Paris. He fought under Condé[1] and Turenne, but his principal success was as a lover. His person, his charm, and his audacity made him almost irre-

---

[1] Louis Condé, II, prince de Bourbon (1621–86): French general, called "The Great Condé"; son of Henri II de Condé. Famous for early victories in the Thirty Years War. Later led a rebel army of princes against France with the support of Spain.

sistible. His recklessness knew no bounds. He even went so far as to make love to a mistress of Louis XIV, Mademoiselle de la Motte. There was *lèse-majesté* with a vengeance, but the Monarch contented himself with banishing the culprit from his Kingdom.

Grammont now came to London, where he was well received at Whitehall. Lady Castlemaine smiled upon him, and many other ladies offered their favours, notably Mrs. Jane Myddleton. However, it was not long before he was enthralled by the virtuous Miss Hamilton, to whom he paid desperate court. Finding her impregnable, and being, anyhow, for the moment, tired of his facile amours, he actually decided to marry the lady — a thing that was easier said than done.

Grammont, sure in his own conceit, was surprised to learn that he had a rival with Mrs. Middleton). He, according to his statement in his *Memoirs*, was informed by Jones, his friend, his confidant, and "his rival, that there was another gentleman very attentive to Mrs. Myddleton: this was Montagu, no very dangerous rival on account of his person, but very much feared for his assiduity, the acuteness of his wit, and for some other talents which are of importance, when a man is once permitted to display them. There needed not half so much to bring into action all the Chevalier's vivacity, in point of competition: vexation awakened in him whatever expedients the desire of revenge, malice, and experience, could suggest, for troubling the designs of a rival, and tormenting a mistress. His first intention was to return her letters, and demand his presents, before he began to tease her; but, rejecting this project, as too weak a revenge for the injustice done him, he was upon the point of conspiring the destruction of poor Mrs. Myddleton, when by accident, he met with Miss Hamilton. From this moment ended all his resentment against Mrs. Myddleton, and all his attachment to Miss Warmestre: no longer was he inconstant: no longer were his wishes fluctuating: this object fixed them all; and, of all his former habits, none remained, except uneasiness and jealousy."

Ralph Montagu was no despicable antagonist, even for Grammont. He was the second son of Edward, second Lord Montagu of Boughton. He was Master of the Horse to Queen Catherine, and after going to France as Ambassador-Extraordinary, was appointed to the sinecure post of Master of the Great Wardrobe. He took part in the prosecution of the Popish plot[2] in 1678; but after the death of his friend, Lord Russell, he returned to Montpellier, where he remained until the death of Charles. He was active during the Revolution, and for his services William created him in 1689 Viscount Monthermer and Earl of Montagu. It was not until sixteen years later that he obtained his especial ambition, and was raised in the peerage to the dignity of Marquis of Monthermer and Duke of Montagu which honour he only enjoyed for a brief period, dying in the spring of 1709 at the age of seventy-two. Enormously wealthy, as the result of his two marriages, he erected Montagu House, in Bloomsbury (on the site of which is now the British Museum) which Boyer stated to be "without comparison the first building in the whole city of London and county of Middlesex, Hampton Court alone excepted." Swift wrote him down as "as arrant a knave as any in his time"; and because of this — or it may be, in spite of it, he was successful in his life. He had his setbacks, however. His quarrel with the Duchess of Cleveland, with whom he was at one time *au mieux*, [on intimate terms] to which reference has already been made, held up his career for a while. Also his attention to Queen Catherine insured for him, temporarily at least, the disfavour of Charles.

Grammont would no doubt have put up a good fight for the possession of Mrs. Myddleton, but for the attraction that Miss Hamilton had for him so soon as he set eyes on her.

"The Chevalier de Grammont," so runs a passage in the *Memoirs*, "was fortunate, without being beloved, and became jealous without having an attachment. Mrs. Myddleton, as we have said, was going to experience what methods he could invent to torment, after having experienced his powers of pleasing. He went in search of her to the

---

[2] The Popish Plot was an alleged Catholic conspiracy. In reality the public scandal was provoked by a conspiracy to discredit Catholics in England. In 1678 a corrupt English clergyman named Titus Oates announced that he had uncovered a "Popish Plot" to murder King Charles II of England and replace him with James, his Roman Catholic brother. Nonconformists rushed to support the Anglican Whigs, who consequently won a great majority in the House of Commons. In 1679 the Whigs passed the "Exclusion Bill" to keep James from the throne, but the act failed to pass the House of Lords. It later developed that Oates had lied, and Whig popularity declined after capitalising off of near-civil-war. (Source: Wikipedia)

Queen's Draw-room, where there was a ball, there she was; but fortunately for her, Miss Hamilton was there likewise. It had so happened, that of all the beautiful women at Court, this was the lady whom he had least seen, and whom he had heard most commended; this, therefore, was the first time that he had had a close view of her, and he soon found that he had seen nothing at Court before this instant. He asked her some questions, to which she replied; as long as she was dancing, his eyes were fixed on her, and from this time he no longer resented Mrs. Myddleton's conduct. Miss Hamilton was at the happy age when the charms of the fair sex begin to bloom, she had the finest shape, the loveliest neck, and most beautiful arms in the world; she was majestic and graceful in all her movements; and she was the original after which all the ladies copied in their taste and aim of dress. Her forehead was open, white, and smooth; her hair was well set, and fell with ease into that natural order which it is so difficult to imitate. Her complexion was possessed of a certain freshness, not to be equalled by borrowed colours; her eyes were not large, but they were lively, and capable of expressing whatever she pleased; her mouth was full of graces, and her contour uncommonly perfect; nor was her nose, which was small, delicate, and turned up, the least ornament of so lovely a face. In fine, her air, her carriage, and the numberless graces dispersed over her whole person, made the Chevalier de Grammont not doubt but that she was possessed of every other qualification. Her mind was a proper companion to such a form: she did not endeavour to shine in conversation by those sprightly sallies which only puzzle; and with still greater care she avoided that affected solemnity in her discourse, which produces stupidity; but without any eagerness to talk she just said what she ought, and no more. She had an admirable discernment in distinguishing between solid and false; and far from making ostentatious display of her abilities, she was reserved, though very just in her decisions: her sentiments were always noble, and even lofty to the highest extent, when there was occasion; nevertheless, she was less prepossessed with her own merit than is usually the case with those who have so much. Formed, as we have described, she could not fail of commanding love, but so far was. she from courting it, that she

was scrupulously nice with respect to those whose merit might enti-
tle them to form any pretensions to her."

At once de Grammont became passionately devoted.

Just before he began to pay his addresses to the lady, John Russell
was a suitor for her hand. "He," so runs the story, "being upon the
point of setting out on a journey, thought it was proper to acquaint
his mistress with his intention before his departure. The Chevalier de
Grammont was a great obstacle to the interview he was desirous of
obtaining of her; but being one day sent for, to go and play at Lady
Castlemaine's, Russell seized the opportunity, and addressing himself to Miss Hamilton, with less embarrassment than is usual on such
occasions, he made his declaration to her in the following manner: I
am brother to the Earl of Bedford: I command the Regiment of
Guards: I have three thousand pounds a year, and fifteen thousand in
ready money: all which, madam, I come to present to you, along with
my person. One present, I agree, is not worth much without the
other, and therefore I put them together. I am advised to go to some
of the watering places for something of an asthma, as I have had it for
these last twenty years: if you look upon me as worthy of the happiness of belonging to you, I shall propose it to your father, to whom I
did not think it right to apply before I was' acquainted with your sentiments: my nephew William is at present entirely ignorant of my
intention; but I believe he will not be sorry for it, though he will
thereby see himself deprived of a pretty considerable estate; for he
has great affection for me, and besides, he has a pleasure in paying
his respects to you since he has perceived my attachment. I am very
much pleased that he should make his court to me, by the attention
he pays to you; for he did nothing but squander his money upon that
coquette Myddleton, while at present he is at no expense, though he
frequents the best company in England.'

"Miss Hamilton," so continues the narrative, "had much difficulty to suppress her laughter during this harangue: however, she
told him that she thought herself much honoured by his intentions
towards her, and still more obliged to him for consulting her, before
he made overtures to her relations. 'It will be time enough,' she said,
'to speak to them upon the subject at your return from the waters; for

I do not think it at all probable that they will dispose of me before that time, and in case they should be urgent in their solicitations, your nephew William will take care to acquaint you therefore, you may set out whenever you think proper; but take care not to impair your health by returning too soon."

Grammont confided his intention to marry Elizabeth Hamilton to his friend, St. Evremond, who endeavoured to persuade him that he had little or no chance of success. The Duke of Russell was at least correct in saying that Grammont was living at no expense to himself in England, for the Count while in this country had practically no means at all. There were those who said that he was supported by his mistresses; but it is more charitable to assume that he depended for his income upon his great skill at play [gambling].

"The Duke of Richmond," St. Evremond, who evidently knew all about the lady, wrote, "paid his addresses to her first; but though he was in love with her, still he was mercenary: however, the King observing that want of fortune was the only impediment to the match, took that article upon himself, out of regard to the Duke of Ormonde, to the merit and birth of Miss Hamilton, and to her father's services; but, resenting that a man who pretended to be in love should bargain like a merchant, and likewise reflecting upon his character in the world, she did not think that being Duchess of Richmond was a sufficient recompense for the danger that was to be feared from a brute and a debauchee Has not little Jermyn, notwithstanding his uncle's great estate, and his own brilliant reputation, failed in his suit to her? And has she ever so much as vouchsafed to look at Henry Howard, who is upon the point of being the first duke in England, and who is actually in possession of all the estates of the house of Norfolk? I confess that he is a clown, but what other lady in all England would not have dispensed with his stupidity and his disagreeable person, to be the first Duchess in the Kingdom, with twenty-five thousand a year?"

Grammont, however, was not to be dissuaded from pursuing his course. Even if wealthy nobles had failed, why should not he, practically penniless as he was, with his advantages, succeed? Anyhow, he was determined to do his utmost, and with splendid braggadocio he replied to St. Evremond: "My friend, thou art a philosopher, *tu con-*

*nais la nature des étoiles du ciel; mais pour les astres de la terre, tu n'y con-
nais rien.* [Thou knowest the nature of heavenly bodies, but of the
stars of the earth, thou knowest nothing.] I have just had a lecture
from the King, of three hours' length upon the same score. "What do
you tell me of these Ostrogoths, my rivals? Think you, if Miss Hamilton had deigned to listen to them, that I should have cared to obtain
her? *Ecoutez, mon ami!* [Listen my friend!] I will marry Miss Hamilton
in spite of them and the world I will have my banishment reversed.
She shall be *Dame du Palais* [Lady of the Bedchamber] to the Queen of
France. My brother shall be pleased to die some day or other for our
particular gratification. Miss Hamilton shall be the mistress of Sé-
meat, the seat of the de Grammont family, Countess de Grammont, to
make her amends for the loss of that oaf Norfolk, that sot Richmond,
and that rake Falmouth. And what have you to say to this, my dear
philosopher."

## To this, St. Evremond replied:

"ÉPÎTRE DE ST. EVREMOND Á M. LE CHEVALIER DE GRAMMONT
À l'occasion de son amour pour Mademoiselle Hamilton.

"EPISTLE FROM ST. EVREMOND TO M. LE CHEVALIER DE GRAMMONT
On the occasion of his love for Mademoiselle Hamilton.

| | |
|---|---|
| Il n'est qu'un Chevalier au monde! | There is in the world but one Knight! |
| Et que ceux de la table ronde, | And I pray that those of the Round Table might, |
| Que les plus fameux aux tournois, | With those in tournaments celebrated, |
| Aux aventures, aux exploits, | In adventures, and deeds most venerated, |
| Me pardonnent si je les quitte | Forgive if I leave their memory to dust, |
| Pour chanter un nouveau mérite; | For to sing of greater valor, I must; |
| C'est celui qu'on vit ala cour, | It is he who at court was often present, |
| Jadis si galant sans amour, | E'en without love so gallant and pleasant, |
| Le meme qui sût à Bruxelles | Here or in Brussels, this noble man |
| Comme ici plaire aux demoiselles; | Pleased the ladies as no other can; |
| Gagner tout l'argent des maris, | The money of their husbands firmly in hand, |
| Et puis revenir à Paris, | He returned to Paris from a foreign land, |
| Ayant couru toute la terre | Having traveled o'er all the earth |
| Dans le jeu, l'amour, et la guerre. | In love, in war, in games and mirth. |
| Insolent en prosperité, | Insolent when prosperity smiles down |
| Fort courtois en necessité, | Most courteous when necessity brings him round, |
| L'âme en fortune libérale, | In fortune a generous soul, |
| Aux créanciers pas trop loyale: | His loyalty to creditors none extoll : |
| Qui n'a changé, ni changera, | He is unchanging, and ever will be, |
| Et seul au monde qu'on verra | And him alone in the world shall we see |
| Soutenir la blanche vieillesse | In white old age pass his days |
| Comme il a passe la jeunesse; | With the vigor of youthful ways ; |
| Rare merveille de nos jours ! | Rare marvel in our time, no doubt ! |
| N'étaient vos trop longues amours, | Were not your loves so long drawn out, |
| N'était la sincere tendresse | Was not the tenderness most sincere |
| Dont vous aimez votre princesse, | With which you love your princess dear, |
| N'était qu'ici les beaux désirs | Is it only now that such precious desires |
| V ous font pousser de vrais soupirs, | From your lips a true sigh inspires |
| Et qu'enfin vous quittez pour elle | And for her at last you lay down |
| Votre mérite d'infidelle- | The mantle of infidelity's renoun |
| Cher et parfait original! | Dear and perfect original ! |
| Vous n'auriez jamais eu d'egal. | You would never have had an equal |
| Il est des heros pour la guerre, | There are of heroes in war |
| Mille grands hommes sur la terre, | A thousand great men both near and far |
| Mais au sens de Saint Evremond | But in Saint Evremond's sense be it known |
| Rien qu'un Chevalier de Grammont; | A Knight of Grammont there is but one alone; |
| Et jamais ne sera de vie, | And never in this life will there be |
| Plus admiré et moins sui vie ! " | One more admired and less followed than he! |

There were other Richmonds in the field. One was the President Tambonneau, the favoured admirer of the beauteous Luynes.

"Miss Hamilton had, at first, the honour of being distinguished by Tambonneau, who thought she possessed a sufficient share of wit to discover the delicacy of his; and, being delighted to find that nothing was lost in her conversation, either as to the turn, the expression, or beauty: of the thought, he frequently did her the favour to converse with her; and perhaps he would never have found out he was tiresome if, contenting himself with the display of his eloquence, he had not thought proper to attack her heart. This was carrying matters a little too far for Miss Hamilton's complaisance, who was of opinion that she had already shown him too much for the trophes of his harangues: he was therefore desired to try somewhere else the experiment of his seducing tongue, and not to lose the merit of his constancy by an infidelity which would be of no advantage to him. He followed this advice like a wise and tractable man; and some time after, returning to his old mistress in France, he began to lay in a store of politics for those important negotiations on which he has since been employed."

A more dangerous rival to Grammont for the hand of Elizabeth Hamilton was Richard Talbot (youngest son of the Irish politician, Sir William Talbot), who was created by James II Duke of Tyrconnel. After serving with distinction under Cvnde, he returned to England at the Restoration, and was in high favour at Court, and was appointed a Gentleman of the Bedchamber to the Duke of York.

The Duke of Berwick gave him a good character on the whole. "Talbot," he says, "had great experience of the world, having been early introduced into the best company, and possessed of an honourable employment in the Household of the Duke of York, who, upon his succession to the Crown, raised him to the dignity of an earl, and, well knowing his great attachment, made him soon after Viceroy of Ireland. He was a man of very good sense, very obliging, but immoderately vain, and full of cunning. Though he had acquired great possessions it could not be said that he had employed improper means, for he never appeared to have a passion for money. He had not a military genius, but much courage. After the Prince of Orange's invasion, his firmness preserved Ireland, and he nobly refused all the others that were made to him to submit. After the battle of the Boyne, he sank prodigiously, being become as irresolute in his mind as unwieldly in his person."

Talbot had an intrigue with Lady Shrewsbury, mother of Charles Talbot, Duke of Shrewsbury; but broke this off to pay attention to Miss Hamilton. "There was not a more genteel man at Court," Anthony Hamilton wrote in the *Memoirs of Grammont*. "He was, indeed, but a younger brother, though of a very ancient family, which, however, was not very considerable either for its renown or its riches; and though he was naturally of a careless disposition, yet, being intent upon making his fortune, and much in favour with the Duke of York, and fortune likewise favouring him at play, he had improved both so well that he was in possession of about £4000 a year in land. He offered himself to Miss Hamilton, with this fortune, together with the almost certain hopes of being made a peer of the realm by his master's credit; and, over and above all, as many sacrifices as she could desire of Lady Shrewbury's letters, pictures, and hair-curiosities which, indeed, are reckoned for nothing in housekeeping, but which testify strongly in favour of the sincerity and merit of a lover. Such a rival was not to be despised; and the Chevalier de Grammont thought him the more dangerous as he perceived that Talbot was desperately in love; that he was not a man to be discouraged by a first repulse; that he had too much good sense and good breeding to draw upon himself either contempt or coldness by too great eagerness. When the Chevalier de Grammont reflected upon all these things, there was certainly ground for uneasiness; nor was the indifference which Miss Hamilton showed for the addresses of his rival sufficient to remove his fears; for being entirely dependent on her father's will, she could only answer for her own intentions; but Fortune, who seemed to have taken him under her protection in England, now delivered him of all uneasiness."

What actually happened was that Talbot was insolent to the Duke of Ormonde, then Lord-Lieutenant of Ireland, who had him committed to the Tower for a while—after which Miss Hamilton would have nothing to do with him. Recovering from his disappointment, Talbot made love to the beautiful Fanny Jennings, elder sister of the Duchess of Marlborough, who coquetted with him, but became the wife of Sir George Hamilton. The disappointed lover ultimately married "the languishing Miss Boynton," daughter of Matthew, second son of Sir Matthew Boynton, of Barmston, in Yorkshire.

Of Talbot's attachment to Miss Boynton, Grammont gave an amusingly malicious account. "About this time Talbot returned from Ireland," thus runs a passage in the *Memoirs*. "He soon felt the absence of Miss Hamilton. A remnant of his former tenderness still subsisted in his heart, notwithstanding his absence, and the promise he had given the Chevalier de Grammont at parting. He now, therefore, endeavoured to banish her entirely from his thoughts by fixing his desires upon some other object; but he saw no one in the Queen's new Court whom he thought worthy of his attention. Miss Boynton, however, thought him worthy of hers. Her person was slender and delicate, to which a good complexion and large motionless eyes gave it at a distance an appearance of beauty that vanished upon nearer inspection. She affected to lisp, to languish, and to have two or three fainting fits a day. The first time that Talbot cast his eyes upon her she was seized with one of these fits. He was told that she swooned away upon his account. He believed it; was eager to afford her assistance; and ever after that accident showed her some kindness, more with the intention of saving her life than to express any affection he had for her. This seeming tenderness was well received, and at first she was visibly affected by it. Talbot was one of the tallest men in England, and in all appearance one of the most robust; yet she showed sufficiently that she was willing to expose the delicacy of her constitution to whatever might happen, in order to become his wife, which event perhaps might have then taken place, as it did afterwards, had not the charms of the fair Jennings at that time proved an obstacle, to her wishes."

St. Evremond had soon to admit that he had been wrong. Grammont triumphed. He proposed to Elizabeth Hamilton, and was accepted. Then, in 1663, his sister, the Marquise de St. Chaumont, wrote to tell him that Louis XIV had cancelled the order for his banishment, and, all agog with excitement, he set out for France. He apparently forgot all about his fiancée, and got as far as Dover, where he was intercepted by her brothers, George and Anthony, who put to him the pertinent question: "Chevalier de Grammont, is there not something you have forgotten to do in London?" With great presence of mind, he replied without hesitation: "My dear Sirs, of course. Pray forgive me, I have forgotten to marry your sister." He returned with them, and the marriage duly took place.

"It was about this time that the Chevalier de Grammont received a letter from the Marchioness de Saint-Chaumont, his sister, acquainting him that he might return to France when he thought proper, the King having given him leave. He would have received this news with joy at any other time, whatever had been the charms of the English Court; but in the present situation of his heart, he could not resolve to quit it. He had returned from Tonbridge Wells, a thousand times deeper in love than ever; for, during this agreeable excursion he had every day seen Miss Hamilton, either in the marshes of melancholy of Peckham, or in the delicious walks of Summerhill, or in the daily diversions and entertainments of the Queen's Court; and whether he saw her on horseback, heard her conversations or observed her in the dance, still he was persuaded that Heaven had never formed an object in every respect more worthy of the love, and more deserving of the affection of a man of sense and delicacy. How then was it possible for him to bear the thoughts of leaving her? This appeared to him absolutely impracticable, however, as he was desirous of making a merit with her of the determination he had made to neglect his fortune rather than to be separated from her charms, he showed her his sister's letter; but this confidence had not the success he expected. Miss Hamilton, in the first place, congratulated him upon his return. She returned him many thanks for the sacrifice he intended to make her; but as this testimony of affection greatly exceeded the bounds of mere gallantry, however sensibly she might feel this mark of his tenderness, she was determined not to abuse it. In vain did he protest that he would rather meet death than part from her irresistible charms, and her inimitable charms protested that he should never see them more, unless he departed immediately. Then, he was forced to obey. However, he was allowed to flatter himself that these positive orders, how harsh soever they might appear, did not flow from indifference; that she would always be more pleased with his return than with his departure, for which she was so urgent; and having generously given him assurance that so far as depended upon herself, he would find upon his return no variation in her sentimerits during his absence, he took leave of his friends, thinking of nothing but his return at the very time he was making preparations for his departure."

The information to Grammont by his sister was inaccurate; but, actually, he and his wife went to France in the winter of 1664, and mainly resided there during the rest of their lives. They often, however, came to England, where they were popular at Court, where Charles welcomed them with open arms. In 1669, the King sent a letter to his sister, the Duchess of Orleans: "I wrote to you yesterday by the Count de Grammont; but I believe this letter will come sooner to your hand, for he goes to Dieppe with his wife and family. And now that I have named her, I cannot choose but again desire you to be kind to her, for besides the merit her family has on both sides, she is as good a creature as ever lived. I believe she will pass for a handsome woman in France, though she has not yet, since her lying-in, recovered that good shape she had before, and I am afraid never will."

Grammont, in 1688, being restored to the royal favour, was sent by Louis XIV as an envoy to congratulate James II on the birth of a son. Whether his wife accompanied him is not clear; but for some reason unknown, he received from the British secret service fund a grant of over a thousand pounds.

In France, the Countess de Grammont was not too popular. Madame de Maintenon said of her, that she was "more agreeable than amiable"; and Madame de Sévigné thought her "a woman by no means agreeable, somewhat affected, and much too inclined to give herself airs." However, she was given the appointment of a Dame du Palais.

Grammont, in 1696, when he was in his seventy-fifth year, was taken ill, and not expected to recover. "At the time when this celebrated libertine was thought to be on his death-bed," the story is told, "the King sent the Marquis Dangeau, a famous devotee of those times, to talk with him of God. The Countess de Grammont, also a professed devotee, and who had been perpetually teasing her husband with repentance, was sitting on the bedside. So after the King's devotee had been haranguing him for some time, he turned to his wife and said, 'Countess, if you don't look about you, Dangeau will smuggle [*escamotera*] my conversion.' St. Evremond, hearing of this, declared himself confident that Grammont would gladly die, to go off with such a bon-mot on his lips. However, he recovered. He was vivacious to the end. "Madame du Coulogne," Ninon de l'Enclos wrote to St. Evremond after the death of Grammont in 1707, "has undertaken to make your compliments to the Count de Grammont, by the Countess de Grammont. He is so young, that I think him as light as when he hated sick people, and loved them after they had recovered their health." The Countess de Grammont survived him but a year. She had borne him two daughters: Claude Charlotte, who in 1694 married Henry Howard, Earl of Stafford; and Marie Louise, who became Superior of Ste. Marie de Poussey in Lorraine.

# CHAPTER VI

## MAIDS OF HONOUR

### GODITHA PRICE; HENRIETTA MARIA BLAGGE; MISS HOBART; AND ELIZABETH, COUNTESS OF FALMOUTH, AFTERWARDS COUNTESS OF DORSET (*née* BAGOT) 1643 (?)-1684

THE first four Maids of Honour of the Duchess of York were Goditha Price, Henrietta Maria Blagge (or Blague), Miss Hobart, and Elizabeth Bagot.

Of these there is not a great amount to say.

Miss Price's history is unknown except in a few details. Granger mentions a Lady Price, a fine woman, who was daughter of Sir Edmond Warcup. Her father had the vanity to think that Charles II would marry her, and there is a letter of his in which he mentions that "his daughter was one night and t'other with the King, and very graciously received by him." Miss Price was fond of fun and frolic, and especially of amorous adventure. It was believed that she had lost her virginity even before she came to Court. In love and passion she was unscrupulous. There was one Dongan who was attached to Miss Blagge, whom Miss Price seduced from his allegiance. Elizabeth Hamilton gave each of these girls a pair of gloves for a masquerade, and Miss Price, who called to thank her, said she would certainly wear them on that occasion. "You will oblige me if you do," said the donor, "but if you mention such a trifle as this comes from me, I shall never forgive you; but do not go and rob poor Miss Blagge of the Marquis Brisacier, as you already have of Dongan. I know very well that it is in your power; you have wit; you speak French; and were he once to converse with you ever so little, the other could have no pretensions to him." This appeal was, of course, well-intentioned, but surely unwise to deliver to a lady already confident enough in her powers of attraction. As Grammont put it, "Miss Blagge was only ridiculous and coquettish; Miss Price was ridiculous, coquettish, and something more besides." The ball took place, and Grammont is the authority for what took place there.

Elizabeth, Countess of Falmouth (*née* Bagot)

"They found that the billet they had conveyed to her on the part of Brisacier had its effect. She was more yellow than saffron; her hair was stuffed with eitron-coloured riband, which she had put there out of complaisance; and to inform Brisacier of his fate, she raised often to her head her victorious hands, adorned with the gloves we have before mentioned; but if they were surprised to see her in a head-dress that made her look more wan than ever, she was very differently surprised to see Miss Price partake with her in every particular of Brisacier's present. Her surprise soon turned to jealousy, for her rival had not failed to join in conversation with him, on account of what had been insinuated to her the evening before; nor did Brisacier fail to return her first advances without paying the least attention to the fair Blagge, nor to the signs she was tormenting herself to make him, to inform him of his happy destiny. Miss Price was short and thick, and consequently no dancer. The Duke of Buckingham, who brought Brisacier forward as often as he could, came to desire him, on the part of the King, to dance with Miss Blagge, without knowing what was then passing in this nymph's heart. Brisacier excused himself, on account of the contempt he had for country dances. Miss Blagge thought it was herself that he despised; and, seeing that he was engaged in conversation with her mortal enemy, she began to dance, without knowing what she was doing. Though her indignation and jealousy were sufficiently remarkable to divert the Court, none but Miss Hamilton and her accomplices understood the joke perfectly." Such were the simple pleasures of the times when Charles II was King.

Miss Price, however, soon went too far. Again to quote Grammont:

"Miss Price was witty, and as her person was not very likely to attract many admirers, which, however, she was resolved to have, she was far from being coy when an occasion offered: she did not so much as make any terms: she was violent in her resentments, as well in her attachments, which had exposed her to some inconveniences; and she had very indiscreetly quarrelled with a young girl whom Lord Rochester admired. This connection, which till then had been a secret, she had the imprudence to publish to the whole world, and thereby draw upon herself the most dangerous enemy in the universe: never did any man write with more ease, humour, spirit, and delicacy; but he was at the same time the most severe satirist.

"Poor Miss Price, who had thus voluntarily provoked his resentment, was daily exposed in some new shape: there was every day some new song or other, the subject of which was her conduct, and the burden her name. How was it possible for her to bear up against these attacks, in a Court where every person was eager to obtain the most insignificant trifle that came from the pen of Lord Rochester?

The loss of her lover, and the discovery that attended it, was only wanting to complete the persecution that was raised against her.

"About this time died Dongan, a gentleman of merit, who was succeeded by Durfort, afterwards Earl of Feversham, in the post of lieutenant of the Duke's Life Guards. Miss Price having tenderly loved him, his death plunged her into a gulf of despair; but the inventory of his effects had almost deprived her of her senses: there was in it a certain little box sealed up on all sides it was addressed in the deceased's own handwriting to Miss Price; but instead of receiving it, she had not even the courage to look upon it. The governess thought it became her in prudence to receive it, on Miss Price's refusal, and her duty to deliver it to the Duchess herself, supposing it was filled with many curious and precious commodities, of which perhaps she might take some advantage. Though the Duchess was not altogether of the same opinion, she had the curiosity to see what was contained in a box sealed up in a manner so particularly careful, and therefore caused it to be opened in the presence of some ladies, who happened then to be in her closet.

"All kinds of love trinkets were found in it; and all these favours, it appeared, came from the tenderhearted Miss Price. It was difficult to comprehend how a single person could have furnished so great a collection; for besides counting the pictures, there was hair of all descriptions, wrought into bracelets, lockets, and into a thousand other different devices, wonderful to see. After these were three or four packets of letters, of so tender a nature, and so full of raptures and languors so naturally expressed, that the Duchess could not endure the reading of any more than the two first."

This was too much even for the very tolerant Duchess of York, who, in effect, told Miss Price that she must really weep her departed lover elsewhere than in the royal ante-chamber. She was removed from the post of Maid of Honour, but was afterwards a frequent visitor, if not actually an ornament of the Court of their Royal Highnesses.

Biographical details of Henrietta Maria Blagge (or Blague) are few and far between. She was the daughter of Thomas Blagge, of Horningsheath, Suffolk, a Royalist colonel and Governor of Wallingford, who on the Restoration became Governor of Yarmouth and Land-guard Fort. Her mother was Mary, daughter of Sir Roger North of Mildenhall. Henrietta's sister, Margaret, was born in 1652. There are many: mentions of her in the memoirs of John Evelyn, with whom she was on"very friendly terms. She was an amiable and accomplished woman, and was much beloved and respected by her many intimates. After a long courtship, she married in 1675 Sidney (afterwards Earl) Godolphin. Three years later, having borne him a son, Francis, she died from a fever contracted in childbirth.

There are references to Henrietta in Grammont's *Memoirs*, where she is thus described: "Miss Blague was another species of ridicule. Her shape was neither good nor bad; her complexion bore the appearance of the greatest insipidity, and her complexion was the same all over; with two little hollow eyes, adorned with white eyelashes as long as one's finger. With these attractions she placed herself in ambuscade to surprise unwary hearts; but she might have done so in vain, had it not been for the arrival of the Marquis de Brisacier. Heaven seemed to have made them for each other. He had in his person and manners every requisite to dazzle a creature of her character. He talked eternally without saying anything, and in his dress exceeded the most extravagant fashions. Miss Blagge believed that all this finery was on her account; and the Marquis believed that her long eyelashes had never taken aim at any but himself. Everybody perceived their inclination for each other; but they had only conversed by mute interpreters, when Miss Hamilton took it into her head to intermeddle in their affairs." The result of the latter lady's intervention has already been given. Another, and less unflattering, description of Miss Blagge, has been given: "Her beauty was the more striking because it was of a style and character very unusual in England. She was a brunette, with fine regular features, black eyes, rather soft than sparkling, and a well-proportioned figure on a large scale. Miss Blagge did not long remain at Court. She married Sir Thomas Yarborough, a Yorkshire baronet, as singularly fair as herself — to show the world, says Hamilton, '*Ce qui produirait une union si blafarde.*'" [ 'What would result from such a pallid union.']

As regards Miss Hobart, of her antecedents nothing is known, but it may be presumed that she was of good family. Scandal was busy with her name, though with what justification cannot now be said. She was clever and mischievous, and this quality made her many enemies. Perhaps it was because of this that the amiable Duchess of York removed her from the post of Maid of Honour, and placed her immediately about her person as a Woman of her Bedchamber.

Grammont had a good deal to say about her. "Miss Hobart's character," he writes, "was at that time as uncommon in England as her person was singular, in a country where to be young and not to be in some degree handsome is a reproach. She had a good shape, rather a bold air, and a great deal of wit, which was well cultivated, without having much discretion. She was likewise possessed of a great deal of vivacity, with an irregular fancy. There was a great deal of fire in her eyes, which, however, produced no effect upon the beholders; and she had a tender heart, whose sensibility some pretended was alone in favour of the fair sex."

Something more, if not very much, is known about Elizabeth Bagot than about the other contemporary Maids of Honour. She was the daughter of Colonel Henry Bagot, of Pipe Hall, in Warwickshire, a younger son of Sir Henry Bagot, Bart., of Blythfield, in Staffordshire, by his wife, Dorothea Arden, of the Ardens of Park Hall, in Warwickshire. The Bagots had suffered heavily in the Stuart cause, and Colonel Bagot, who had distinguished himself by his gallantry in the Civil Wars was at the Restoration given the post of Gentleman Pensioner, while the girl was appointed a Maid of Honour to the Duchess of York. Grammont had a kind word for her: "Miss Bagot was the only one who was really possessed of virtue and beauty among the Maids of Honour. She had beautiful and regular features, and that sort of brown complexion which, when in perfection, is so particularly fascinating, and more especially in England, where it is uncommon. There is an involuntary blush almost continually upon her cheek, without having anything to blush for." This is praise indeed, considering the source from which the tribute comes.

So lovely a creature must have been wooed, honourably or dishonourably, by many at Court. She preserved her heart intact, until she met Sir Charles Berkeley, the second son of Sir Charles Berkeley, of Bruton, in Gloucestershire. He was created by Charles II Baron Berkeley and Viscount Fitzharding in the peerage of Ireland, and in 1664, Baron Bottecourt and Earl of Falmouth in England. Clarendon wrote of him: "A young man of dissolute life, and prone to all wickedness in the judgment of all sober men.... One in whom few men (except the King) had ever seen any virtue or quality which they did not wish their best friends without. He was young, and of an unstable ambition; and a little more experience might have taught him all things which his weak parts were capable of." This is indeed severe; but the Lord Chancellor had not—and never did forgive him for the attitude he had taken up in the matter of the marriage of Anne Hyde and the Duke of York—an attitude so scandalous as to make forgiveness impossible by a devoted father. More kind than Clarendon was Burnet: "Berkeley was generous in his expense; and it was thought that if he had outlived the lewdness of that time, and come to a more sedate course of life, he would have put the King on great and noble designs."

Berkeley had lost his heart to Elizabeth Hamilton. "Lord Falmouth has told me himself," St. Evremoud put on record, "that he always looked upon Miss Hamilton as the only acquisition wanting to complete his happiness: but that even at the height of the splendour of his fortune, he never had had the assurance to open his sentiments to her; that he either felt in himself too much weakness, or too much pride, to be satisfied with obtaining her solely by the persuasion of her relations; and that, though the first refusals of the fair on such occasions are not much minded, he knew with what an air she had received the addresses of those she did not like." Berkeley, then, coming to the conclusion that he had no chance whatever with Miss Hamilton, turned his attention to Elizabeth Bagot, who ultimately accepted him. In spite of his admiration for Elizabeth Hamilton, it would seem that his marriage was inspired by love, for though Miss Bagot was beautiful indeed, she was not of high rank, nor had she any dowry worth consideration. This is the view taken also by Mrs. Jameson: "We have reason to believe that Elizabeth Bagot was, at this period of her life, a beloved and happy wife as well as a worshipped beauty; for, whatever might be the faults of Lord

Falmouth, his attachment to her must have been passionate and dis-interested, since she had no portion, and there was scarcely an unmarried woman of any rank pr fortune that would have rejected his suit. Perpetual constancy, perhaps, had been too much to expect from a man of his temperament and morals; but he was not long enough her husband to forget to be her lover. Rich in all the gifts of nature and fortune, young and thoughtless in the gayest of Courts, 'round like the ring that made them one, the golden pleasures circled without end' — that is, for a few short months, for so long did this eternity of happiness endure, and no longer."

The marriage between Elizabeth Bagot and Lord Falmouth took place in 1663. They remained together, being frequently at Court, where both were great favourites, for two years. Then the Earl volun-teered for the fleet which the Duke of York was taking against the Dutch. In the action of June 2, 1665, he was killed, the cannon ball that knocked his head off, killing also Lord Muskerry and Robert Boyle, a son of the Earl of Burlington. Of him, Andrew Marvell [1] wrote brutally:

> "Falmouth was there, I know not what to act,
> Some say, 'twas to grow Duke by contract;
> An untaught bullet, in its wanton scope,
> Dashes him all to pieces, and his hope:
> Such was his rise, such was his fall unpraised;
> A chance shot sooner took him than chance raised;
> His shattered head the fearless Duke disdains,
> And gave the last final proof that he had brains."

Others, however, were more kind. "The King, it seems, is much troubled at the fate of Lord Falmouth," Pepys noted; "but I do not meet with I any man else that so much as wishes him alive again, the world conceiving him a man of too much pleasure to do the King any good, or offer any good advice to him. But I hear of an hands he is confessed to have been a man of great honour, that did show it in this

---

[1] Andrew Marvell (1621-1678): was an English metaphysical poet, and the son of an Anglican clergyman. As a metaphysical, he is associated with John Donne, George Herbert, and Ben Jonson. He was the first assistant of John Milton. He wrote prose satires (anonymously, of course) criticizing the monarchy, defending Puritan dis-senters, and denouncing censorship. (source: Wikipedia)

his going with the Duke, the most that ever man did." Charles's grief was beyond question sincere. "No sorrow," Clarendon said, "was equal—at least, no sorrow so remarkable, as the King's was for the Earl of Falmouth. Those who knew his Majesty best, and had seen how unshaken he had stood in other very terrible assaults, were amazed at the floods of tears he shed on this occasion." Nor was the Duke of York less distressed.

Of the widow's feelings nothing is known. She, of course, went into retirement for a while, but in 1667 she was back at Court, and there were unfounded rumours that she was engaged to marry Henry Jermyn. When the Duke of York lost his first wife, it was thought possible that Lady Falmouth might be her successor. "I doubt," the French Ambassador in London wrote to Louis XIV, "whether this Prince's passion for her is so great as to lead him to marry her." It was not.

Then came upon the scene Charles Sackville, sixth Earl of Dorset and first Earl of Middlesex, who was born in 1638. A rake-helly fellow, he was patriotic enough, however, to take part in the naval action that cost Lord Falmouth his life. About 1667 he acquired notoriety as a lover of Nell Gwyn, before she was taken into keeping by the King. He had a taste for literature. His song, "To all you ladies now at land "is an accepted masterpiece. He was also a patron of men of letters, and numbered among his friends Prior, Dryden, Wycherley, and Waller. Dryden, however, was not kind to him:

> "Thus Dorset purring like a thoughtful cat,
> Married, but wiser puss ne'er thought of that.
> And first he worried her with railing rhyme,
> Like Pembroke's mastiffs at his kindest time;
> Who for one night, sold all his slavish life,
> A teeming widow but a barren wife;
> Swelled by contact of such a fulsome toad,
> He lugged about a matrimonial load ;
> Till fortune, blindly kind as well as he,
> Has ill restored him to his liberty;
> Which he would use in his old sneaking way,
> Drinking all night, and dozing all the day;

Dull as Ned Howard, whom his brisker times
Has famed for dulness in malicious rhymes."

More pleasant it is to read Burnet: "Dorset was a generous, good-natured man. He was so oppressed with phlegm, that, till he was a little heated with wine, he scarce ever spoke; but he was, upon that exaltation, a very lively man. Never was so much ill-nature in a pen as in his, joined with so much good-nature as was in himself, even to excess; for he was against all punishing, even of malefactors. He was bountiful, even to run himself into difficulties, and charitable to a fault; for he commonly gave all he had about him when he met an object that moved him. But he was so lazy, that, though the King seemed to count him to be a favourite, he would not give himself the trouble that belonged to that post. He hated the Court, and despised the King, when he saw he was neither generous nor tender-hearted."

Horace Walpole, in his *Royal and Noble Authors*, was pleasant, even generous about him: "He was the finest gentleman of the voluptuous Court of Charles II, and in the gloomy one of King William. He had as much wit as his royal master, or his contemporaries, Buckingham and Rochester, without the royal want of feeling, the Duke's want of principles, or the Earl's want of thought. The latter said, with astonishment, that he did not know how it was, but Lord Dorset might do anything, and yet was never to blame.' It was not that he was free from the failings of humanity, but he had the tenderness of it too, which made everybody excuse whom everybody loved; for even the asperity of his verses seems to have been forgiven to 'The best good man, with the worst-natur'd Muse.'"

The date of the marriage of the widowed Countess of Falmouth with the Earl of Dorset is not precisely known-one authority, however, gives it as 1674, when the bridegroom was in his thirty-seventh year. Lady Dorset died in 1684, without having issue by either husband. In the following year Lord Dorset married Mary, daughter of James Compton, third Earl of Northampton, a lady famous for beauty and wit. He survived until 1706.

# CHAPTER VII

## HENRIETTA, COUNTESS OF ROCHESTER (née BOYLE) 1643 (?)-1687.
## MRS. JANE MYDDLETON (née NEEDHAM), 1645-1692

LADY HENRIETTA BOYLE was the youngest daughter of Richard, second Earl of Cork, who in 1663 was created Earl of Burlington in the peerage of England. Her mother was Lady Elizabeth, sole daughter and heiress of Henry Clifford, Earl of Cumberland. Her eldest sister married the Earl of Thanet; her second sister, the Earl of Roscommon; the third, Lord Hinchinbroke, afterwards Earl of Sandwich.

Lady Henrietta was a beauty. According to Grammont, she was "of a middle size, had a skin of a dazzling whiteness, fine hands, and a foot surprisingly beautiful, even in England. Long custom had given such a languishing tenderness to her looks, that she never opened her eyes but like a Chinese; and, when she ogled, one would have thought she was doing something else." Laurence Hyde, second son of Edward, first Earl of Clarendon, was entranced by her and married her in 1665. He had entered Parliament five years earlier, and in 1662 was given the appointment at Court of Master of the Robes[1], which he held for thirteen years. He had been trained carefully and thoroughly by his father, and was well equipped for diplomacy and politics. His chief defect was an ungovernable temper. "I never knew a man," Lord Dartmouth wrote, "who was so soon put in a passion, that was so long before he could bring himself out of it, in which he would say things that were never forgot by anybody but himself. He therefore had always more enemies than he thought, though he had as many professedly so as any man of his time." For his services to his country he was in 1681 created Viscount Hyde and Earl of Rochester the latter title having become extinct on the death of John Wilmot, the second Earl in the previous year.

---

[1] Master of the Robes: an officer of the English royal household (when the sovereign is a king) whose duty is supposed to consist in caring for the royal robes.

Henrietta, Countess of Rochester (*née* Boyle)

The marriage was successful, and husband and wife were devoted. At one time, however, it looked as if there might be trouble.
"Mrs. Hyde," Grammont relates, "was one of the first of the beauties
who were prejudiced with a blind prepossession in favour of Jermyn.
She had just married a man whom she loved: by this marriage she
became sister-in-law to the Duchess of York, brilliant by her own na-
tive lustre, and full of pleasantry and wit. However, she was of
opinion that so long as she was not talked of on account of Jermyn,

all her other advantages would avail nothing for her glory: it was, therefore, to receive this finishing stroke that she resolved to throw herself into his arms. Jermyn accepted of her at first; but being soon puzzled what to do with her, he thought it best to sacrifice her to Lady Castlemaine. The sacrifice was far from being displeasing to her; it was much to her glory to have carried off Jermyn from so many competitors; but this was of no consequence in the end."

This was Lady Rochester's one adventure. Afterwards, she settled down to a life so domestic that mention of her name, even in her husband's correspondence, is rare. During the first years of her married life she gave her husband two sons and four daughters. It may have been this that impaired her health, but for the rest of her life — she died when she was about forty-five — she was very delicate. "God Almighty preserve you and my sister," Henry Hyde, second Earl of Clarendon, wrote to his brother, Lord Rochester. "I am very much afraid lest this change should make impression on my sister's tender health; but she has seen such variety of changes in our poor family that I doubt not her wisdom and resolution, if her strength do not fail her."

The eldest daughter of the marriage, Lady Anne Hyde, was the favourite of her mother and father. Nevertheless, when she was fifteen they married her to the Earl of Ossory, grandson of the great Duke of Ormonde, who was only four years her senior. Like her mother, her constitution was weak, and perhaps being a wife at such an early age may have impaired her health. Her death took place at Dublin Castle in January 1685. Mrs. Jameson repeats a tale that was current at the time: "Some fancies might possibly contribute to this calamity; for the young lady was impressed with the common superstitious notion as to thirteen people sitting at table. A short time previous to her death, Dr. John Hough (afterwards Bishop of Worcester) was going to sit down, when, perceiving that he made the thirteenth, he stopped short and declined taking his place. She immediately guessed at his reason, and said: 'Sit down, Doctor; it is too late. It is the same thing, if you sit or go away.' He believed that the circumstance affected her, as she was in very indifferent health, and had been subject for some time to hysterical and fainting fits. The poor lady's imagination seems to have been peculiarly susceptible of such impressions, for another story is related, that may perhaps have accelerated the fatal event. Upon the death of the Countess of Kildare, Lady Ossory, being then only seventeen, dreamed that some one came and knocked at her chamber-door; and that calling to her servant to see who was there, and nobody answering, she went to the door herself and opening it, saw a lady mumed up in a hood, who, drawing it aside, she saw it was Lady Kildare. Upon this, she cried out, 'Sister, is it you? What makes you come in this manner?' 'Don't be frightened,' replied she, 'for I come on a very serious affair, and it is to tell you that you will die very soon.' Such was her dream as she related it to Dr. Hough."

"It pleased God," Lord Rochester wrote, "to take my daughter away, as it might be on this day, and I lived on almost a week longer deceived in my vain expectations that I should hear better of her, and that the worst was passed, till here comes the dismal news, a week after the blow was given! A week's time I had spent, after her lyiftg cold and breathless, in the ordinary exercises of my life; —nay, I think I had wrote from hence to her after the time she was dead; with the hopes that my letter should find her better, with expressions of tenderness for the sickness she had endured; of wishes for her recovery; of hopes of being in a short time happy in her company; of joy and comfort to myself, in being designed to go to live again in the same place with her — I say I had written all this — to whom? — to my poor dead child! Oh, sad and senseless condition of human life!... In the midst of this I had my wife lying weak and worn with long and continual sickness, and now as it were, knocked quite on the head with this cruel blow — a wife for whom I had all the tenderness imaginable; with whom I had lived long and happily, and had reason to be well pleased; whose fainting heart and weak spirits I was to comfort and keep up when I had none myself."

Second to none in looks at the Court of Charles II was Mrs. Jane Myddleton. "What pleased me," Pepys wrote in June 1666, "was to have the fair Mrs. Myddleton at our Church, who indeed is a very beautiful lady." A year later, he said: "Mrs. Myddleton

Mrs. Myddleton (*née* Needham)

has a very excellent face and body." People flocked to the theatre and to the Park to gaze upon her. Even in 1680, when she was thirty-five which in those days was regarded as quite elderly it is related that Courtin had to take the Duc de Nevers then on a mission to the English Court, together with his suite, in two coaches to see the celebrity; and that Louvois was so impressed by the account that he sent over for a portrait of her.

Jane Myddleton was a daughter of Sir Robert Needham, and related through his first wife to John Evelyn, who in his diary referred to her as "that famous and incomparable beauty." Her mother, the second wife of Sir Robert, was Jane, a daughter of William Cockayne and the widow of a Mr. Worfield. The child was born in the latter part of 1645.

The younger Jane was married at Lambeth Church on June 18, 1660, to Charles Myddleton of Ruabon, third surviving son of Sir Thomas Myddleton of Chirk, by whom she had two daughters. Beyond this, little or nothing is known of Charles, who faded away into the obscurity of "the beauty's husband." This married couple seem to have lived, on nothing a year: at least for some years they subsisted almost entirely on the generosity of their relatives. When Lady Needham died in 1666, she left some money to her daughter, and on the death in the same year of Sir Thomas Myddleton they came into another legacy, which, though not considerable, was peculiarly acceptable.

Jane Myddleton's morals were quite in keeping with those of her time, and it is to be feared that her lovers furnished the greater part of her income. She was, sad to relate, rather promiscuous in the bestowal of her favours. Grammont was early attracted by her after he came to England.

"Mrs. Myddleton was the first whom he attacked: she was one of the handsomest women in town, though then little known at Court: so much of the coquette as to discourage no one; and so great was her desire of appearing magnificently, that she was ambitious to vie with those of the greatest fortune, though unable to support the expense. All this suited the Chevalier de Grammont; therefore, without trilling away his time in useless ceremonies, he applied to her porter for admittance, and chose one of her lovers for his confidant. This lover, who was not deficient in wit, was at that time a Mr. Jones, afterwards Earl of Ranelagh: what engaged him to serve the Chevalier de Grammont, was to traverse the designs of a dangerous rival, and to relieve himself from an expense which began to lie too heavy upon him. In both respects the Chevalier answered his purpose. Immediately spies were placed, letters and presents flew about: he was received as well as he could wish: he was permitted to ogle: he was even ogled again; but this was all. He found that the fair one was very willing to accept, but was tardy in making returns. This induced him, without giving up his pretensions to her, to seek his fortune elsewhere.

"Among the Queen's Maids of Honour there was one called Warmestre: she was a beauty very different from the other. Mrs. Myddleton was wellmade, fair, and delicate; but had in her behaviour and discourse something precise and affected. The indolent, languishing airs she gave herself did not please everybody: people grew weary of those sentiments of delicacy, which she endeavoured to explain without understanding them herself, and instead of entertaining, she became tiresome. In these attempts she gave herself so much trouble, that she made the company uneasy, and her ambition to pass for a wit, only established for her the reputation of being tiresome, which lasted much longer than her beauty."

It was unkindly said of Mrs. Myddleton that she talked her lovers to sleep with the most irreproachable sentiments. She was, indeed, as Jesse put it, "a silly and sentimental beauty — not so silly, it may be added, as not to have an eye to the main chance."

According to a contemporary pasquinade, Mrs. Myddleton was sometime mistress of one of the Hydes — probably Lawrence Hyde, Earl of Rochester:

> "Not for the Nation, but the fair,
> Our Treasury provides;
> Bulkeley's Godolphin's only care,
> As Myddleton is Hyde's."

De Grammont was, only one admirer among many. Richard Jones, first Earl of Ranelagh, was another. Of him Burnet said: "Lord Ranelagh was a young man of great parts and as great vices." He had a pleasantness in his conversation that took much with the King [Charles], and he had a great dexterity in business. Born in 1638, he entered the Irish Parliament at the age of twenty-three, and sat for county Roscommon until the death of his father raised him to the Upper House in 1669 as third Viscount Ranelagh. His morality as Paymaster-General of the Army, to which post he was appointed by William III, was such that, after holding office for twelve years, he was expelled from Parliament in 1703 and faced with a prosecution for defalcations amounting to more than £70,000. However, his influence at Court was sufficient to avert the action. He survived until 1712, and Swift, giving an account of his death to Archbishop King, wrote, "He was very poor and needy, and could hardly support himself for want of a pension which used to be paid him, and which his friends solicited as a thing of perfect charity. He died hard, as the term of art here is to express the woeful state of men who discover no religion at their death."

Mrs. Myddleton's name was associated with Colonel William Russell, son of the Hon. Edward Russell, a brother of the Earl of Bedford, and standard-bearer in the first regiment of foot-guards; and with the Duke of York. Povy says on June 24, 1667, "that the Duke of York hath not got Mrs. Myddelton, as I was told the other day, but says he wants her not, for he hath others, and hath always had." Of all the others mentioned in connection with this exquisite creature, it is not necessary to mention Edmund Walier, the poet. In one of the letters from the Countess of Sunderland (Waller's "Sacharissa"), she thus alludes incidentally to Mrs. Myddleton:

"Mrs. Myddleton and I have lost old Waller, he is gone away frightened." Last, but not least, no less a person than the King himself. It is said that at one time she threatened to be a serious menace in Charles's affection to Lady Castlemaine. The latter, however, soon again dominated the situation.

With this famous beauty, as with others of her class, a youth of folly was succeeded by an old age at cards. According to Mrs. Jameson, who wrote an account of her, "she was frequently one of the society of the Duchess Mazarin, whose house at Chelsea was maintained on the footing of one of the modern gambling houses, with this exception, that it was the resort of the dissipated and extravagant of both sexes." "Many of the women," the biographer says, "who were occasionally seen in this society, were women of amiable character and spotless reputation, led thither by fashion and the lax opinions and habits of the time; and probably more attracted by the fascinating manners of the Duchess, and the wit and gaiety of St. Evremond, and by the *petits soupers où régnait la plus grande liberté du monde et une égale discrétion,* [little suppers where there reigned the greatest liberty in the world and equal amounts of discretion] if we may trust St. Evremond, than by the bassett-table. It appears, for instance, that Lady Rochester, Lady Arlington, the Duchess of Grafton, Lady Derby were visitors, if not *habituées* [regulars] but Mrs. Myddleton was one of the latter."

Among the occasional poems of St. Evremond there is "*Une Scéne de Bassette,*" [A Bassett Scene] in which little piece the interlocutors are Jane Myddleton, the Duchess Mazarin, and the Hon. Francis Villiers. Mrs. Myddleton is discussing the charms of some rival beauties:

MRS MYDDLETON

"Dites nous qui des deux vous semble la plus belle

Tell us who seems most beautiful to you?

De Mesdames Grafton et Litchfield?*— laquelle?"

Miss Grafton or Litchfield?— which of the two?

THE HON. FRANCIS VILLIERS

"Commencez: dites nous, Madame Myddleton,
Votre vrai sentiment sur Madame, Grafton."

Begin, then: tell us, Madam Myddleton, Your true feelings for Madam Grafton.

MRS. MYDDLETON

"De deux doigts seulement faites-la moi plus grand,
Il faut qu'à. sa beauté toute beauté se rende."

Of two fingers, only accord her for me the greatest splendor, To her beauty all beauty must surrender.

THE HON. FRANCIS VILLIERS

"L'autre n'a pas besoin cette faveur-là"

Of such a favor as this, the other has no need.

MRS. MYDDLETON

"Elle est grande, elle est droite-----"

She is tall, she is straight----

THE HON. FRANCIS VILLIERS

"Après cela? "

What more, indeed?

MRS. MYDDLETON

"Madame Litchfield un peu plus animée    Madam Litchfield's more vibrant demeanor
De tout ceux qu'elle voit se verrait fort    Would endear her greatly to all those
aimée."    who meet her.

This somewhat dreary, forced conversation is stopped by the Duchess Mazarin, who is angry because it is interrupting the play at the bassett-table close by:

"Vos beaux discours d'appas, de grace,    Your lofty praises of beauty, pomp and
de beauté,    grace,
Nous contant notre argent—il ne m'est    Tell us nothing new—I fear them out of
rien resté."    place.

*To which Mrs. Myddleton replies:*

"Nous n'avons pas appris à garder le    We did not learn to hold our tongue
silence
Comme vous avez fait dans vos couvens    As you did in French convents when
de France,    you were young,
Monsieur, Monsieur Villiers, allons nous    O Monsieur Villiers, let us depart at our
consoler;    ease;
Il est d'autres maisons où l'on pourra    There are other houses where we can
parler."    converse as we please.

* Lady Isabella Bennet, Duchess of Grafton; and Charlotte Fitzroy, Countess of Litchfield, a natural daughter of Charles II.

Of Jane Myddleton's later years there is little to relate. She, and presumably her husband, had a house in Charles Street, Mayfair, and a cottage at Greenwich. She spent some time at Clevedon, a seat of George Villiers, second Duke of Buckingham, where Edmund Waller was a frequent visitor. Their only visible means of subsistence was £400 a year which Myddleton drew a place in the Prize Office. After the accession of her old admirer, the Duke of York, to the throne, their means were slightly improved by an annual pension of £500 a year from the Secret Service funds. Myddleton died in 1691, and his wife a year later. They lie buried side by side in Lambeth Church.

Her epitaph was written by St. Evremond:

"Ici git Myddelton, illustre entre les belles,

Here lies Myddelton, among beauties most celebrated,

Qui de notre commerce a fait les agrémens:

By her presence, the sweeter part in all relations:

Elle avait des vertus pour les amis fidèles,

Among faithful friends, her virtues venerated,

Et des charmes pour les amants.

And charms praised in lovers' ovations.

Malade avec inquietude,

Sick under the weight of anxiety's toll,

Resolue à mourir sans peine, sans effort,

Resolved without pain, without effort to die,

Elle aurait ptl faire l'étude

She played perchance the worthy role

D'un philosophe dans la mort,

Of noble philosopher as death cometh nigh,

Le plus indifférent, Ie plus dur, Ie plus sage,

Determined with indifference and wisdom to play

Prennant part au malheur qui nous afflige tous,

Her part in the misfortune that afflicts us all,

Passant, interromps ton voyage,

Traveler, your voyage for a moment delay,

Et te fais un mérite à pleurer avec nous."

Show your merit, let your tears with ours fall.

# CHAPTER VIII

## FRANCES, LADY WHITMORE (*née* BROOKE), BORN 1645 (1). ELIZABETH, LADY DENHAM (*née* BROOKE), 1647 (1)-1667

THE beautiful Brooke sisters, Frances and Elizabeth, were brought to London and taken to Court at an early age.

Their grandfather was George Brooke, younger brother of Henry, eighth Lord Cobham. The latter was attainted for his share in Raleigh's plot [1], and although found guilty, James I did not allow him to be executed, and even made him a modest allowance. He was, except for a brief interval, confined in the Tower from his trial in 1603 until his death in 1619. Having no issue, his estates passed to William, the son of his brother, George. William was "restored in blood" in 1610, but was not allowed to assume the title, which in 1645 Charles I conferred on a royalist supporter, Sir John Brooke, grandson of George, sixth Lord Cobham, and second cousin of Henry, the eighth baron. William, who was made a Knight of the Bath, married Penelope, third daughter of Sir Moyses Hill, of Hillsborough Castle in Ireland, the ancestor of the Marquises of Downshire. His widow married Edward Russell, youngest son of Francis, fifth Earl of Bedford, whose sister was Countess of Bristol.

The girls were nieces of Digby, Earl of Bristol, and, according to Mrs. Jameson, "Their profligate uncle, who was at this time intriguing against the influence of Lady Castlemaine, introduced them at Court, in the hope that one or both would capture the versatile Charles. How far these young girls, and both were then very young, lent themselves to this project, or were acquainted with his purposes, is not clear, but Lady Castlemaine interfered in good time to prevent the accomplishment of the Earl's hopes; and the King, who had just

---

[1] The Main Plot was a conspiracy by English Catholics, allegedly led by lay Catholic Lord Cobham, to remove King James I of England from the English throne, replacing him by aid of Spain with his cousin Arabella (or Arbella) Stuart. The plot involved George Brooke and Lord Grey of Wilton raising a regiment and marching on London to take over the government. Henry Brooke, 8th Lord Cobham, was to act as a negotiator.

Frances, Lady Whitmore (*née* Brooke)

purchased a peace at the usual hard price, was not inclined to ex-
change it for the sake of Miss Brooke."

The elder daughter, Frances, escaped the temptations of the Court
by espousing Sir Thomas Whitmore, Bart., of Apley. It is believed
that Frances and her husband led an uneventful life in the country;
but little or nothing is known of them, except that their daughter
married William, grandson of Sir George Whitmore, of Balmes, who
is mentioned by Pepys.

Dryden wrote her epitaph:

> "Fair, kind, and true, a treasure each alone,
> A wife, a mistress, and a friend, in one;
> Rest in this tomb, raised at thy husband's cost,
> Here sadly summing, what he had, and lost.
>   Come, virgins, ere in equal bands ye join,
> Come first and offer at her sacred shrine;
> Pray but for half the virtues of this wife,
> Compound for all the rest, with longer life;
> And wish your vows, like hers, may be returned
> So loved when living, and, when dead, so mourned."

The younger daughter of William Brooke, Elizabeth, was a much more prominent figure in Society. Born in 1647, she at the age of eighteen became the second wife of Sir John Denham, the marriage taking place on May 25, 1665, in Westminster Abbey. The persistent report that Denham was seventy-three at this time may be dismissed, since there is authority for the fact that he was born in 1615.

Denham had had a somewhat adventurous career. The only son of Sir John Denham, an Irish judge, by his second wife, Eleanor, daughter of Garrett More, Viscount Drogheda, he was born at Dublin and educated in London. He went to Oxford — there is no record that he took a degree — and thence was entered as a student at Lincoln's Inn. At nineteen he married his first wife, Ann Cotton, of a Gloucester family, who was fairly well dowered. His passion for gaming was nearly his undoing, for he seems to have been more than ordinarily unlucky. His father frequently protested, but did not go so far as to disinherit him, and the son, on the death of Sir John in 1638, inherited the paternal acres. Even this did not sober him, and much of his not over-robust patrimony was lost at the tables.

There is a curious sketch of Denham by the antiquarian Aubrey in his *Letters and Lives of Eminent Persons*. "I have heard Mr. James Howe say that he was the dreamingest young fellow; he never expected such things from him as he hath left the world. When he was there, he would game extremely, when he had played away all his money, he would play away his father's cappes wrought with gold. His father was Sir John Denham, one of the Barons of the Exchequer; he had been one of the Lord Justices in Ireland. He married Ellanor, one of the daughters of Sir Garrett Moore, Knight, Lord Baron of Mellifont, in ye Kingdome of Ireland, whom he married during his service in Ireland, in ye place of Chief justice there. Sir John was not supposed to be a witt. At last, viz. in 1640, his play of *The Sophy* came out, which did take extremely. Mr. Edmund Walter sayd of him that he broke out like the Irish Rebellion three score thousand strong, when nobody expected it. He was much rooked by gamesters, fell acquainted with that unsanctified crew, to his ruine. His father had some suspicion of it, and chid him severely; whereupon his son John (only child) wrot a little Essay in 8$^{vo}$, pointed against gaming, and to shew the vanities and inconveniences of it, which he presented to his father, to let him know his detestation of it: but shortly after his father's death (1638), (who left 2000 or 1500 lib. in ready money, two houses well furnished, and much plate), the money was played away first, and next the plate was sold. I remember, about 1646, he lost 200 lib. one night at Newcutts." The title of the "Essay," which was published in 1651, was, "The Anatomy of Play, Written by a worthy and learned gent. Dedicated to his father to show his detestation of it." Even at that time Denham had a nice sense of humour.

Sir John Denham, when the Civil War began, was High Sheriff of Surrey, and threw in his lot with the Royalists. Of his adventures during that period, this is not the place to write in detail, except, perhaps, to mention that during the Civil Wars, when the Prince was a mere boy, Denham at the risk of his life conveyed him out of England, and carried him to the Queen at Paris. His estates were sold. "In the time of the Civil Wars," Aubrey relates, "George Withers, the poet, begged Sir John Denham's estate of the Parliament, in whose cause he was a captain of horse. It happened that Withers was taken prisoner, and was in danger of his life, having written severely against the King. Sir John Denham went to the King, and desired his Majesty not to hang him, for that whilst George Withers lived, he should not be the worst poet in England." Withers may have been grateful for Denham's intervention in his favour, but would, no doubt, have preferred another reason to have been given.

During the Civil War, Denham's estates were sold, and he was practically penniless. At the Restoration, however, he was in some measure rewarded for his loyalty by financial grants. Also he was appointed to the lucrative post of Surveyor-General of Works. According to Sir Sidney Lee, Denham claimed to have received the reversion to this office from Charles I in the life-time of its latest holder, Inigo Jones, who died in 1651. Inigo Jones's assistant, John Webbe, protested, stating that "though Denham may have, as most gentry, some knowledge of architecture, he can have none of the practice." He asked for the appointment for himself, but was compelled to content himself with the reversion. What Denham knew about architecture has not transpired. "I went to London," Evelyn wrote in October 1661, "to visit my Lord of Bristol, having been with Sir John Denham (his Majesty's Surveyor), to consult with him about the placing of his Majesty's Palace at Greenwich, which I would have had built between the river and the Queene's house, so as a large square cut should have let in the Thames like a bay; but Sir John was for setting it on piles at the very brink of the water, which I did not assent to, and so came away, knowing Sir John to be a better poet than architect, though he had Mr. Webbe (Inigo Jones's man) to assist him." Presently Sir John Denham had the extraordinary good fortune to secure as his deputy Christopher Wren.

Denham had, apart from the stage, a dramatic sense, and was entrusted with the management of the Coronation ceremonies, for which service he was knighted. He now entered Parliament and sat for Old Sarum for the rest of his life, though it is not on record that he took any considerable part in the proceedings of the House of Commons.

Sir John Denham is thus described by Aubrey: "He was of the tallest, but a little uncurvetting at his shoulders, not very robust. His hair was but thin and flaxen, with a moist curl. His gait was slow, and was rather a stalking (he had long legs). His eye was a kind of light goose gray, not big, but it had a strange piercingness, not so to shining and glory, but (like a Momus) when he conversed with you, he looked into your very thoughts."

When Elizabeth Brooke came to Court, her appearance caused her to be much remarked: "The two Brookes," Grammont says, "were always of those parties [given by their relation, the Earl of Bristol]; they were both formed by nature to excite love in others, as well as to be susceptible of it themselves; they were just what the King wanted: the Earl, from this commencement, was beginning to entertain a good opinion of his project, when Lady Castlemaine, who had lately gained entire possession of the King's heart, was not in a humour, at that time, to share it with another, as she did very indiscreetly afterwards, despising Miss Stuart. As soon, therefore, as she received intimation of these secret practices, under pretence of attending the King in his parties, she entirely disconcerted them; so that the Earl obliged to lay aside his projects, and Miss Brooke to discontinue her advances. The King did not dare to think any more on this subject; but his brother was pleased to look after what he neglected; and Miss Brooke accepted the other of his heart, until it pleased Heaven to dispose of her otherwise, which happened soon after in the following manner. Sir John Denham, loaded with wealth as well as years, had passed his youth in the midst of those pleasures which people at that age indulge in without restraint; he was one of the brightest geniuses England ever produced, for wit and humour, and for brilliancy of composition: satirical and free in his poems, he spared neither frigid writers, nor jealous hJ1sbands, nor even their wives: every part abounded with the most poignant wit, and the most entertaining stories; but his most delicate and spirited raillery turned generally against matrimony."

The Duke of York was, according to Grammont, attracted to her in the following way: "The Duchess of York, being desirous of having the portraits of the handsomest persons at Court, Lely painted them, and employed all his skill in the performance; nor could he ever exert himself upon more beautiful subjects. Every picture appeared a masterpiece, and that of Miss Hamilton appeared the highest finished. Lely himself acknowledged that he had drawn it with a particular pleasure. The Duke of York took a delight in looking at it, and began again to ogle the original. He had very little reason to hope for success; and at the same time that his hopeless passion alarmed de Grammont, Lady Denham thought proper to renew the negotiation which had so unluckily been interrupted. It was soon brought to a conclusion, for, when both parties are sincere in a negotiation, no time is lost in cavilling. Everything succeeded prosperously on one side; yet I know not what fatality obstructed the pretensions of the other."

After a while, as was his wont, he neglected the lady; but when she returned to London after her marriage, he again became assiduous: "Here [at Whitehall]," Pepys wrote on September 26, 1666, "I had the hap to see my Lady Denham: and at night went into the dining-room, and saw several fine ladies, among others, Castlemaine, but chiefly Denham again; and the Duke of York taking her aside and talking to her in the sight of all the world, all alone; which was strange, and what also I did not like. Here I met with good Mr. Evelyn, who cries not against it, and calls it bitchering, for the Duke of York talks to her a little, and then she goes away, and then he follows her again like a dog." On the following October 8, he noted, "The Duke of York is wholly given up to this bitch of Denham." There were rumours in December that his interest was waning. "They," said Pepys, "talked for certain, that now the King do follow Mrs. Stuart wholly, and my Lady Castlemaine not above once a week; that the Duke of York do not haunt my Lady Denham so much; that she troubles him with matters of state, being of my Lord Bristol's faction, and that he avoids." In fact, the liaison was the talk of the town. The lady was at no pains to disguise the situation: in fact, she at all times insisted on the Duke acknowledging her publicly as his mistress, and visiting her every day at her husband's house in Scotland Yard.

The situation in which Lady Denham was held is indicated in a passage from Grammont's *Memoirs*, which passage also throws light on the morals of the Court in general at this time:

"'It is strange,' he said, 'that the country, which is little better than a gallows or a grave for young people, is allotted in this land for the unfortunate, and not for the guilty! Poor Lady Chesterfield for some unguarded looks, is immediately seized upon by an angry husband

Elizabeth, Lady Denham (*née* Brooke)

who will oblige her to spend her Christmas at a country house, a hundred and fifty miles from London; while here there are a thousand ladies who are left at liberty to do whatever they please, and who indulge in that liberty, and whose conduct, in short, deserves a daily bastinado. I name no person—God forbid I should; but Lady Myddleton, Lady Denham, the Queen's and Duchess's Maids of Honour, and a hundred others, bestow their favours to the right and left, and not the least notice is taken of their conduct. As for Lady Shrewsbury, she is conspicuous. I would take a wager she might have a man killed for every day, and she would only hold her head the higher for it. One would suppose she imported from Rome plenary indulgences for her conduct. There are three or four gentlemen who wear an ounce of her hair made into bracelets, and no person finds any fault; and yet such a cross-grained fool as Chesterfield be permitted to exercise an act of tyranny, altogether unknown in this country, upon the prettiest woman in England, and all for a mere trifle; but I am his humble servant; his precautions will avail him nothing; on the contrary, very often a woman who had no bad intentions when she was suffered to remain in tranquility, is prompted to such conduct by revenge, or reduced to it by necessity.

This is as true as Gospel: hear now what Francisco's Saraband says on the subject:

> "'Tell me, jealous-pated swain,
>     What avail thy idle arts,
>     To divide united hearts?
>     Love, like the wind, I trow,
>     Will, where it listeth, blow;
>
> So, prithee, peace, for all thy cares are vain.
>
> "'When you are by,
>
> Nor wishful look, be sure, nor eloquent sigh,
>     Shall dare those inward fires discover,
>     Which burn in either lover;
>
> Yet Argus' self, if Argus were the spy,
>     Should ne'er, with all his mob of eyes, Surprise.
>
> " 'Some joys forbidden, Transports hidden,
>     Which love, through dark and secret ways,
>     Mysterious love, to kindred souls convey.'"

The Duke was very urgent with the Duchess to put Lady Denham in possession of the place which was the object of her ambition; but as she was not guarantee for the performance of the secret articles of the treaty, though till this time she had borne with patience the inconstancy of the Duke, and yielded submissively to his desires; yet, in the present instance, it appeared hard and dishonourable to her, to entertain near her person a rival, who would expose her to the danger of acting but a second part in the midst of her own Court. However, she saw herself upon the point of being forced to it by authority, when a far more unfortunate obstacle for ever bereft poor Lady Denham of the hopes of possessing that fatal place, which she had solicited with such eagerness. Old Denham, naturally jealous, became more and more suspicious, and found that he had sufficient ground for such conduct: his wife was young and handsome, he old and disagreeable: what reason then had he to flatter himself that Heaven would exempt from the fate of husbands in the like circumstances? This he was continually saying to himself; but when compliments were poured in upon him from all sides, upon the place his lady was going to have near the Duchess's person, he formed ideas of what was sufficient to have made him hang himself, if he had possessed the resolution. The traitor chose rather to exercise his courage against another. He wanted precedents for putting in practice his resentments in a privileged country: that of Lord Chesterfield was not sufficiently bitter for the revenge he meditated: besides he had no country-house to which he could carry his unfortunate wife. This being the case, the old villain made her travel a much longer journey without stirring out of London. Merciless fate robbed her of life, and of her dearest hopes, in the bloom of youth. As no person entertained any doubts of his having poisoned her, the populace of his neighbourhood had a design of tearing him in pieces, as soon as he should come abroad; but he shut himself up to bewail her death, until their fury was appeased by a magnificent funeral, at which he distributed four times more burnt wine[2] than had ever been drunk at any burial in England."

Pepys records on November 9, 1666, that he heard that my Lady Denham is exceeding sick, even to death, and that she says, and everybody else discourses that she is poisoned. Lady Denham died the following January 6, and on the next day he wrote:

"My Lady Denham is at last dead. Some suspect her poisoned, but it will be best known when her body is opened, which will be to-

---

[2] Burnt wine is a colloquial name for brandy because its distillation required boiling.

day, her dying yesterday morning. The Duke of York is troubled for her; but hath declared he will never have another public mistress again; which I shall be glad of, and wish the King would do the same." The lampoons of the day by Andrew Marvell and others hint very definitely at the suspicion that she was poisoned by a mixture infused into her chocolate. Sir John Denham was not the only suspect. The slander of the times attributed Lady Denham's death to the jealousy of the Duchess of York, who by some was thought to be the instigator of the crime. Aubrey, however, accuses Henrietta, Countess of Rochester, of being responsible for the crime. As a matter of fact there was no crime, for a post-mortem examination, showed no trace of poison. It is said that Lady Denham suffered from internal trouble that gave her pain, which, as a contemporary put it, "if true, is sufficient to clear both the Duchess from poison and the Duke from lying with her."

Late in 1666 or early in the following year Sir John Denham was thought to be suffering from a fit of madness, though whether real or feigned is uncertain. By some it was attributed to the distress he felt at the disgraceful conduct of his wife; but it is more likely that it was the effect of an accidental blow on the head. "The Duke of York fell deeply in love with Lady Denham," Aubrey wrote. "This occasioned Sir John's distemper of madness in 1666 which first appeared when he went to London to see the famous free-stone quarries at Portland, in Dorset. When he came within a mile of it, turned back to London and would not see it. He went to Hounslowt and demanded rents of lands he had sold many years before; went to the King, and told him he was the Holy Ghost; but it pleased God that he was cured of this distemper, and wrote excellent verses, particularly on the death of Abraham Cowley, afterwards:

> "'His fancy and his judgment such,
> Each to the other seemed too much:
> His severe judgment, giving law,
> His modest fancy kept in awe;
> As rigid husbands jealous are,
> When they believe their wives too fair.'"

"Sir John Denham is fallen to the ladies also," Lord Lisle wrote to Sir William Temple. "He is at many of the meetings at dinners, talks more than ever he did, and is extremely pleased by those who seem willing to hear him, and, from that obligation exceedingly praises the Duchess of Monmouth and my Lady Cavendish. If he had not the name of being mad, I believe in most companies he would be thought wittier than ever he was. He seems to have fewer extravagances besides that of telling stories of himself, which he was always inclined to. Some of his acquaintances say, that extreme vanity was the cause of his madness, as well as it is an effect." The attack of madness did not, however, last long. He survived until March 1669, and was buried near Chaucer's monument in Westminster Abbey.

# CHAPTER IX

HORTENSIA, DUCHESS MAZARIN (née MANCINI) 1646-1699

"THE Duchess Mazarin," says Jesse in the *Memoirs of the Court of England during the Reign of the Stuarts*," was unquestionably the most remarkable woman who languished in the seraglio of Charles II. In her youth she was considered the most beautiful woman and the wealthiest heiress in Europe. During the King's early days of poverty and exile, when the almost infant niece of the powerful Mazarin was courted by the most illustrious families in Europe for their sons, Charles had been an eager suitor for her hand. The offer, however, was rejected by the haughty Cardinal. The fact is singular that she should have afterwards become the mistress of her admirer, and indebted to his bounty for the ordinary luxuries, if not the necessaries, of life."

When the Duchess came to England in 1676, she created a sensation. Nell Gwyn, who, on her own lines and in her own place, was always able to hold her own, regarded her with rather amused interest; but the Duchess of Portsmouth was roused to fury by the attention that Charles paid to the newcomer. She was, indeed, a dangerous rival, if St. Evremond's description of her is accurate: "She is one of those Roman beauties who in no way resemble your dolls of France. The colour of her eyes has no name; it is neither blue, nor grey, nor altogether black, but a combination of all the three; they have the sweetness of blue, the gaiety of grey, and above all, the fire of black. There are none in the world so sweet. There are none in the world so serious and so grave when her thoughts are occupied with any serious object. They are large, well-set, full of fire and intelligence.

"All the movements of her mouth are full of charm, and the strangest grimaces become her wonderfully, when she imitates those who make them. Her smiles would soften the hardest heart and ease the most profound depression of mind; they almost entirely change her expression, which is naturally haughty, and spread over it a certain tincture of sweetness and kindness, which reassures those hearts which her charms have alarmed.

"Her nose, too, which without doubt is incomparably well turned and perfectly proportioned, imparts a lofty air to her whole physiognomy. The tone of her voice is so harmonious and agreeable that none can hear her speak without being sensibly moved. Her complexion is so delicately clear that I cannot believe that anyone who examined it closely can deny it to be whiter than the driven snow. Her hair is of a glossy black, with nothing harsh about it. To see how naturally it curls as soon as it is let loose, one would say it rejoiced to shade so-lovely a head. She has the finest turned countenance that a painter ever imagined."

Hortensia was the youngest and most beautiful of the three daughters of Lorenzo Mancini, an Italian nobleman, who had married Jeromina, sister of Cardinal Mazarin. She was educated under the direction of the great man, about whose severity when she was a child Hortensia complained bitterly.

Her attraction for men was undoubted. She was not much more than ten years old when Charles II asked for her hand, and only three years older when she married Armand Charles de la Ponte, Duke de Meilleraye, and a Peer of France. The Cardinal had intended that this nobleman should marry his niece, Mary, but the Duke fell so desperately in love with Hortensia that he declared that if she was refused him, he was sure he would die in three months. In the end, the Cardinal gave his consent, on condition that de Meilleraye and his heirs should for ever adopt the name, title, and arms of Mazarin. When the alliance was concluded, the girl-bride received a cabinet containing ten thousand pistoles[1]. "One day," she wrote, "wanting other divertisement, we threw above three hundred pistoles out of the window of the Palace Mazarin to have the pleasure of seeing the servants that were in the court scramble and fight for them. This prodigality being told the Cardinal, it caused so much displeasure with him, that it is believed it hastened his end; but whether it was so or no, he died within eight days after, and left me the richest heiress, but the unhappiest woman, in Christendom. Upon the first tidings of his death, my brother and sister, instead of being sorry, cried to one another,

---

[1] 10,000 pistoles equals 5000£ in 17$^{th}$ C. currency. This would be about £475,000 ($0.9 million) in 2002.

'God be thanked, he is gone.' To tell the truth I was not much more afflicted. It is a remarkable thing that a man of that merit, who all his life had laboured to raise and enrich his family, should never receive thanks from them than apparent signs of hatred and aversion even after his death." Hortensia had married on February 28, 1661. From Mazarin, who died on the following March 9 she inherited over a million sterling.

The marriage was from the first unhappy. The Duke was narrow-minded. He was not only a devotee, but believed himself inspired. To such an extent, it is related, did he carry his devotional prejudices, that, having taken under his charge an infant child of Madame de Richelieu, he actually forbade the nurse to give it suck on the fasting days of the Church! As St. Evremond put it, "Piety poisoned all the talents that Nature had bestowed on him." He was most unhealthily prurient. He would not let the women servants milk the cows, lest it put ideas into their heads; and he himself broke up with a hammer the nude statues and painted out the nude figures in the pictures in his gallery. "Madame de Mazarin was very wretched," says St. Evremond. "She used to long for the approach of night, which brings succour to the most unhappy by drowning the sense of their miseries. But even this comfort was denied her. No sooner did she close her beautiful eyes, but Monsieur de Mazarin, the amiable husband, used to wake his best-beloved — you would never guess for what — to make her partake of his midnight visions.... Nature has set reason and Monsieur de Mazarin so far apart, that it was almost impossible they could ever come together." In fact the man was half mad.

The Duke's jealousy made his wife's life a misery. "I could not speak to a servant but he was dismissed the same day," she wrote in her memoirs. "I could not receive two visits but he was forbidden the house. If I showed any preference for one of my maids, she was at once taken away from me. He would have liked me to see no one in the world except himself. Above all, he could not endure that I should see either his relations or my own — the latter because they had begun to take my part; his own, because they no more approved of his conduct than did mine." For nearly six years Hortensia put up with this life; but then she accepted the advice of friends to apply to the court for a separation. Jesse has summarised her pleadings: his jealous disposition, his rigorous sanctity, his forcing her to accompany him on the most harassing journeys even when on the eve of confinement, the large amount of her wealth which he distributed in alms, and his having insulted her by charging her with having been guilty of familiarities with one of her nearest relations." As regards the last the Duchess says that when her brother, the Duc de Nevers, came to visit her at a country house at Sedan, Mazarin was jealous of him. "He had," she remarked, referring to her husband, "an implacable hatred against all those I loved or loved me; an indefatigable care to bring into my presence all those I hated mortally, and to corrupt those of my servants whom I most trusted to betray my secrets if I had any; a studious application to cry me down everywhere and make my actions odious to all people."

Before the suit she had instituted was heard, she went for a while into voluntary retirement at the Abbey de Celles; but her husband withdrew her from there, and placed her in the very strict Couvent des Filles de Sainte-Marie. There, to her great happiness, she found the Marquise de Courcelles, and these two frivolous young people gave the nuns the most exciting time of their lives. "As Madame de Courcelles was very amiable and entertaining, I had the complacency to join with her in some pleasantries which she played upon the nuns," the Duchess related. "A hundred ridiculous stories were carried to the King, who was told that we put ink in the holy water-basin to bespatter the good ladies, that we ran through the dormitories, accompanied by a pack of hounds, crying, 'Tayaut! Tayaut!' ['Tallyho! Tallyho!'] and such-like things, all of which were absurdly false or grossly exaggerated. For example, having asked for some water to wash our feet, the nuns disapproved and refused our request, just as if we were there to observe the regulations." Mark the sequel. "It is true that we filled with water a large coffer which stood in our dormitory, and the boards of the floor being very loosely joined together, the water which overflowed leaked through the wretched floor and wetted the beds of the good sisters. This accident was talked about as if it had been something which we had done of design." After a time the Abbess petitioned the powers that were to take away this distressing visitor, who was then allowed to retire to Celles.

The Duke soon heard of this. "Some few days after," says the lady, "Monsieur de Mazarin comes with a guard of three-score horse, with leave from the Archbishop of Paris to enter the nunnery, and carry me away by force, if necessary. But the Abbess not only refused him entrance, but put all the keys of the house in my hands, to free me from the suspicion of the evil she might have done me; with this condition only, that I would speak with Monsieur Mazarin. I asked him, what he would have? But, he still replied, I was not the Abbess. I answered him, that I was the Abbess for him that day, since all the keys of the house were in my power, and there was no getting in for him, but by my favour. He turned his back, and went his way.... A gentleman that the Countess de Soisson (the Duchess's sister, Plympia) sent to know how I did, carried the news to Paris, and said it was reported at Celles, that Monsieur Mazarin went off only with design to return again in the night. You have heard without doubt, how Madame de Bouillon (the Duchess's sister, Mary), the Count de Soissons, the Duke de Bouillon, and the best and greatest people about the Court got on horseback, to come to my rescue. At the noise they made, Madame de Courcelles and I took them for my enemies, but our fear was not so great but that we thought upon an expedient to hide ourselves. There was a hole in the grate of our parlour big enough for a great dish to pass, and we never till then thought one could creep through it. Yet we both got into that hole, but it was with so much difficulty, that if Monsieur Mazarin had been in that parlour he would never suspect that place, and would have looked for us anywhere else than there. But when we found our error, the shame and confusion we were in, made us resolve to shoot that gulph once more without calling anybody to our aid. Madame de Courcelles got through easily enough, but I was above a quarter of an hour between two bars of iron, and almost squeezed to death, without being able to get in or out. But though I was so horribly pinched, I would not consent that anyone should be called to help us; and Madame de Courcelles never left tugging until she had me out. I went to thank them all, and after they had joked a while upon Monsieur Mazarin's attempt to catch nothing, they all returned back."

The King of France was anxious to avoid all unnecessary scandal, and he exerted his influence to bring the Duke and Duchess together.

At last he had his way. The lady yielded to his wish, on condition that she should have a separate suite of apartments in the Palace Mazarin — a condition which her husband granted, but with an ill grace. This arrangement might have continued, but when Hortensia was preparing for a theatrical performance, which was to take place on a holy day, the Duke, hearing of this, had the stage pulled down. Then, the Duchess heard that her husband was applying for a decree for restoration of conjugal rights. That was the end: she decided to take refuge in flight.

On June 14, 1668, Hortensia early in the morning secretly left the Palace Mazarin. When she had got some distance away, she discovered that she had forgotten her money and jewels, and sent back for them. This exhibition of nerve delighted Charles II when he heard of it, and he wrote to his sister, the Duchess of Orleans: "The sudden retreat of Madame Mazarin is an extraordinary action as I have heard. She has exceeded Lady Shrewsbury by robbing her husband. I see wives do not love devout husbands, which means this woman had, besides many more, as I hear, to be rid of her husband, upon any terms, and so I wish her a good journey."

The Duchess has herself told the story of her flight from France. "My train," she has written, "consisted of a maid I had but six months, called Nannon, dressed in man's apparel, as I was; a man of my brother's called Narcissus, with whom I had no acquaintance; and a gentleman, belonging to Monsieur de Rohan, called Courbeville, whom I had never seen before. My brother desired Monsieur de Rohan not to leave me until he had seen me out of the city. I parted with him without the Gate of Saint Anthony, and drove on, in a coach with six horses, to a house belonging to the Princess of Guimene, his mother, ten leagues from Paris. From thence, I went six or seven leagues in a caleche, but these kind of carriages were too slow for my fears, therefore, I took horse, and arrived at Bar the Friday following about noon; from there, seeing myself out of France, I went no further than Nancy that night. The Duke of Lorraine, hearing of my arrival, and desiring to see me, was so civil as not to press it when he heard I was unwilling. The Resident of France was very earnest to have me stopped there, but in vain; and the Duke to complete his generosity to me, gave me a lieutenant and twenty of his guard to conduct me into Switzerland. We were almost everywhere known to be women; and Nannon still, through forgetfulness, called me 'Madame.' Whether for this reason, or that my face gave some cause of suspicion, the people watched us through the keyhole when we had shut ourselves in, and saw our long tresses, which, as soon as we were at liberty, we untied, because they were very troublesome to us under our periwigs. Nannon was extremely low of stature, and so unfit to be clothed in man's apparel, that I could never look upon her without laughing. The night that I lay at Nancy, where we resumed our woman's apparel, I was so overjoyed to see myself out of danger, that I gave myself the liberty of diverting me a little at my ordinary sports, and as I ran after to laugh at her I fell upon my knee and hurt it. I did not feel it then, but some days after, having caused a bed to be made in a sorry village in Franche-Comté, in order to rest myself while dinner was preparing, such a grievous pain took me of a sudden in that knee that I was not able to rise. But on I must go I Therefore, having been let blood by a woman, for want of another chirurgeon, I followed my journey in a litter till I came to Neufchatel, where the people persuaded themselves I was Madame de Longueville. You can imagine the joy the people expressed to see me, being not used to see women of quality of France pass through their country; nor could they comprehend that any other but the Duchess of Longueville could have business that way. I know some would have laid hold of this occasion and made use of their kindness to taste of the sweetness of sovereignty. After all, the mistake was advantageous to me, and what I wanted in age, I gained in quality. But power and authority seemed to me too great and good for a fugitive. I was so skilfully handled there that my pain grew worse, insomuch that I had once thoughts of returning to Paris; and were it not that Milan was nearer, and that I hoped to be sooner and safer there, I had pursued my first thought."

The Duchess stayed at Chambéry for three years, where Charles Emmanuel II, who had wanted to marry her, lent her a palace there. She took into her service one César Vichaud, who, for some reason unknown, styled himself the Abbé de Saint-Real, thereby occasioning much scandal, so much so that when the King died in 1675, it was intimated to her that her presence in Savoy was no longer desired.

Thereupon she came to England. "The Duke of York received at his house yesterday the Duchess Mazarin, who received at the same time the compliments of the King of England through the Earl of Sunderland," Ruvigny[2] wrote to Pomponne. "Everyone here is in expectation of some important changes, and it is believed that a lady so extolled cannot fail to be the cause of adventures. M. de Grammont, who has undertaken the care of this lady's conduct, considers her as beautiful as ever. For myself, who have seen her since the first days of her marriage, and who have retained the recollection of what she was then like, I have observed some alteration, which, however, does not prevent her being more beautiful than ever... She is to all appearances a finely developed young girl. I never saw anyone who so well defies the power of time and vice to disfigure. At the age of fifty she will have the satisfaction of thinking, when she looks at her mirror, that she is as lovely as she ever was in her life." She was then, however, but thirty years of age. At this time St. Evremond wrote an account of her appearance. "Her complexion was soft-toned, yet warm and fresh," he said. "It was so harmonious that, although dark, she appeared to be of beautiful freshness. Her jet-black hair rose in strong waves above her forehead, as if proud to shade and adorn so lovely a head. Even an artist could not determine the colour of her eyes, which had the sparkle of black, but the liveliness of grey and the sweetness of blue. They were neither languishing nor passionate in expression, as if nature had maliciously designed them only to express love and veneration, while being susceptible to neither."

The Duchess Mazarin landed at Torbay, and rode to London in male attire, accompanied by no less than nine servants. She went to St. James's Palace where accommodation was provided for her by her kinswoman, Mary of Modena, who had married the Duke of York in 1673, when she was in her sixteenth year. The Duke of York interested himself in Hortensia to the extent of purchasing Lord Windsor's house in the Park, and lending it her during her sojourn in

---

[2] Henry de Massue (1648-1720), a.k.a. the Marquis de Ruvigny (later Viscount and Earl of Galway), a distinguished French diplomatist, and a relative of Rachel, the wife of Lord William Russell. He saw service under Turenne, who thought very highly of him. Probably on account of his English connections he was selected in 1678 by Louis XIV. to carry out the secret negotiations for a compact with Charles II, a difficult mission which he executed with great skill.

England. "I was in Cheapside," Lady Chaworth wrote after the Lord Mayor's Show, "and had the good luck to escape the squibs, which were plentiful, especially directed to the balcony over against me where the Duchess Mazarin, Lady Sussex [daughter of the Duchess of Cleveland], the Prince of Monaco, and the Portuguese Ambassador stood; one of them lighting such on Lady Sussex's forehead which forced her presently to put on a huge patch. They say her husband and she will part unless she leave the Court and be content to live with him in the country, he disliking much her converse with Madam Mazarin and the addresses she gets in that company."

When the Duchess came to Court, she created a furore. All the gallants, with one accord, threw themselves at her feet. If poets raved about her, lampooners allowed themselves the licence customary in that day. To take one example:

> "When through the world fair Mazarin had run
> Bright as her fellow-traveller, the sun, I
> Hither at length the Roman eagle flies,
> As the last triumph of her conquering eyes,
> As heir to Julius, she may pretend
> A second time to make this nation bend;
> But Portsmouth, springing from the ancient race
> Of Britons, which the Saxons here did chase,
> As they great Cæsar did oppose, makes head,
> And does against this new invader lead."

Charles was again attracted by her. "The arrival," wrote Miss Strickland, "of the Duchess Mazarin in England, who, when Hortensia Mancini, had inspired the King with a passion so intense that he had offered to make her his wife, must have been an alarming event to the Queen, who naturally apprehended a formidable rival in one whom he had thus regarded. The lapse of fifteen years, however, had banished every particle of romance from the heart of Charles—love was with him no longer a sentiment. He gave Hortensia a residence at Chelsea and a pension of £4000 a year, and visited her occasionally; but her influence never equalled that of the Duchess of Portsmouth."

The Duchess of Portsmouth, anyhow for a while, was of a different opinion. She was furious at the attentions paid to the Duchess Mazarin by Charles. Very wisely, however, knowing her man, she said little, and bided her time. Charles begged Louis XIV to insist on the Duke Mazarin making his wife a suitable allowance. "I have just learnt," de Ruvigny wrote to Louis on March 12, 1676, "that there is certain and secret intelligence between the King of England and the Duchess Mazarin. She carries on her intrigue very quietly with him. Those who had hoped to share in the triumph have not yet had the opportunity they expected."

In December of the same year Honoré Courtin[3] wrote to Louvois a letter which has been summarised by Forneron, the Duchess Mazarin's biographer: "Courtin pitied Charles, who wanted to be well with everybody—a hard problem to solve, surrounded as he was by jealous women. He had to face the anger of the Duchess of Portsmouth for drinking twice in twenty-four hours to the health of Nell Gwyn, with whom he still often supped, and who still made the Duchess of Portsmouth the butt of her tickling sarcasms. The rakes of the Town met the King at her supper table, and said freely before him whatever came uppermost in their heads. As for the Duchess Mazarin, the Court of Versailles was informed by the watchful Ambassador that Charles went regularly through the going-to-bed ceremony at Whitehall; and when his gentlemen and servants had left his chamber, he got up, dressed, stole oft to St. James's Palace, where he arrived after the Duchess's cardparties were over, and did not return to his Palace until after five in the morning. It was evident, then, that he did not spend his nights with the Duchess of Portsmouth. He went to see her often in the daytime when he knew she had company with her; but that was all."

How the Duchess of Portsmouth took the situation may be deduced from the following letter from the French Ambassador in London to Louvois. "I witnessed yesterday evening," he wrote, "an incident which aroused in me the greatest pity imaginable, and which would perhaps have touched you, all wise and virtuous though you be. I went to Madame de Portsmouth's apartments. She

---

[3] Honoré Courtin was the French ambassador stationed in London at this time.

opened her heart to me, in the presence of two of her waiting-maids. The two maids remained glued against the wall, with downcast eyes. The mistress shed a torrent of tears, and her sighs and sobs interrupted her words. In short, never has a spectacle appeared to me more sad or touching. I remained with her until midnight, and I neglected nothing to restore her courage, and to make her understand how much it was to her interest to dissemble her grief."

The Duchess of Portsmouth temporarily accepted the supremacy of the Duchess Mazarin with the King, who, it may be mentioned, supplied the latter with unlimited funds. "She has had a livery made," Courtin wrote, "more magnificent than any with which you are acquainted. The lace costs three livres, fifteen sols the French ell, and the coats are quite hidden by it. There are nine of them with which to array two porters, six lackeys, and a page; and they cost, with the cravat, two thousand six hundred livres. She keeps an excellent table. In a word, her expenditure far exceeds the two thousand crowns which she receives from her husband. With the appetite which God has given her, she would certainly devour double the income that she has.... I do not know how she does it, but these extraordinary expenses appear to me a little suspicious."

The Duchess Mazarin, for her part, was not in the least doubt about her personal attractions, which, however, she reviewed critically. "I am tall," she said. "I have an admirable figure. I have rather fine eyes, which I never quite open, and this is a charm that renders my glance the sweetest and most tender in the world. I have a well-formed bosom. I have divine hands, passable arms — that is to say, a little thin; but I find consolation for this misfortune in the pleasure of having the most beautiful legs in the world." There was no false modesty about her Grace.

The Duchess Mazarin might have held her own against the Duchess of Portsmouth to the end of the life of Charles II, but her vanity and her love of adventure betrayed her. She fell in love with the Prince of Monaco, and so annoyed the King. Her house at Chelsea was the centre of a distinguished social circle. "Freedom and discretion are equally to be found there," St. Evremond wrote. "Every one is made more at home than in his own house, and treated with more respect than at Court. It is true there are frequent disputes there, but they are those of knowledge and not of anger. There is play there, but it is inconsiderable, and only practised for its amusement. You discover in no countenance the fear of losing, nor concern for what is lost. Some are so disinterested, that they are reproached for expressing joy when they lose, and regret when they win. Play is followed by the most excellent repasts in the world. There you will find whatever delicacy is brought from France, and whatever is curious from the Indies. Even the commonest meats have the rarest flavours imparted to them. There is neither a plenty which gives a notion of extravagance, nor a frugality that discovers penury or meanness. Her guests see nothing but her. They never come soon enough, or depart late enough: they go to bed with regret to have left her, and they rise with a desire to see her again."

Evelyn saw the Duchess Mazarin at Whitehall in 1685, a few days before the death of the King. James II treated her with great attention, if not with affection, and she was received at his Court. William III, it can only be said, tolerated her. She fell upon evil times during the last years of her life, her allowance from her husband being withdrawn. At her death she was in debt over £8000, and her body was actually seized by her creditors. She died in her house at Chelsea on June 2, 1699, in her fifty-third year.

"Now died the famous Duchess Mazarin, who had been the richest lady in Europe," Evelyn wrote a few days later. "She was niece to Cardinal Mazarin, and was married to the richest subject in Europe, as is said. She was born in Rome, educated in France, and was of extraordinary beauty and wit, but dissolute and impatient of matrimonial restraint, so as to be abandoned of her husband and banished, when she came to England for shelter. She lived on a pension given her here, and is reported to have hastened her death by intemperate drinking of strong spirits. She has written her own story and adventures, and so has her other extravagant sister, wife of the noble family of Colonna." St. Evremond, who was whole-heartedly devoted to her, lamented her in a characteristic strain: "Had the poor Duchess Mazarin been alive, "he wrote to M. Silvestre, "she would have had peaches, of which I should not have failed to have shared; she would have had truffles, which we should have eat together; not to mention the carp of Newhall. I must make up the loss of so many advantages, by the Sundays and Wednesdays of Montagu House." A curious lament!

# CHAPTER X

## FRANCES TERESA, DUCHESS OF RICHMOND AND LENNOX
(née STUART), 1647-1702

THE appearance at the Court of Charles II of Frances Teresa Stuart (or Stewart) created a tremendous sensation. Nothing so beautiful or so graceful had been seen there, though it was a haunt of lovely women. She was at once christened "la belle Stuart."

Frances was born on July 8, 1647. She was the elder daughter of the Hon. Walter Stuart (or Stewart), third son of Walter, first Lord Blantyre. Stuart, who was a doctor of medicine, fled to France in 1649, and was given a post in the Household of Queen Henrietta Maria. Frances' younger sister, Sophie, married Henry Bulkeley, Master of the Household to Charles II and James II; and, it is worthy of note here, that Sophie's daughter, Anne, became the wife of James Fitzjames, Duke of Berwick, a natural son of James, Duke of York, by Arabella Churchill.

Young as Frances was, she attracted the attention of Louis XIV, who, according to Pepys, "would fain have had her mother, who is one of the most cunning women in the world, to let her stay in France," as "an ornament to the Court — or in some other and more lucrative capacity." However, Queen Henrietta Maria, who seems to have made herself responsible for the young girl, would have none of this, and sent her to England with a letter of introduction to her son, in which she described her as "la plus jolie fille du monde." ["The prettiest girl in the world"] The French King took his disappointment well, and gave her a parting present.

Frances arrived in England at the beginning of the year 1663, and was soon afterwards appointed a Maid of Honour to Queen Catherine.

Whitehall was not the best place for "la plus jolie fille du monde," who desired to preserve her virtue. The licentiousness of the Court was notorious, and adultery and concubinage for the most part open and unashamed. Frances Stuart, only sixteen years of age, had a difficult time and a troublous; but, so far as is known, held all comers at a sufficient distance.

Frances, Duchess of Richmond (*née* Stuart)

Lady Castlemaine almost at once took the girl under her protection, but knowing this lady's character, this was probably less to
protect her than to keep her away from the King, or, rather, the King
from her. "Miss Stuart's beauty began at this time to be celebrated,"
says Grammont. "The Countess of Castlemaine perceived that the
King paid attention to her; but, instead of being alarmed at it, she favoured as far as she was able, this new inclination, whether from an
indiscretion common to all those who think themselves superior to
the rest of mankind, or whether she designed, by this pastime, to di-
vert the King's attention from the commerce which she held with

Jermyn. She was not satisfied with appearing without any degree of uneasiness at a preference which all the court began to remark: she even affected to make Miss Stuart her favourite, and invited her to all the entertainments she made for the King; and in confidence of her own charms, with the greatest indiscretion, she often kept her to sleep. The King, who seldom neglected to visit the Countess before she rose, seldom failed likewise to find Miss Stuart in bed with her. The most indifferent objects have charms in a new attachment: however, the imprudent Countess was not jealous of this rival's appearing with her, in such a situation, being confident that whenever she thought fit, she could triumph over all the advantages which these opportunities could afford Miss Stuart; but she was quite mistaken."

Charles, very soon after Frances Stuart arrived in England, cast amorous eyes at her. He, from his charm of manner, backed by his position, found few to say him nay. It was, therefore, early assumed that the girl would do as others did. "Above all," Pepys wrote on May 18, 1663, "Mrs. Stuart is a fine woman, and they say now a common mistress of the King, as my Lady Castlemaine is, which is a pity." During the next month he clearly was still of this opinion. "In Hall to-day Dr. Pierce tells me that the Queen begins to be brisk, and play like other ladies, and is quite another woman from what she was, of which I am glad. It may be, it makes the King like her better, and forsake his two mistresses, my Lady Castlemaine and Stuart."

It was in July of the same year that the diarist noted that "the King had been besotted with Miss Stuart, and will be half an hour kissing her." If Pepys's description of the girl when visiting with the Court at Windsor about this time is accurate, Charles's passion is not to be wondered at: "Mrs. Stuart in this riding dress, with her hat cocked and a red plume, with her sweet eye, little Roman nose, and excellent taille, is now the greatest beauty I ever saw I think in my life; and, if ever woman can, do exceed my Lady Castlemaine, at least in this dress: nor do I wonder if the King changes, which I believe is the reason of his coldness to my Lady Castlemaine." Grammont gives a somewhat different account. "It was hardly possible for a woman to have less wit or more beauty," he wrote. "All her features were fine and regular; but her shape was not good; yet she was slender, straight enough and taller than the generality of women. She was very graceful, danced well, spoke French better than her mother tongue. She was well-bred, and possessed in perfection that air of dress which is so much admired, and which is very rarely attained, unless acquired when young in France."

"The fair Stuart, then in the meridian of her glory, attracted all eyes, and commanded universal respect and admiration," Grammont wrote. "The Duchess of Cleveland endeavoured to eclipse her at this fête by a load of jewels, and by all the artificial ornaments of dress; but it was in vain: her face looked rather thin and pale, from the commencement of a third or fourth pregnancy, which the King was still pleased to place to his own account; and, as for the rest, her person could in no respect stand in competition with the grace and beauty of Miss Stuart. It was during this last effort of her charms, that she would have been Queen of England, had the King been as free to give his hand as he was to surrender his heart: for it was at this time that the Duke of Richmond took it into his head either to marry her, or to die in the attempt."

"At this time," Grammont continues, "the King's attachment to Miss Stuart was so public, that every person perceived, that if she was but possessed of art, she might become as absolute a mistress over his conduct as she was over his heart. This was a fine opportunity for those who had experience and ambition. The Duke of Buckingham formed the design of governing her, in order to ingratiate himself with the King: God knows what a governor he would have been, and what a head he was possessed of, to guide another; however, he was the properest man in the world to insinuate himself with Miss Stuart: she was childish in her behaviour, and laughed at everything, and her taste for frivolous amusements, though unaffected, was only allowable in a girl about twelve or thirteen years old. A child, however, she was, in every other respect, except playing with a doll: blind-man's-buff was her most favourite amusement: she was building castles of cards, while the deepest play was going on in her apartments, where you saw her surrounded by eager courtiers, who handed her the cards, or young architects, who endeavoured to imitate her.

"She had, however, a passion for music, and had some taste for singing. The Duke of Buckingham, who built the finest towers of cards imaginable, had an agreeable voice: she had no aversion to scandal: and the Duke was both the father and the mother of scandal, he made songs, and invented old women's stories, with which she was delighted; but his particular talent consisted in turning into ridicule whatever was ridiculous in other people, and in taking them off, even in their presence, without their perceiving it; in short, he knew how to act all parts with so much grace and pleasantry, that it was difficult to do without him, when he had a mind to make himself agreeable; and he made himself so necessary to Miss Stuart's amusement, that she sent all over the town to seek for him, when he did not attend the King to her apartments. He was extremely handsome, and still thought himself much .more so than he really was: although he had a great deal of discernment, yet his vanity made him mistake some civilities as intended for his person, which were only bestowed on his wit, and drollery: in short, being seduced by too good an opinion of his own merit, he forgot his first project and his Portuguese mistress, in order to pursue a fancy in which he mistook himself; for he no sooner began to act a serious part with Miss Stuart, then he met with so severe repulse that he abandoned, at once, all his designs upon her: however, the familiarity she had procured him with the King, opened the way to those favours to which he was afterwards advanced."

Frances Stuart's conduct in public was most ingenious — she was, indeed, still more of a child than a woman. "I went yesterday to Miss Stuart's after the audience of those damned Muscovites, "Lord Chesterfield said. "The King arrived there just before me; and as if the Duke had sworn to pursue me wherever I went that day, he came in just after me. The conversation turned upon the extraordinary appearance of the Ambassadors. I know not where that fool Crofts had heard that all these Muscovites had handsome wives; and that all their wives had handsome legs. Upon this the King maintained that no woman ever had such handsome legs as Miss Stuart; and she, to prove the truth of his Majesty's statement, with the greatest imaginable ease, immediately shewed her leg above the knee. Some were ready to prostrate themselves in order to adore its beauty; for indeed none can be handsomer; but the Duke alone began to criticise upon it. He contended that it was too and that as for himself he would give nothing for a leg that was not thicker and shorter, and concluded by saying that no leg was worth anything without green stockings. Now, this, in my opinion, was a sufficient demonstration that he had just seen green stockings, and had them fresh in his remembrance."

Pepys, with his usual thoroughness, watched the progress of the amour:

August 11, 1663. "Dr. Pierce tells me that the King comes to town this day from Tunbridge, to stay a day or two, and then fetch the Queen from thence, who, he says, is grown a very debonnaire lady, and now hugs, him, and meets him galloping upon the road, and all the actions of a fond and pleasant lady that can be, that he believes has, a chat now and then of Mrs. Stuart, but there is no great danger of her, she being only an innocent, young, raw girl; but my Lady Castlemaine, who rules the King in matters of state, and do what she list with him, he believes is now falling out of favour."

Frances Stuart held her own against the King, but it is probable that he would have prevailed in the end. "She," Grammont says, "was now of opinion that she was capable of being the mistress of her own conduct: she had done all that was necessary to inflame the King's passions, without exposing her virtue by granting the last favours; but the eagerness of a passionate lover, blessed with favourable opportunities, is difficult to withstand, and still more difficult to vanquish; and Miss Stuart's virtue was almost exhausted, when the Queen was attacked with a violent fever, which soon reduced her to extreme danger. Then it was that Miss Stuart was greatly pleased with herself for the resistance she had made, though she paid dearly for it: a thousand hopes of greatness and glory filled her heart, and the additional respect that was universally paid her, contributed not a little to increase them."

Charles was ready to go any lengths to obtain possession of Frances Stuart. When in November Queen Catherine was thought to be on her death-bed, it was generally believed that, in the event of the demise of his Consort, he would offer to share his throne with his favourite, let the opposition to that project be what it might. However, Catherine recovered, and the idea had to be abandoned.

The belief that this was the King's intention is supported by an entry in Pepys's Diary:

November 9, 1663. "Mr. Pierce told me how the King is now become besotted upon Mrs. Stuart, that he gets into corners, and will be with her half an hour together, kissing her to the observation of all the world; and she now stays by herself and expects it, as my Lady Castlemaine used to do; to whom, he says, the King is still kind, so as now and then he goes to have a chat with her as he believes, but with no such fondness as he used to do. But yet it is thought that this new wench is so subtle, that she lets him do anything that is safe to her, but yet his doting is so great, Pierce tells me, it is verily thought that if the Queen had died, he would have married her."

Charles showered jewels upon the girl, and these she accepted with alacrity. He offered her titles; but these she declined. She would not yield her person to his Majesty; but she gave him enough encouragement to keep him dangling. This conduct exasperated him, but he could not cut himself adrift; but one day he lost his temper with her and expressed the pious hope that he might live to see her "ugly and willing" — at which outburst the girl roared with laughter.

There seems to be no doubt that Miss Stuart resisted all the King's importunities. Grammont, however, hints that this was not so and mentions, in his *Memoirs* an amusing incident. "Coaches with glasses were then a late invention: the ladies were afraid of being shut up in them: they greatly preferred the pleasure of showing almost their whole persons, to the convenience of modern coaches: that which was made for the King not being remarkable for its elegance, the Chevalier de Grammont was of opinion that something ingenious might be invented, which should partake of the ancient fashion, and likewise prove preferable to the modern; he, therefore, sent away Termes privately with all the necessary instructions to Paris: the Duke of Guise was likewise charged with this commission; and the courier, having by the favour of Providence escaped the quicksand, in a month's time brought safely over to England the most elegant and magnificent calash that had ever been seen, which the Chevalier presented to the King. The Chevalier de Grammont had given orders that fifteen hundred louis[1] should be expended upon it; but the Duke of Guise, who was his friend, to oblige him, laid out two thousand. All the Court was in admiration at the magnificence of the present; and the King, charmed with the Chevalier's attention to everything which could afford him pleasure, failed not to acknowledge it: he would not, however, accept a present of so much value, but upon condition that the Chevalier should not refuse another from him. The Queen, imagining that so splendid carriage might prove fortunate for her, wished to appear in it first, with the Duchess of York. Lady Castlemaine, who had seen them in it, thinking that it set off a fine figure to greater advantage than any other, desired the King to lend her this wonderful *caléche* to appear in it the first fine day in Hyde Park: Miss Stuart had the same wish, and requested to have it on the same day. As it was impossible to reconcile these two goddesses, whose former union was turned into mortal hatred, the King was very much perplexed. Lady Castlemaine was with child, and threatened to miscarry if her rival was preferred; Miss Stuart threatened that she never would be with child, if her request was not granted. This menace prevailed, and Lady Castlemaine's rage was so great, that she had almost kept her word; and it was believed that this triumph cost her rival some of her innocence."

So the game went on, and its progress is duly recorded in the pages of Pepys's Diary:

January 20, 1664. "Mr. Pierce tells me that my Lady Castlemaine is not at all set by the King, but that he do doat upon Mrs. Stuart only; and that to the leaving of all business in the world, and to the open slighting of the Queen; that he values not who sees him or stands by him while he dallies with her openly; and then privately in her chamber below, where the very sentries observe his going in and out; and that so commonly, that the Duke or any of the nobles, when they would ask where the King is, will continually say, 'Is the King above, or below?' meaning with Mrs. Stuart."

---

[1] 1500 louis is the equivalent of £160,000 ($300,000) in 2002 currency.

January 15, 1664. "In one of the galleries (at St. James's Palace), she comes into the room, in a most lovely form, with her hair all about her ears, having her picture taken there. There was the King and twenty more, I think, standing by the while, and a lovely creature she in this dress seemed to be."

Pepys, however, did not waver in his allegiance to Lady Castlemaine, whose loveliness had made a deep impression on him. "At the theatre was Mrs. Stuart, who is indeed very pretty, but not like my Lady Castlemaine for all that," he wrote on May 2, 1664; and a few weeks later remarked, "After sermon among the ladies on the Queen's side; where I saw Mrs. Stuart, very fine and pretty, but far beneath my Lady Castlemaine." Two years later Pepys says of Mrs. Stuart that she "is grown a little too tall, but is a woman of most excellent features." She evidently improved in looks as she grew up, and Pepys appreciated this. "I saw Mrs. Stuart this afternoon," he wrote when she was nineteen, "methought the beautifullest creature that ever I saw in my life, more than ever I thought her so, often as I have seen her; and I begin to think do exceed Lady Castlemaine, at least now."

The King did not, as time passed, relax his attentions. He had his affairs, as a matter of course; there was always Lady Castlemaine; but he really seems to have been in love with Frances Stuart. In the autumn of 1666, Pierce, the Court surgeon, told Pepys, "that all the people about the King do lie with Mrs. Stuart, who, he says, is a most excellent natured woman."

When Frances Stuart was about twenty, she, though flattered by them, became weary, and frightened, of the King's persistent attentions. In confidence, she told her fears to a friend, who repeated it in confidence to John Evelyn, who told this in confidence to Pepys, who duly recorded it on April 3, 1667:

"Mr. Evelyn told me the whole story of Mrs. Stuart going away from Court, he knowing her well; and believes her, up to her leaving the Court, to be as virtuous as any woman in the world: and told me, from a Lord that she told it to but yesterday, with her own mouth, and a sober man, that when the Duke of Richmond did make love to her, she did ask the King, and he did the likes also; and that the King did not deny it, and she told this Lord that she was come to that pass to resolve to have married any gentleman of £1500 a year that would have had her in honour; for it was come to that pass, that she could not longer continue at Court without prostituting herself to the King, whom she had so long kept off, though he had liberty more than any other had, or ought to have, as to dalliance. She told this Lord that she had reflected upon the occasion she had given the world to think her a bad woman, and that she had no way but to marry and leave the Court, rather in this way of discontent than otherwise, that the world might see that she sought not anything but her honour; and that she will never come to live at Court more than when she comes to town to kiss the Queen her mistress's hand: and hopes, though she hath little reason to hope, she can please her Lord so as to reclaim him; that they may yet live comfortably in the country on his estate. She told this Lord that all the jewels she ever had given her at Court, or any other presents, more than the King's allowance; of £700 a year out of the Privy Purse for her ,clothes, were, at her first coming the King did give her a necklace of pearls of about £1,100 [which Lord Braybroke says she returned to him], and afterwards, about seven months since, when the King had hopes to have obtained some courtesy of her, the King did give her some jewels, I have forgot what, and I think a pair of pendants. The Duke of York, being once her Valentine, did give her a jewel of about £800; and my Lord Mandeville, her Valentine this year, a ring of about £300; and the King of France would have had her mother, who, he says, is one of the most cunning women in the world, to have let her stay in France, saying that he loved her not as a mistress, but as one that he could marry as well as any lady in France; and that, if she might stay, for the honour of the Court, he would take care she should not repent. But her mother, by command of the Queen-Mother, thought rather to bring her into England; and the King of France did give her a jewel; so that Mr. Evelyn believes that she may be worth in jewels about £6,000, and that that is all that she hath in the world: and a worthy woman; and in all this hath done as great an act of honour as ever was done by woman."

"Miss Stuart, realising her danger," says Mr. Davidson, the biographer of Catherine of Braganza, "now sought the support of Catherine. She went to her rooms, and flinging herself on her knees before her, bathed in tears, confessed her folly and unworthy conduct in allowing Charles's attentions to single her out from the Court, and earnestly begged Catherine's forgiveness. She told her she knew she had caused her own trouble by her vanity and love of admiration, and assured the Queen that that was all she could be charged with. Catherine implicitly believed her and was grieved at her trouble. She raised her and comforted her, and promised her her protection, which to the end of both their lives she continued, together with the friendship. She kept Frances Stuart constantly in her own presence, and people believed she helped on the marriage with the Duke of Richmond, though there is no proof whatever of it. Frances assured her that she had never accepted anything from the King, but a few jewels of little value, given on New Year's days and the like, and that the Duke of York had presented her with a jewel worth £800 when he drew her for his valentine — an event in which presents were always given."

Frances Stuart would not have had far to seek for "a gentleman of £1,500 a year that would have her in honour," for Charles was not the only one to woo her, though courtiers fought a little shy of paying overt duty to the lady he delighted to honour. The Duke of Buckingham, as has been said, laid siege to her until he was very definitely rebuffed. Count de Grammont lost his heart to her, with fervour unusual for him, since it was usually he who was pursued. Anthony Hamilton nearly won her by holding in his mouth two lighted candles longer than anyone at Court could hold one. George Digby, second Earl of Bristol, was passionately in love with her. John Rottiers, the medallist, cherished a hopeless attachment—he paid desirable tribute by taking her as the model for Britannia. "At my goldsmith's," Pepys wrote, "did observe the King's new medal, where, in little, there is Mrs. Stuart's face as well done as ever I saw anything in my whole life 1 think; and a pretty thing it is, that he should choose her face to represent Britannia by." Nathaniel Lee (1653-1692), the dramatist, would gladly have taken her to wife; in fact, he dedicated to her his *Theodosius*, produced at Dorset Gardens in 1680. Lee is almost forgotten, but he lives in literary history as the author of the worst line in verse that probably has ever been written:

"O Sophonisba! Sophonisba O! "

Nathaniel Lee addressed a dedication to her, couched in terms extravagant even for the period in which it was written: "Something there is in your mien so much above what we vulgarly call charming, that to me it seems adorable, and your presence almost divine, whose dazzling and majestic form is a proper mansion for the most elevated soul; and let me tell the world, nay, sighing, speak it to a barbarous age (I cannot help calling it so, when 1 think of Rome and Greece), your extraordinary love for heroic poetry is not the least argument to show the greatness of your mind and fulness of perfection. To hear you speak, with that infinite sweetness and cheerfulness of spirit that is natural to your Grace, is, methinks, to hear our titular angels; 'tis to bemoan the present malicious times, and remember the Golden Age; but to behold you, too, is to make prophets quite forget their heavens, to blind a poet with eternal rapture."

Another in the field was Charles Stuart, third Duke of Richmond and sixth Duke of Lennox, to which titles he had succeeded in 1660 on the death of his cousin, Esmé Stuart. He was Hereditary Great Chamberlain of Scotland, and Hereditary Great Admiral of Scotland, and held in addition other high offices. His second wife died in December 1666, and he at once offered his hand to Frances Stuart.

There were no secrets at Court; and the King, of course, came to hear of this proposal. There was nothing he was not prepared to do. He was, in fact, desperate, as well as helpless. He begged Frances Stuart to let him make her a duchess. She declined. He offered to dismiss Lady Castlemaine. She was not interested. At this time he actually asked Archbishop Sheldon if the Church of England would allow of a divorce in a case when both parties were in consent and one was barren. The Primate tactfully asked for time for consideration.

Burnet refers to this in his *History of my Own Times*: "The King had grown very weary of the Queen: and it was believed he had a great mind to be rid of her. The load of that marriage was cast on the Lord Clarendon, as made on design to raise his own grandchildren. Many members of the House of Commons, such as Clifford, Osborne, Carr, Lyttelton, and Seymour, were brought to the King, who all assured him that upon his Restoration they intended both to have raised his authority and to have increased his revenue, but that the Earl of Clarendon had discouraged it, and that all his creatures had possessed the House with such jealousies of the King, that they thought it was not fit to trust him too much nor too far. This made a deep impression on the King, who was weary of Lord Clarendon's imposing way, and had a mind to be freed from the authority to which he had been so long accustomed, that it was not easy to keep him within bounds. Yet the King was so afraid to engage himself too deep in his own affairs, that it was a doubt whether he would dismiss him or not, if a concern of one of his amours had not sharpened his resentments. What other considerations could not do, was brought about by an ill-grounded jealousy. Mistress Stuart had gained so much ground on the King, and yet had kept her ground with so much firmness, that the King seemed to design, if possible, to legitimate his addresses to her, since he saw no hope of succeeding any other way. The Duke of Richmond, being a widower, courted her. The King seemed to give way to it; and pretended to take such care of her, that he would have good settlements made for her. He hoped by that means to have broke the matter decently, for he knew the Duke of Richmond's affairs were in disorder. So the King ordered, Lord Clarendon to examine the estate he pretended to settle. But he was told, whether true or false I cannot tell, that Lord Clarendon told her that the Duke of Richmond's affairs, it is true, were not very clear, but that a family so nearly related to the King could never be left in distress, and 'that such a match would not come in her way every day; so she had best consider well before she rejected it. This was carried to the King, as a design he had that the Crown might descend to his own grandchildren; and that he was afraid lest strange methods should be taken to get rid of the Queen, and to make way for her. When the King saw that she had a mind to marry the Duke of Richmond, he offered to make her a Duchess, and to settle an estate on her. Upon this she said, she then saw that she must either marry him, or suffer much in the opinion of the world."

It is related by Grammont that Charles first learnt of the Duke of Richmond's desire to marry Frances Stuart from Lady Castlemaine (afterwards Duchess of Cleveland):

"Miss Stuart continued to torment, and almost to drive the King to distraction; but his Majesty soon after found out the real cause of this coldness.

"This discovery was owing to the officious Duchess of Cleveland, who ever since her disgrace, had railed most bitterly against Miss Stuart as the cause of it, and against the King's weakness, who, for an inanimate idiot, had treated her with so much indignity. As some of her Grace's creatures were still in the King's confidence, by their means she was informed of the King's uneasiness, and that Miss Stuart's behaviour was the occasion of it: and as soon as she had found the opportunity she had so long wished for, she went directly into the King's cabinet, through the apartment of one of his pages called Chiffinch. This way was not new to her.

"The King was just returned from visiting Miss Stuart, in a very ill humour: the presence of the Duchess of Cleveland surprised him, and did not in the least diminish it: she perceiving this, accosted him in an ironical tone, and with a smile of indignation: 'I hope,' said she, 'I may be allowed to pay you my homage, although the angelic Stuart has forbid you to see me at my own house. I will not make use of reproaches and expostulations, which would disgrace myself: still less will I endeavour to excuse frailties which nothing can justify, since your constancy for me deprives me of all defence, considering I am the only person you have honoured with your tenderness, who has made herself unworthy of it by ill conduct. I come now, therefore, with no other intent than to comfort and to condole with you upon the affliction and grief into which the coldness, or new-fashioned chastity of the inhuman Stuart have reduced your Majesty.' These words were attended by a fit of laughter, as unnatural and strained as it was insulting and immoderate, which completed the King's impatience: he had, indeed, expected that some bitter jest would follow this preamble; but he did not suppose she would have given herself such blustering airs, considering the terms they were then upon; and, as he was preparing to answer her: 'be not offended,' said she, 'that I take the liberty of laughing at the gross manner in which you are imposed upon: I cannot bear to see that such particular affectation should make you the jest of your own Court, and that you should be ridiculed with such impunity. I know that the affected Stuart has sent you away, under pretence of some indisposition, or perhaps some scruple of conscience; and I come to acquaint you that the Duke of Richmond will soon be with her, if he is not there already. I do not desire you to believe what I say, since it might be suggested either through resentment or envy: only follow me to her apartment, either that, no longer trusting calumny and malice, you may honour her with a just preference, if I accuse her falsely; or, if my information be true, you may no longer be the dupe of a pretended prude, who makes you act so unbecoming and ridiculous a part.'

"As she ended this speech, she took him by the hand, while he was yet undecided, and pulled him away towards her rival's apartments. Chiffinch, being in her interest, Miss Stuart could have no warning of the visit; and Babiani, who owed all to the Duchess of Cleveland, and who served her admirably well upon this occasion, came and told her that the Duke of Richmond had just gone into Miss Stuart's chamber. It was in the middle of a little gallery, which, through a private door, led from the King's apartments to those of his mistresses. The Duchess of Cleveland wished him good night, as he entered her rival's chamber, and retired, in order to wait the success of the adventure, of which Babiani, who attended the King, was charged to come and give her an account.

"It was near midnight: the King, in his way, met his mistress's chambermaid, who respectfully opposed his entrance, and in a very low voice whispered his Majesty that Miss Stuart had been very ill since he left her: but that, being gone to bed, she was, God be thanked, in a very fine sleep. 'That I must see,' said the King, pushing her back, who had posted herself in his way. He found Miss Stuart in bed, indeed, but far from being asleep. The Duke of Richmond was seated at her pillow, and in all probability was less inclined to sleep than herself. The perplexity of the one party, and the rage of the other, were such as may easily be imagined upon such a surprise. The King, who, of all men, was one of the most mild and gentle, testified his resentment to the Duke of Richmond, in such terms as he had never before used. The Duke was speechless, and almost petrified: he saw his master and his King justly irritated. The first transports which rage inspires on such occasions are dangerous. Miss Stuart's window was very convenient for a sudden revenge, the Thames flowing close beneath it: he cast his eyes upon it; and, seeing those of the King more incensed and fired with indignation than he thought his nature capable of, he made a profound bow, and retired, without replying a single word to the vast torrent of threats and menaces that were poured upon him.

"Miss Stuart, having a little recovered from her first surprise, instead of justifying herself, began to talk in the most extravagant manner, and said everything that was most capable to inflame the King's passion and resentment; that, if she were not allowed to receive visits from a man of the Duke of Richmond's rank, who came with honourable intentions, she was a slave in a free country; that she knew of no engagement that could prevent her from disposing of her hand as she thought proper; but, however, if this was not permitted her in his dominions, she did not believe that there was any power on earth that could hinder her from going over to France, and throwing herself into a convent, to enjoy there that tranquility which was denied her in his Court. The King, sometimes furious with anger, sometimes relenting at her tears, and sometimes terrified at her menaces, was so greatly agitated, that he knew not how to answer, either the nicety of a creature who wanted to act the part of Lucretia under his own eye, or the assurance with which she had the effrontery to reproach him. In this suspense, love had almost entirely vanquished all his resentments, !and had nearly induced him to throw himself upon his knees, and entreat pardon for the injury he had done her, when she desired him to retire, and leave her in repose at least for the remainder of that night, without offending those who had either accompanied him, or conducted him to her apartment, by a longer visit.

This impertinent request provoked and irritated him in the highest degree: he went out abruptly, vowing never to see her more, and passed the most restless and uneasy night he had ever experienced since his restoration.

"The next day the Duke of Richmond received orders to quit the Court, and never more to appear before the King; but it seems he had not waited for those orders, having set out early that morning for his country seat.

"Miss Stuart, in order to obviate all injurious constructions that might be put upon the adventure of the preceding night, went and threw herself at the Queen's feet; where, acting the new part of an innocent Magdalen, she entreated her Majesty's forgiveness for all the sorrow and uneasiness she might have already occasioned her. She told her Majesty that a constant and sincere repentance had induced her to contrive all possible means for retiring from Court: that this reason had inclined her to receive the Duke of Richmond's addresses, who had courted her a long time; but since this courtship had caused his disgrace, and had likewise raised a vast noise and disturbance, which perhaps might be turned to the prejudice of her reputation, she conjured her Majesty to take her under her protection, and endeavour to obtain the King's permission for her to retire into a convent, to remove at once all those vexations and troubles her presence had innocently occasioned at Court. All this was accompanied with a proper deluge of tears. It is a very agreeable spectacle to see a rival prostrate at our feet, entreating pardon, and at the same time justifying her conduct. The Queen's heart not only relented, but she mingled her own tears with those of Miss Stuart. After having raised her up, and most tenderly embraced her, she promised her all manner of favour and protection, either in her marriage, or in any other course she thought fit to pursue, and parted from her with the firm resolution to exert all her interest in her support but being a person of great judgment, the reflections which she afterwards made, induced her to change her opinion."

"Little Mademoiselle de la Garde," Grammont relates, "was charged to acquaint Miss Stuart that the Duke of Richmond was dying of love for her, and that when he ogled her in public, it was a certain sign that he was ready to marry her, as soon as ever she would consent. "There is no reason to believe that the girl was vastly attracted by the Duke, but she was tremendously anxious to get away from Court. The Duke's second wife had died in December 1666, and a few weeks after he asked his "fair cousin" to marry him. Towards the end of March she, "on a dark and stormy night," fled from her apartments at Whitehall, met his Grace at the Bear Inn by London Bridge, and went with him into Kent, where she married him privately. From there, the new Duchess returned to the King the jewels with which he had loaded her. For a short time the bride and bridegroom remained in retirement in the country. Charles was full of anger and regret., He wrote to his sister, Henrietta, Duchess of Orleans: "You may think me ill-natured, but if you consider how hard a thing it is to swallow an injury done by a person I had so much tenderness for, you will in some degree excuse the resentment I use towards her: you know my good-nature enough to believe that I could not be so severe if I had not had great provocation. I assure you her carriage towards me has been as bad as a breach of faith and friendship can make it, therefore I hope you will pardon me if I cannot so soon forget an injury which went so near my heart." His Majesty believed that the Earl of Clarendon was privy to the marriage, and believed he had urged it to frustrate the design to divorce the Queen. These suspicions engendered, says Burnet, led to the King's resolve to take the seals from him.

"Mr. Pierce," Pepys mentions on July 17, 1667, "told me the story of Mrs. Stuart, much after the manner I was told it long ago by Mr. Evelyn; only he says it is verily believed that the King did never intend to marry her to any but himself, and that the Duke of York and the Lord Chancellor Hyde were jealous of it; and that Mrs. Stuart might be got with child by the King, or someone else, and the King own a marriage before his contract, for it is but a contract, as he tells me so this day with the Queen, and so wipe their noses of the Crown; and that, therefore, the Duke of York and Chancellor did all they could to forward the match with the Duke of Richmond, that she might be married out of the way; but, above all, it is a worthy part that this good lady hath acted."

Again on December 26, Pepys notes: "I hear that Mrs. Stuart do at this day keep a great court at Somerset House[2], with her husband the Duke of Richmond, she being visited for her beauty's sake by people, as the Queen is, at nights, — they say also that she is likely to go to Court again, and there put my Lady Castlemaine's nose out of joint.

---

[2] http://www.somerset-house.org.uk/

God knows that would make a great turn." And on the following day he adds: "Mr. Povy tells me that the business of getting the Duchess of Richmond to Court is broke off, the Duke not suffering it; and thereby great trouble is brought among the people that endeavoured it, and thought that they had compassed it." A couple of weeks later he mentions the Duchess again: "Mrs. Cornwallis tells me that the Duchess of Richmond do not yet come to the Court, nor hath seen the King, nor will not, nor do he own his desire of seeing her, but hath used means of getting her to Court, but they do not take."

The Duchess, however, had a friend at Court in the person of the Queen, who seems to have liked her well, probably because of her resistance to the King's will. Anyhow, Catherine prevailed — at least so far as to have her, in July 1688, appointed a Lady of her Bedchamber. Just before this, her Grace had had an illness. "Word was brought," says Pepys on March 26, "that the Duchess of Richmond is pretty well, but mighty full of the smallpox, by which all do conclude she will be wholly spoiled, which is the greatest instance of the uncertainty of beauty that could be in this age; but then she hath had the benefit of it to be first married, and to have kept it so long, under the greatest temptations in the world from a King, and yet without the least imputation." After her recovery, Pepys (in May) says: "There are great disputes like to be at Court between the factions of the two women, my Lady Castlemaine and Mrs. Stuart, who is well again, and the King hath made several public visits to her, and like to come to Court: the other is to Berkeshire House." In the same month he mentions: "Since my Lord Ormonde's coming over, the King begins to be mightily reclaimed and sleeps every night with great pleasure with the Queen: and yet it seems he is mighty hot upon the Duchess of Richmond, insomuch that upon Sunday se'n-night at night, after he had ordered his guards and coach to be ready to carry him to the Park, he did, on a sudden, take a pair of oars or scullers, and all alone, or but one with him, go to Somerset House, and there, the garden door not being open, himself clamber over the wall to make a visit to her, which is a horrid shame."

The Queen in May 1670 took the Duchess of Richmond in her suite to Calais to meet the Duchess of Orleans; and in the following

October the Duchess accompanied her on a visit to Audley End, where, as is recorded in the Past on Letters, they indulged in a "frolic." "There being a fair at Audley End, the Queen, Duchess of Richmond, and Duchess of Buckingham had a frolic to disguise themselves like country lasses, in red petticoats, waistcoats, etc., and to go see the fair. Sir Bernard Gascoigne, on a cart-jade, rode before the Queen, another stranger before the Duchess of Buckingham, and Mr. Roper before Richmond. They had all so overdone it in their disguise, and looked so much more like antiques than country folk, that as soon as they came to the fair the people began to go after them: but the Queen going to a booth to buy a pair of yellow stockings for her sweetheart, and Sir Bernard asking for a pair of gloves stitched with blue for his sweetheart, they were soon by their gibberish found to be strangers, which drew a bigger stock about them, — one amongst them had seen the Queen at dinner, knew her, and was proud of his knowledge. This soon brought all the fair into a crowd to stare at the Queen. Being thus discovered, they as soon as they could got to their horses; but as many of the fair as had horses got up, with wives, sweethearts, and neighbours behind them to get as much gape as they could, till they brought thein to the Court gate. Thus was a merry frolic turned into a penance."

Charles became reconciled to Frances, but he could not bring himself to forgive the Duke of Richmond. He was still enamoured of her Grace, and the gossip of the day has it that she was more kind to him after her marriage than before. He sent the Duke out of the way, in honourable exile — first, in 1670, to Scotland, and, in the following year, on an embassy to Denmark, where in December 1672 he died. He left no issue, and most of his titles went to the King, who was the nearest collateral male heir. The dukedom he presently bestowed on his natural son, Charles, by Louise de Kéroualle, whom he had created Duchess of Portsmouth.

The Duchess, after her husband's death, was much at Court. She received many offers of marriage, but declined them. As she grew older, she became more staid, and retained the countenance of the Queen to the end. She was received into the Roman Catholic Church, and when she died on October 15, 1702, she was buried in Westminster Abbey, in the Duke of Richmond's vault in Henry VII's Chapel.

# CHAPTER XI

## ELIZABETH, COUNTESS OF NORTHUMBERLAND, AFTER-WARDS DUCHESS OF MONTAGU (née WRIOTHESLEY), 1647-1690.
## ANNE, COUNTESS OF SUNDERLAND (née DIGBY), 1644-1716

"HERE [at Whitehall] I saw my Lady Percy, a beautiful lady indeed." Thus Pepys on March 31, 1667.

Lady Elizabeth Wriothesley, who was born in 1647, was the third and youngest daughter of Thomas, first and last Earl of Southampton, by his second wife, Elizabeth, eldest daughter and heiress of Francis Leigh, Lord Dunsmore (afterwards Earl of Chichester). She was half-sister to the better known Rachel, the wife of William, Lord Russell, "The Patriot." Her elder sister, Lady Audrey, was betrothed to Josceline, Lord Percy, who, born in 1644, succeeded his father twenty-four years later as (eleventh) Earl of Northumberland. The bride elect, however, died in her fourteenth year, and was regretted anyhow by the Earl of Northumberland who would have been her father-in-law: "she was," he wrote to Lord Leicester, "of a nature, temper, and humour likely to make an excellent wife." However, the death of Lady Audrey was not allowed to interfere in the family plans. Lady Elizabeth, on the death of her sister, became sole heiress to the estates of her maternal grandfather, Lord Chichester, and it was arranged that she should marry Lord Percy. The marriage took place in 1662, when the bride was fifteen, and the husband eighteen. After the ceremony Lord Percy continued his studies, and his bride stayed with her family at Titchfield, in Hampshire. About two years later the young couple resided together at Petworth. There was issue: in 1667, Lady Elizabeth, who was afterwards Duchess of Somerset; in 1668, Lord Henry, who, dying in 1669, predeceased his father by a year; and, in 1669, Lady Henrietta, who died in infancy.

The Earl and Countess of Northumberland, much distressed by these bereavements, went abroad for the benefit of their health. At Paris Lady Northumberland remained in the care of John Locke, the philosopher, who acted as her physician; and her husband went to Italy, where he caught a fever, and died at Turin in May 1670, in his twenty-seventh year.

Elizabeth, Countess of Northumberland
(*née* Wriothesley)

According to another account, the reason why the Countess went to France was to escape the amorous attentions of Charles II, which were not welcomed by her.

The widowed Lady Northumberland was one of the greatest matches of the day, not only by virtue of her powerful connections, but because she had a fortune of some £6000 a year in her own right[1]. Harry Savile now wooed her, and so did many others; but without success. Rumour had it that she was reserving herself for the Duke of York, whose first wife, Anne Hyde, died in March 1671. In the *Life of James II* there is an entry dated July 13, 1672: "Buckingham proposed to the King to get Lady Percy (the infant heiress of Earl Josceline) for Lord Harry (the King's natural son, afterwards Duke of Grafton). Buckingham at the same time offered to the Countess of Northumberland to get the King to consent that he should command the Duke to marry her." That nothing came of the latter scheme is, of course, a matter of history. It may be that the Duke of York, who had been worried to death by marrying a commoner, decided definitely to choose as his second wife a lady of the blood royal, so that there should be no further complications at Court.

Ralph Montagu made love to the Countess of Northumberland, and presently outdistanced his rivals. He was, according to Grammont, "no very dangerous rival on account of his person, but very much to be feared for his assiduity, the acuteness of his wit, and for some other talents which are of importance, when a man is once permitted to display them." Ralph, who was the second son of Edward, second Lord Montagu of Boughton, was a man of parts, and he showed marked ability both in politics and diplomacy: also, he had had much experience as a man of the world, and he knew that in love perseverance is half the battle. Montagu followed Lady Northumberland to Aix in the winter of 1672. Madame de Sévigné was then in Provence on a visit to her daughter, and Madame de la Fayette wrote to her there from Paris: [translations follow below]

"Voilà un pacquet que je vous envoie pour Madame de Northumberland. On dit ici si M. de Montagu n'a pas un heureux succès de

---

[1] A sum worth approximately £650,000 (or about $1.2 million) in today's money.

son voyage, il passera en Italie, pour faire voir que ce n'est pas pour les beaux yeux de Madame de Northumberland qu'il court le pays: mandez nous un peu ce que vous verrez de cette affaire, et comme il sera traité."

["Here is a packet sent to you for Madame de Nothumberland. They say here that if Monsieur de Montagu hasn't met with great success in his voyage, he will go to Italy to show that it is not for the beautiful eyes of Madam de Northumberland that he is running about the country: write a little to us to tell what you see in this affair, and how it might proceed."]

The same correspondent wrote on April 15, 1673, from Paris, where Montagu had come in pursuit of the lady:

"Madame de Northumberland me vint voir bier; j'avais été la chercher avec Madame de Coulanges: elle me parut une femme qui a été fort belle, mais qui n'a plus un seul trait de visage qui se soutienne, ni où il soit resté le moindre air de jeunesse: j'en fus surprise; elle est avec cela mal habillée, point de grâce, enfin je n'en fus point de tout éblouie. Elle me parut entendre fort bien tout ce qu'on dit, ou pour mieux dire tout ce que je dit, car j'étais seule. M. de la Rochefoucauld et M. de Thianges, qui avaient envie de la voir, ne vinrent que comme elle sortait. Montagu m'avait mandé qu'elle viendrait me voir, je lui ai fort parlé d'elle i il ne fait aucune façon d'être embarqué à son service, et paraît très rempli d'esperance."

["Madame de Northumberland came to see me yesterday; I had been to get her with Madame de Coulanges: she seemed to me a woman who had been most beautiful, but who no longer possesses a single facial feature which holds up of its own accord, nor where there remains the least air of youth: I was surprised; moreover, she is poorly dressed, has no grace, and in fine, I was not at all impressed. She appeared to be very much aware of all that is said, or better yet all that I said, for I was alone. Monsieur de la Rochefoucauld and Monsieur de Thianges, who had desired to see her, came only as she was leaving. Montagu had asked that she should come to see me, and I spoke at great length to him of her and he does not seem in the least indisposed to place himself at her service, and appears quite full of hope."]

Lady Northumberland was, apparently, jealous at this time of the attentions paid by her suitor to the Duchess de Brissac, to whom he had once been passionately attached, and Madame de la Fayette thought that consequently he stood no chance with the Countess.

"Montagu s'en va," she wrote to Madame de Sévigné in the following May, "on dit que ses espérences seront renversées; je crois qu'il y a quelque chose de travers dans l'esprit de la nymphe."

["Montagu is leaving," she wrote to Madame de Sévigné in the following May, "for they say his hopes will be dashed; I think there to be something amiss in the mind of the nymph."]

However, events proved her wrong, for, despite the opposition of her first husband's family, Lady Northumberland married Montagu privately on August 24, 1673, at Titchfield, in Hampshire, the country seat of ' the Wriothesleys. The lady, it may be remarked, retained her title, and was known as the Countess of Northumberland.

The alliance was not a success, and after a short time a separation was seriously considered. Also, the Countess had trouble with the Dowager-Countess of Northumberland, who, after her daughter-in-law's second marriage, claimed the entire control of Lady Elizabeth Percy, the daughter of the first marriage. "The two Lady Northumberlands," wrote Rachel, Lady Russell, "have met at Northumberland House after some propositions offered by my sister to the other, which were discussed first yesterday before my Lord Chancellor, between the elder lady and Mr. Montagu. Lord Suffolk, by my sister, offers to deliver up the child, upon condition he will promise she shall have her on a visit for ten days or a month sometimes, and that she will enter into bonds not to marry the child without her mother's consent, nor till she is of years to consent; and on her part, Mr. Montagu and she will enter into the same bonds, that when she is with them, at no time they will marry or contract any marriage for her without the grandmother's consent: but she was stout yesterday, and would not hear patiently, yet went to Northumberland House and gave my sister a visit: I hope for an accommodation. My sister urges, it is hard that her child (that if she have no other children must be her heir) should be disposed of without her consent, and in my Judgment it is hard; yet I fancy I am not very apt to be partial." Actually, Lady Elizabeth Percy was married in her fourteenth year to Henry Cavendish, Earl of Ogle, only son of the Duke of Newcastle, who was about the same age. He, however, died a few months later, in 1680. She was then attracted by the notorious adventurer, Count Konigsmarck, whereupon, to prevent any disaster, she was engaged to Thomas Thynne of Longleat; but before the marriage took place, Thynne was murdered in Pall Mall by three ruffians in the pay of the Count. The three assassins were apprehended and duly executed; but Konigsmarck escaped abroad. A few months later, on May 20, 1682, she married Charles Seymour, sixth Duke of Somerset, who figures in social history as "the proud Duke." [2]

Montagu went to Paris in 1676, for the second time as Ambassador to Louis XIV. There he committed a disgraceful indiscretion, mentioned elsewhere in this book, which was exposed by the Duchess of Cleveland, whose lover he had been and with whom he had quarrelled. This led to his recall, and for some time he was in dire disgrace. He became a partisan of the Duke of Monmouth, whom he wished to be proclaimed as Prince of Wales. As regards the rest, he succeeded to his father's barony in 1684; was created an earl by William III, whose cause he had heartily espoused at the time of the Revolution; and a duke by Anne.

In Lady Russell's correspondence there are, of course, references to Lady Northumberland. "I hear," she wrote on July 11, 1686, "by my sister Montagu, she found a sickly family at Paris; her daughter in a languishing condition, worn to nothing with a fever which has hung round her for the last six weeks. The doctors apprehend a hectic; but youth, I hope, will overcome it." Within a year Lady

---

[2] Charles Seymour, Duke of Somerset (1662-1748) was a British statesman of great influence during the reign of Queen Anne and the early Georgian era. He was largely responsible for the Revolution of 1688 and the accession of George I in 1714 thus securing the Hanoverian dynasty. He was also known as "The Proud Duke" because of his arrogance. He "would never suffer his children to sit in his presence, and would never speak to his servants except by signs". One daughter dared to sit in the room while she thought he was dozing and was penalised for it in his will! One of Henry XVIII's six wives, Jane Seymour, was from this family.

Northumberland lost her eldest son at the age of twelve. "I believe she takes it heavily," Lady Russell wrote, "for truly I have not seen her since the child died on Sunday morning. Now my own sad trials making me know what a mean comforter I can be, I think the best service is to take some care of her two children, who are both well now; and I hope God will be pleased to keep them so, and teach her to be content." Lady Russell's trouble was the execution of her husband for high treason[3] in 1683. When William and Mary came to the throne, the attainder was reversed, whereupon Lady Northumberland, who was now known under the style of Countess of Montagu, wrote:

"BOUGHTON,
"December 23, 1689.

"I am very sorry, my dear sister, to find by yours, which I received by the last post, that your thoughts have been so much disturbed with what I thought ought to have some contrary effect. It is very true, what is once taken from us in that nature can never be returned; all that remains of comfort (according to my temper) is the bringing to punishment those who were so wickedly and unjustly the cause of it. I confess it was a great satisfaction to me to hear that was the public care; it being so much to the honour, as well as what in justice was due to your dead Lord, that I do not doubt, when your sad thoughts will give you leave to recollect, you will find comfort. I heartily pray God you may, and that you may never have the addition of any other loss, which is, and ever shall be, the prayer of

"Your entirely affectionate,
"E. MONTAGU."

---

[3] On the breaking out of the Rye House Plot, of which neither Lord William Russell, Essex, nor Sidney had the slightest knowledge, he was accused by informers of promising his assistance to raise an insurrection and compass the death of the king. Refusing to attempt to escape, he was brought before the council, when his attendance at the meeting referred to was charged against him. He was sent on June 26, 1683 to the Tower, and, looking upon himself as a dying man, betook himself wholly to preparation for death. (Source: Wikipedia)

Lady Montagu died at Boughton in 1690, at the age of forty-three. "She was my last sister, and I ever loved her tenderly," Lady Russell wrote to the Bishop of Salisbury. "It pleases me to think that she deserves to be remembered by all those who knew her; but after forty years' acquaintance with so amiable a creature, one must needs, in reflecting, bring to remembrance so many engaging endearments as are at present embittering and painful."

Lady Anne Digby was much in the public eye after her marriage, more perhaps because of her husband's notoriety as a politician than for her beauty, her wealth, and her charm.

Evelyn wrote of her in very high terms; but her husband had many bitter enemies, and some of the obloquy that was showered upon him fell also on her devoted head. Particularly Princess Anne disliked the couple, and wrote of them to her sister, the Princess of Orange: "Lady Sunderland plays the hypocrite more than ever, for she is at church half an hour before other people come, and half an hour after everyone else is gone, at her private devotions. She runs from church to church after the famoustest preachers, and keeps such a clatter with her devotion, that it really turns one's stomach. Sure there never was a couple so well matched as she and her husband, for as she is the greatest jade that ever was, so is he the subtillest workingest villain that is on the face of the earth."

Lady Anne was the third child of George Digby, second Earl of Bristol, by his wife, Lady Anne Russell, second daughter of Francis, fourth Earl of Bedford. Her elder brother, John, succeeded his father in the earldom, but died childless in 1698, when the title became extinct, and the estates passed to Lady Anne; while the other brother, Francis, was killed at sea in 1672. Her elder daughter, following in her father's footsteps, became a member of the Roman Catholic Church, and married Baron Moll, a Flemish nobleman. The second Earl of Bristol, politician and soldier, has his niche in Horace Walpole's *Catalogue of Royal and Noble Authors*, where it is written of him: "A singular person, whose life was one contradiction. He wrote against Popery, and embraced it; he was a zealous opposer of the Court, and a sacrifice for it; was conscientiously converted in the midst of his prosecution of Lord Stafford, and was most unconsci-

Anne, Countess of Sunderland (*née* Digby)

entiously a persecutor of Lord Clarendon. With great parts, he always hurt himself and his friends; with romantic bravery, he was always an unsuccessful commander. He spoke for the Test Act, though a Roman Catholic, and addicted himself to astrology on the birthday of true philosophy."

At the Restoration, Lord Bristol's estates, which had been confiscated by Cromwell, were recovered to him, and he was able to make a figure at Court. Lady Anne was then in her seventeenth year, and has been described as being at this time "exceedingly fair, with a profusion of light brown tresses, tinged with a golden hue; she had a complexion of the most dazzling transparency, small regular features, and a slight delicate figure, yet with a certain dignity of presence that is said to have characterised the Digbys of that age." About the same time that Lady Anne came to London, there returned to England Robert Spencer, second Earl of Sunderland, who in 1643, when he was three years old, had succeeded his father, killed at the first battle of Newbury, in the title and estates. His mother was Lady Dorothy Sidney (Waller's "Sacharissa"). When he was twenty-three he began to pay his addresses to Lady Anne Digby. A marriage was arranged. Then there was a hitch.

Pepys, of course, knew of this, and on July 1, 1663, noted in his Diary: "My Lord of Sunderland (whom I do not know) was as near to the marriage of his daughter as that the wedding-clothes were made, and portion and everything agreed on and ready; and the other day he goes away nobody yet knows whither, sending her the next morning a release of his right or claim to her, and advice to his friends not to enquire into the reason of this doing, for he hath enough for it; but that he gives them liberty to say and think what they will of him, so that they do not demand the reason of his leaving her, being resolved never to have her, but the reason desires and resolves not to give." About the same time the Count de Comminges, French Ambassador at London, wrote to M. de Lionne at Paris: [translation follows below]

"Je vous avais mandé que le Comte de Sunderland épousait la fille du Comte de Bristol. Il se retira le soir qu'on devoit l'epouser, et donne ordre à un de ces amis de rompre le mariage. Le procédé surprit toute la cour, et le Roi même s'en est moqué, et la blamé au dernier point."

["I had asked you if the Count of Sunderland married the daughter of the Count of Bristol. He departed the night that he was to marry her, and left the order with one of his friends to break off the marriage. These proceedings surprised the entire court, and the King himself joked of it, and blamed him in the end."]

Thomas Seccombe thought that the trouble was that "the young Earl's fears were due to a suspicion that he had met his match in duplicity," and that if this were so, his fears were probably not unfounded. "His bride," he went on to say, "was *'born intrigante'* ['born devious] and her *'commerce de galanterie'* ['commerce in gallantry'] with her husband's uncle, Henry Sidney, was somewhat later to afford a congenial theme to Barillon and his fellow-reporters of Court intrigue." If Sunderland had already found out his bride, it was early days indeed — even if the marriage was only *de convenance* [marriage of convenience].

The following account is, perhaps, more worthy of credence: "The Earl of Bristol, in consequence of some extravagance of language, was called up before the House of Commons to justify himself; he made a most eloquent speech, but with so much heat and gesticulation, that he was compared to a stage-player; and, what was worse, his rhetoric did not appear to have much effect on the Commons, while the Lords were incensed at his appearing before the other House without their express permission: in short, his disgrace or ruin was impending, and Lady Anne had nearly been the innocent victim of her father's misconduct or indiscretion." The marriage was, however, delayed until June 10, 1665.

In 1689 Sunderland, who was exiled from England, was arrested in Holland by order of the States-General, but was released at the request of William III: whereupon his wife wrote to the King:

"AMSTERDAM,

"March 11, 1689.

"The relief I had by your Majesty's justice and grace from the sharpest apprehensions I ever lay under, may, I hope, be allowed a sufficient plea for the liberty I now take to present you my most humble acknowledgments for that great charity of yours. I dare not impute it to any other motive; but however unfortunate my present circumstances are, I have this to support me, that my thought, as well as actions, have been and are, and I dare to say ever will be, what they ought to be to your Majesty; and not only upon the account of the duty I now owe you, but long before your glorious undertaking, I can't but hope you remember how devoted I was to your service, which Was founded upon so many great and estimable qualities in you, that. I can never change my opinion, whatever my fortune may be in this world; and may I but hope for so much of your Majesty's favour as to live quietly in a country where you have so much power, till it shall please God to let me end my days at my own home, I shall ever be most truly and humbly grateful."

On the following day, and on the same matter, the Countess wrote to John Evelyn:

"Under all the misfortunes I have gone through of late, I cannot but be sensible of that of not having heard a word from you. Indeed, I have sometimes need of your letters, as well for to help me as to please me; and, indeed, my good friend, they do both: wherefore pray make amends. I am sure you have heard of the unusual proceedings my Lord met with in this country; but by the King's grace and justice he is released. I here enclose you a paper which was writ by your advice and another very good friend. If it be not what you like, I hope the sincerity will make amends, for it is actually true, every little I dare say. I thank God, my Lord is come to a most comfortable frame of mind, and a serious consideration of his past life, which is so great a comfort to me that I must call upon you, my good friend, to thank God for it and to pray that I too may be truly thankful. As to what relates to this world, we desire nothing but to live quietly in Holland, till it please God we may end our days at Althorpe: that were a great blessing to us '; but it will not be thought of such an inestimable price by others as we esteem it; and therefore I hope in God it will not be envied us. I am sure nothing else in our fortune deserves envy; and yet, having reduced my Lord to the thoughts he has, it is for ever to be acknowledged by me to Almighty God as the greatest of mercies. Pray for me, and love me, and let me hear from you. Do enclose your letters to this merchant. Farewell.

"Pray remember to urge that, desiring to live in Holland till we can be allowed to live at Althorpe, is neither a sign of a Frenchman nor a Papist; and I thank God my Lord is neither. He has no pretentions and will have none; and therefore interest cannot make him say it; but he never did anything but suffer. it to be said, besides going to chapel, as hundreds did, who now value themselves for good Protestants. God knows that was so much to my soul's grief; but more had been wrong, and I daresay he is most heartily and most Christianly sorry for what he has done."

Soon after this, the Sunderlands were allowed to return to England, and from this time to the end the history of the wife was that of the husband.

# CHAPTER XII

## LOUISE, DUCHESS OF PORTSMOUTH (*née* KÉROUALLE), 1649-1734

IT is a hard thing to say of any woman, but Louise de Kéroualle was a "baggage," though whether she was at the beginning more sinned against than sinning it is at this time of day impossible to say. That she had beauty, however, is undeniable; though not of the highest kind, her face suffered from a want of expression. Evelyn talks of her: "a famous beauty, but in my opinion of a childish, simple baby face," and a contemporary poem describes her:

> "That baby face of thine, and those black eyes,
> Methinks should ne'er a hero's love surprise;
> None that had eyes, e'er saw in that French face
> O'er much of beauty, form, or comely grace."

[Sir John] Revesby speaks of her as "a very fine woman "; but others were not of that opinion. When she was little more than thirty the following lines were written about her:

> "Who can on this picture look,
> And not straight be wonder-struck,
> That such a sneaking, dowdy thing
> Should make a beggar of a King?
> Three happy nations turn to tears.
> And all their former love to fears.
> Ruin the great, and raise the small,
> Yet will by turns betray them all.
> Lowly born, and meanly bred,
> Yet of this nation is the head:
> For half Whitehall make her their court,
> Though th' other half make her their sport.
> Monmouth's tamer, Jeffrey's advance,
> Foe to England, spy to France;
> False and foolish, proud and bold,
> Ugly, as you see, and old."

"Louis XIV," says Hume, "in order to fix him to the French interests, resolved to bind by the ties of pleasure, the only ones which
with him were irresistible; and he made him a present of a French
mistress, by whose means he hoped for the future to govern him.
This, of course, was a reference to Louise de Kéroualle. Louise Renée
de Kéroualle, who was born in 1649, was the elder daughter of Guil-
laume de Penancöet, Sieur de Kéroualle, a Breton gentleman of very
ancient lineage, whose wife was through her mother connected with
the noble house of De Rieux. While in her teens she was appointed a
Maid of Honour to Henrietta, Duchess of Orleans, the sister of
Charles II. She accompanied that royal lady to Dover in 1670, and
met the English King when he came to Dover to negotiate with Colbert de Croissy the Treaty of Dover. Charles was always attracted by
a fresh face, and was particularly susceptible at the time, being more
than usually weary of Lady Castlemaine and her demands upon him,
and wished to keep the girl in England. Sir Adolphus Ward has gone
so far as to suggest that the negotiations preceding the Treaty were
deliberately prolonged by the King, in order that he might see more
of his latest charmer. The Duchess of Orleans, with more of decency
than might have been expected of a Stuart, refused her brother's request, and took Louise back with her to Paris. What the girl's wish
was has not been revealed, but it may be guessed at, for her subsequent career shows that 'she was ambitious and self-seeking. "Her
parents," says Saint-Simon, "intended her to be Louis XIV's mistress,
and she obtained the place of Maid of Honour to Henrietta of England (the Duchess of Orleans). Unfortunately for her, Mlle. de la
Vallière was also Maid of Honour to the Princess, and the King preferred that lady. If the latter had little intelligence, she was gentle,
good-natured, and obliging, and made herself popular at the Court.
It may be said, therefore, without attaching any importance to the
libellous pamphlets, that, whether owing to indiscretions or ambitious words Mademoiselle de Kéroualle had succeeded in giving the
impression that she would not have objected to the position of a
King's Favourite." So, anyhow, her sense of morality would probably
not have prevented her accepting Charles's proposal. The Duchess
died shortly after her return to France, and Charles, who was devoted to her, was greatly distressed, and not the less so because it
was rumoured that she had been poisoned. "The King of England is

inconsolable," Colbert de Croissy [1] wrote to Lionne on July 2, 1670, "and what still further increases his infliction and his sorrow, is that there are many people who do not refrain from asserting that Madame was poisoned, and this malicious rumour is spreading so rapidly in the town that some of the rabble have declared that violent hands ought to be laid upon the French. Nevertheless, neither his Britannic Majesty nor any member of the royal family have said anything to show that they attach any credence to reports so extravagant and so far removed from the truth. I await impatiently your news respecting the details of this death 'and the measures which will have to be taken in order to be able to restrain the principal people of this Court from the inclination they have evinced to believe evil and to receive the sinister impressions that have been given them. God give me grace to overcome this outburst of anger, which to tell the truth, Monsieur, is not a little to be feared!... The Duke of Buckingham is in the transports of a madman, and if the King were not more wise and prudent and my Lord Arlington very reasonable and well-intentioned affairs here would be carried to the last extremities."

Charles still hankered after Louise, and the Duke of Buckingham was, for his own political ends, at pains to inflame his passion. "The Duke of Buckingham told him that it was a decent piece of tenderness for his sister to take care of some of her servants. So she was the person the King easily consented to invite over," Burnet wrote. "That Duke assured the King of France that he could not reckon himself sure of the King but by giving him a mistress that should be true to his interests. It was soon agreed to. So the Duke of Buckingham sent her with a part of his equipage to Dieppe, and said he would presently follow."

---

[1] Colbert de Croissy (1625-1696). In 1668 he represented France at the conference of Aix-la-Chapelle; and in August of the same year was sent as ambassador to London, where he was to negotiate the definite treaty of alliance with Charles II. He arranged the interview at Dover between Charles and his sister Henrietta of Orleans, gained the king's personal favour by finding a mistress for him, Louise de Kéroualle, maid of honour to Madame, and persuaded him to declare war against Holland.

"The Duke of Buckingham has taken with him Mdlle. de Kéroualle, who was attached to her late Highness," the Marquis de Saint-Maurice, Savoy's Ambassador, wrote to Duke Charles Emmanuel II on September 19. "She is a beautiful girl and it is thought that the plan is to make her mistress to the King of England. The Duke of Buckingham would like to dethrone Lady Castlemaine, who is his enemy and His Most Christian Majesty will not be sorry, for it is said the ladies have great influence over the mind of the King of England." Immediately upon the arrival of Louise de Kéroualle in England, she was appointed a Maid of Honour to Queen Catherine, and given a handsome suite of apartments in Whitehall. It would appear, however, that the lady did not at once yield herself to her royal admirer.

"It is certain," Colbert de Croissy wrote to Louvois[2] at Paris, "that the King of England shows a warm affection for Mademoiselle de Kéroualle, and perhaps you may have heard from other sources that a richly-furnished lodging has been given her at Whitehall.

"His Majesty repairs to her apartment at nine every rooming and never stays there less than an hour, and sometimes two. He remains much longer after dinner, shares at her card-table in all her stakes and never allows her to want for anything.

"All the Ministers court eagerly the friendship of this lady, and My Lord Arlington said to me quite recently that he was very pleased to see that the King was becoming attached to her; and that, though His Majesty was not the man to communicate affairs of state to ladies, nevertheless, as it was in their power on occasion to render ill services to those whom they disliked and defeat their plans, it was much better for the King's servants that his Majesty should have an inclination for this lady, who is not of a mischievous disposition, and is a gentlewoman, rather than for actresses and such-like unworthy creatures, of whom no man of quality could take the measure; that when he went to visit the young lady every one was able to see him

---

[2] François Michel le Tellier, Marquis de Louvois (1641-1691), was the French war minister under Louis XIV. He was born in Paris to Michel le Tellier. Under the younger Tellier, France raised an army of 400,000 soldiers; this army would fight four wars between 1667 and 1713. The marquis is commonly known as "Louvois".

enter and leave and to pay court to him; and it was necessary to counsel this lady to cultivate the King's good graces, so that he might find with her nothing but pleasure, peace and quiet.

"He added that, if Lady Arlington took his advice, she would urge this young lady to yield unreservedly to the King's wishes, and tell her that there was no alternative but a convent in France, and that I ought to be the first to impress this on her.

"I told him jocularly that I was not so wanting in gratitude to the King or so foolish as to tell her to prefer religion to his good graces; that I was also persuaded that she was not waiting for my advice but that I would, none the less, give it to her, to show how much both he and I appreciated her influence, and to inform her of the obligation she was under to My Lord.

"I believe that I can assure you that if she had made sufficient progress in the King's affection to be of use in some way to His Majesty, she will do her duty."

It was thought by those interested in the matter that the time had come for the lady to surrender. When the King was at Newmarket in October 1671, she was invited to the Arlington's country seat at Euston, where the French Ambassador also was a guest. "It was universally reported," writes Evelyn, who was one of the guests at Euston Hall[3], "that the fair lady was bedded one of these nights, and the stocking flung after the manner of a married bride. I acknowledge that she was for the most part in her undress all day, and that there was fondness and toying with the young wanton. Nay, it was said that I was at the former ceremony, but that is utterly false. I neither saw nor heard of any such thing whilst I was there, though I had been in her chamber and all over that apartment late enough, and was observing all passages with much curiosity. However, it was with confidence believed that she was first made a *Miss*, as they call these unhappy creatures, with solemnity at the time."

This is confirmed by a letter from Colbert de Croissy, written at the end of that month: "The King comes frequently [to Euston] to

---

[3] http://www.eustonhall.co.uk/

take his repasts with us, and afterwards spends some hours with Mlle. de Kéroualle. He has already paid her three visits. He invited us yesterday to the races at Newmarket, where we were entertained very splendidly, and he showed towards her all the kindness, all the little attentions and all the assiduities that a great passion can inspire. And since she has not been wanting, on her side, in all the gratitude that the love of a great King can deserve from a beautiful girl, it is believed that the attachment will be of long duration and that it will exclude all others. "It really is not surprising that Madame de Sévigné should have written to her daughter in the following spring: "Don't you like to hear that little Kéroualle, whose star was divined before she left, had followed it faithfully. The King of England, on seeing her, straightway fell in love, and she did not frown at him when he declared his passion. The upshot is, that she is in an interesting state. Is it not all astounding? Castlemaine is in disgrace. England truly is a droll country."

Louise de Kéroualle gave birth to a son on July 29, 1672, the paternity of which Charles gladly accepted. He showered honours upon the boy, who was christened Charles Lennox. In August 1675, he was created Baron of Settrington, Yorkshire, Earl of March and Duke of Richmond, Yorkshire, in the peerage of England, and as if this were not enough, in the next month, Baron Methuen of Tarbolton, Earl of Darnley and Duke of Lennox, in the peerage of Scotland. Louis XIV also gave him the dignity of Duke d'Aubigny. At the age of nine he was made a Knight of the Garter, and also Governor of Dumbarton Castle, and a year later he was appointed Master of the Horse, vacant by reason of the removal of the Duke of Marlborough, the office during his minority being put in commission.

Mrs. Palmer had been created Duchess of Cleveland, and Louise de Kéroualle saw no reason why she should remain a commoner when there were titles for the asking. The trouble was that she was a French subject, but this difficulty was overcome by the consent of Louis XIV to her being naturalised in England "as" (the French Ambassador in London put it) "a necessary means to profit by the gifts which the King of England might have the kindness to bestow upon her." Following the naturalisation she was created Duchess of Portsmouth, and appointed a Lady of the Bedchamber to the Queen

In the year in which Louise de Kéroualle was raised to the peerage, Catherine was ill, and hopes rose in the mind of the Lady of the Bedchamber that in the event of her Majesty departing this life, Charles might ask her to share his throne. For aught that is known, this might have happened, for at this time Charles was head over heels in love with her, and was behaving as if he was really much indebted to her for presenting him with a son. "The King," wrote Colbert de Croissy, "is going to sup and dance at Lord Arlington's, and I am to be of the party. So also is the Duchess of Richmond. Her great talent is dancing. Mademoiselle de Kéroualle may be taken in by all those parties, and all the more so because she does not keep her head sober, since she has got into it that it is possible she may be Queen of England. She talks from morning till night of the Queen's ailments as if they were mortal."

Louise de Kéroualle had been sent to England to do her best to further the interests of France, and this she did, in an increasingly lukewarm manner, whenever it was not likely to affect her personal objects. What she desired above all things was a *tabouret* of a French duchess in the Presence Chamber at Versailles. It was nearly as difficult, though not quite, to secure this privilege as to obtain permission to drive through the arch on the Horse Guards Parade in London. She used all her charm to induce Charles to take a hand in the game. He did so, and opened the ball by expressing to the French Ambassador in England his desire that Louise should be granted the ducal fief of Aubigny. "I own I find her on all occasionally so ill-disposed for the service of the [French] King and showing such ill-humour against France (whether because she feels herself despised there, or whether from an effect of caprice), that I really think she deserves no favour of, his Majesty," Colbert wrote on July 17 to the new French Foreign Minister, Arnauld de Pomponne. "But as the King of England shows her much love and so, visibly likes to please her, His Majesty can judge whether it is best not to treat her according to her merits. Any attention paid to her will be taken by the King of England as one paid to himself. I have, however, told him upon what conditions alone the fief could be granted, and, what he asks is just the contrary."

That letter was written in 1673, and in the following year the lady was granted the estate, with remainder to such of her natural children by Charles as he should designate. Louise was glad enough to have the estate; but was disgusted that the title carrying with it the right of a *tabouret* was withheld. [4]

"Mrs. Carwell," as Louise de Kéroualle was usually called in this country [the UK] — that being the nearest to her family name that most people could get — was as unpopular as the Duchess of Cleveland had been in the heyday of her reign. More money was spent by her than was given by Charles to any other of his mistresses. Her extravagance was wanton. Her splendid apartments at the end of the gallery at Whitehall was, according to John Evelyn, "twice or thrice pulled down and rebuilt to satisfy her prodigal and expensive pleasures. She was allowed £10,000 a year out of the Privy Purse. In 1681 she actually drew from the Treasury the sum of £136,668!"

The King could deny her nothing, especially after the summer of 1671. "I have a thing to tell you, Monsieur, for the French King's information, which should remain secret as long as it pleases his Majesty to keep it so, because if it gets out it might be a source of unseemly raillery," Count de Ruvigny wrote to de Pomponne on May 14, 1674. "Whilst the King was winning provinces, the King of England was catching a malady which he has been at the trouble of communicating to the Duchess of Portsmouth. That Prince is nearly cured; but to all appearances the lady will not so soon be rid of the virus. She had been, however, in a degree consoled for such a troublesome present by one more suitable to her eharmsa pearl necklace worth four thousand jacobus, and a diamond worth six thousand, which have so rejoiced her that I should not wonder if, for the price she were not willing to risk another attack."

Having as a contemporary put it delicately, "suffered through the miscellaneous nature of the King's amours," she went for a cure to Tonbridge to take the waters, and, these proving ineffectual, then to Bourbon — though some there were who thought she went abroad to

---

[4] Right of the tabouret: the privilege of sitting on a tabouret [stool with no arms or back] in the presence of the sovereign, formerly granted to certain ladies of high rank at the French court.

meet Philip, the Grand Prior of Vendôme, whose acquaintance she had made when, he came on a mission to England. He was at first well received by Charles, but his attentions to the Duchess of Portsmouth became so marked that he was dismissed the Court. There is reference to this incident in "The Duchess of Portsmouth's Garland":

> "When Portsmouth did from England fly, to follow her Vendôme,
> Thus all along the Gallery the monarch made his moan,
> O Châtillon, for charity, send me my Cleaveland home!
> Go, Nymph, so foolish and unkind, your wandering Knight pursue,
> And leave a love-sick King behind, so faithful and so true,
> You Gods, when you made Love so blind, you should have lam'd him too."

Another lampoon is the "Dialogue between Two Horses," by Andrew Marvell:

*Woodchurch.*
"That the King should send for another French whore;
When one already has made him so poor."

*Chorus.*
"The misses take place, each advanced to be duchess
With pomp great as queens in their coach and six horses; Their
bastards made dukes, earls, viscounts and lords.
And all the title that honour affords."

*Woodchurch.*
"While those brats and their mothers do live in such plenty,
The nation's impoverished and the 'Chequers quite empty,
And though was pretended when the money was lent,
More on whores, than in ships or in war hath been spent."

*Chorus.*
"Enough, my dear brother, although we speak reason,
Yet truth many times being punished for treason."

After the death of Charles II his brother James and Louis XIV promised their protection to the Duchess of Portsmouth. However, she grew uneasy, being fully aware of the general hatred against her in England and, further, being, according to Ward, apprehensive of a direct attack in Parliament, she crossed the Channel in August 1685. Her reception at the French Court was cold, and soon she returned to England and remained at Whitehall until July 1688, when she settled permanently in her own country. She lived mostly on her estate at Aubigny, but as her English pension was withdrawn, she was soon financially embarrassed. In her old age, she was, according to Saint-Simon, "*fort vieille, trèsconvertie et pénitente, et très-mal dans ses affaires.*" ["very old, most converted and penitent, and very unfortunate in her affairs"] George Selwyn, who saw her so late as the year before her death, told Sir Nathaniel Wraxall that she was even then "possessed of many attractions, though verging towards fourscore." She died at Paris on November 14, 1734, and was buried in the Church of the Barefooted Carmelites, in the chapel belonging to the De Rieux family. Her son, the Duke of Richmond, had predeceased her by eleven years.

The Duchess of Portsmouth seems to have learnt wisdom from the fate of her sister of Cleveland. While Lady Castlemaine ruled, it may almost be said, by force, Louise de Kéroualle enslaved Charles not only by her childish beauty, but also by tears, coaxings, and affectations of jealousy. Certainly, she kept her hold over him until the end. She was in despair when he was near his death, and perhaps not entirely for selfish reasons. However, the Queen and the Duchess of York refused her admittance to the royal chamber. "I went to the apartments of the Duchess of Portsmouth," Barillon[5] wrote to Louis XIV, "and found her overwhelmed with grief, the physicians having deprived her of all hope. She took a great interest in her soul and in that of Charles. She was one of the few who knew that the King had embraced the Roman Catholic Church, and she was in terror lest he should die without partaking of the Last Sacrament." "I have a thing of great moment to tell you," she said to Barillon at this juncture. "If it were known, my head would be in danger. The King is really and truly a Catholic; but he will die without being reconciled to the Church. His bedchamber is full of Protestant clergymen. I cannot enter it without giving scandal. The Duke is thinking only of himself.

---

[5] Barillon was the French Ambassador posted to England.

Speak to him. Remember that there is a soul at stake. He is master now. He can clear the room. Go this instant, or it will be too late."

One of the most amusing incidents in the life of Louise de Kéroualle — though it was probably no joke to her — was Nell Gwyn's running fight with her. Madame de Sévigné has set out the situation in a letter written in 1675: "With regards to England, Mademoiselle de Kéroualle has been disappointed in nothing; she wished to be the mistress of the King, and she is so. He takes up his abode with her almost every night in the face of the whole Court: she has had a son who has been acknowledged, and presented with two duchies. She amasses treasure and makes herself feared and respected as much as she can.

"But she did not foresee that she should find a young actress in her way, whom the King doats on; and she has it not in her power to withdraw him from her. He divides his care, his time, and his health between these two.

"The actress is as haughty as the Duchess of Portsmouth; she insults her, makes faces at her, attacks her, frequently steals the King from her, and boasts of his preference to her. She is young, indiscreet, confident, meretricious, and pleasant; she sings, dances, and acts her part well. She has a son by the King, and wishes to have him acknowledged: she reasons thus: 'This Duchess,' says she, 'pretends to be a person of quality; she says she is related to the best families in France; whenever any person of distinction dies, she puts herself in mourning. If she be a lady of such quality, why does she demean herself to be a courtesan? She ought to be ashamed of herself.

"As for me, it is my profession, I do not pretend to be anything better. The King maintains me, and I am constant to him at present. He has a son by me: I say he ought to acknowledge him, and I am sure he will, for he loves me as well as he does Portsmouth.'

"This creature gets the upper hand, and discountenances and embarrasses the Duchess extremely. I like these original characters — I could find nothing better to send you from Orleans; but this is at least truth."

The pamphleteers and lampoonists were not slow to seize the opportunity. An anonymous writer was responsible for "A Pleasant Battle between Two Lapdogs of the Utopian Court."

The two curs, Tutty and Snap-short—the former the property of Nell Gwyn, the other of the Duchess of Portsmouth—enter into a ludicrous and snarling discussion respecting the merits of their respective mistresses. This dispute is about to end in a fray, when the rival ladies sweep into the room, and conclude a diverting scene with the following dialogue:

"*Duchess of Portsmouth:* 'Pray, Madam, give my dog fair play; I protest you hinder him with your petticoats; he cannot fasten Madam, fair play is fair play.'

"*Madam Gwyn:* 'Truly, Madam, I thought I knew as well what belonged to dog-fighting as your Ladyship; but since you pretend to instruct me in your French dog-play, pray, Madam, stand a little farther, as you respect your own flesh, for my little dog is mettle to the back and smells a Popish Miss at a far greater distance. Pray, Madam, take warning, for you stand on dangerous ground.' 'Haloo, haloo, haloo! Be brave, Tutty. Ha, brave Snap-short. A guinea on Tutty—two to one on Tutty.'

"'Done,' quoth Monsieur, 'begar, begar me have lost near tousand pounds.'

"Tutty it seems beat Snap-short, and the bell
Tutty bears home in Victory: farewell!"

DIALOGUE BETWEEN THE DUTCHESS OF PORTSMOUTH AND MADAM GWIN AT PARTING.

*Madam Gwin.*
"You never suffer'd Nell to come in Play
Whilst you had left but one Meridian-Ray,
And yet by turns I did myself that right,
If you enjoy'd the day, I rul'd the night.
Let Fame that never yet Spoke well of Woman,

Give out I was a Stroling Whore and Common,

Yet have I been to him since the first hour,
As Constant as the Needle to the Flower;
Whilst you to your Eternal Praise and Fame
To Foreign Scents betray'd the Royal Game.

My name, thou Jezebel of Pride and Malice,
Whose father had a hog-stey for his Pallace,
In my clear Viens but British Bloud does flow,
Whilst thou like a *French* Tode-stool first did grow,
And from a Birth as poor as they delight,
Sprang up a Mushroom-Dutchess in a Night."

*The Duchess of Portsmouth.*
" 'Think not i'th. Respeit of this short Remove
To sit sole Empress on the Throne of Love.
I was thy Rival once, and will Return
To be thy Rival still, and thou my Scorne."

*Madam Gwin.*
"The peoples Hate much less their Curse I fear,
I do them Justice with less Sums a Year.
I neither run in Court nor City's Score.
I pay my Debts, Distribute to the Poor.
Whilst thou with ill-kept Treasure does Resort
T' uphold thy splendor in the *Gallick* Court.
But France is for thy Lust too Kind a Clime,
In Africk with some Wolf or Tyger Lime;
Or in the Indies make a new Plantation
And ease us of the Grievance of the Nation."

## A PLEASANT DIALOGUE BETWIXT TWO WANTON LADIES OF PLEASURE

*The Dutchess of Por[t]smouths woful Far[e]wel to her former Felicity.*

One Lady she Courageously stands to her own defence;

The other now doth seem to bow, her Colours are display'd,
Assuredly none can deny the Words she speaks are sence:
She is content her mind is bent, still maintain her Trade.

Tune of *Tan tarra rara, tan tive*.[6]

"Brave Gallants, now listen and I will tell you,
  With a fa, la, la, la,fa, la, la.
A pleasant discourse that I heard at *Pell Mell*,
  With a fa, la, la, la,fa, la, la.
Between two fair Ladys of the wanton strain,
The one to the other did sigh and complain,
I wish I was over in France now again.
  With a fa, la, la, la,la, la, la.

Quoth Nelly, I prithee, who sent for thee here,
  With a fa, la, la, la, fa, la, la.
'Tis you with a shame that put in for a share,
  With a fa, la, la, la, fa, la, la.
O do you remember when I was dismay'd
When you in attire was richly array'd,
Alas O poor *Nelly* was wrong'd in my trade,
  With a fa, la, la, la,la, la, la.

I pray now could you not your honour advance,
  With a fa, la, la, la,fa, la, la.
With some noble peer in the Nation of *France*,
  With a fa, la, la, la, fa, la, la.
Forsooth you must needs leave your Country, dear,
To utter your fine French Commodity here,
But sorrow and trouble will bring up the rear,
With a fa, la, la, la,fa, la, la.

Dear *Nelly*, be loving and do not reflect
With a fa, la, la, la,fa, la, la.
But prithee now show me some civil respect

---

[6] fairly common tune used for broadside ballads, particularly bawdy Portsmouth ballads,

With a fa, la, la, la,fa, la, la.

For now I am in a most pitiful case,
For shame will not let me uncover my face,
My honour is turn'd to a wail of disgrace,
With a fa, la, la, la,fa, la, la.

Quoth Nelly, pray send for the treasure again,
With a fa, la, la, la,fa, la, la.
That you did send over while you were in fame:
With a fa, la, la, la, fa, la, la.

Come, come, I must tell ye that you was too bold
To send from this nation such parcels of gold,
In such kind dealings you must be controul'd,
With a fa, la, la, la, fa, la, la.

No, sweet Madam Nelly, you cannot deny,
With a fa, la, la, la, fa, la, la.
But you have had the treasure as often as I,
With a fa, la, la, la, fa, la, la.
And yet must lonely be run down
By you that I value the least in the Town,
If I come in favour upon thee i'le frown.
With a fa, la, la, la, fa, la, la.

You drab of a Miss, I do hold you.in scorn,
With a fa, la, la, la, fa, la, la.
I'de have you know I am this Nation born,
With afa, la, la, la,fa, la, la.
Your coming to England I heartily rue,
Of many a good bout I've been cheated by you,
For which may a Thousand vexations issue,
With a fa, la, la, la, fa, la, la.

No matter for that, it was all my delight,
With a fa, la, la, la, fa, la, la.

But now I am in a most pittiful plight,
With a fa, la, la, la,fa, la, la.
Unfortunate Lady that now am deny'd,
In this vail of sorrow my patience is try'd,
Sure this may be termed the downfall of pride,
With a fa la, la, la, fa, la, la.

I'le warrant you thought it would ever be day,
With afa, la, la, la,fa, la, la.
But now you are utterly fell to decay,
With a fa, la, la, la, fa, la, la.
You are in a sad and deplorable state,
You wander alone for' want of a Mate,
You're like an old Almanack quite out of date,
With a fa, la, la, la, fa, la, la.

No, Nelly, I will not be clearly dismay'd
With a fa, la, la, la,ja, la, la.
I'le set a good face and will follow my trade,
With afa, la, la, la,la, la, w.
I, shall have some trading I do make no doubt,
I'le have youthful damosels to ply on the scout,
I'le play a small Game now before I'le stick out,
*With a fa, la, la, la, fa, la, la.*"

# CHAPTER XIII

## ELEANOR ("NELL") GWYN, 1650-1687

"And once Nell Gwyn, a frail young sprite
Look'd kindly when I met her;
I shook my head perhaps—but quite
Forgot to quite forget her."

THERE has never been a royal mistress more popular than Nell Gwyn. There was no false pride about her. She was just as she was, and did not pretend to be anything more. When driving one day through the City, the London apprentices, thinking that her coach was that of the Duchess of Portsmouth, another mistress of Charles II, hooted her. Whereupon she put her pretty, saucy face out of the window, and cried: "Pray, good people, be civil, I am the Protestant whore."

A very pretty wench Nell Gwyn must have been—beautiful she never was. Exquisite, rather full figure, and short in stature; she had reddish-brown hair and delightful twinkling eyes that almost closed when she smiled; the tiniest feet possible and the smallest hands. She had an immense vitality and a robustious Cockney humour. These qualities, together with her invariable good temper and her merry fooling, and a freedom of speech that was more than Rabelaisian, made her a delight to the gallants of the day.

She was born in February, 1650, at some place unknown; but at a very early age came with her mother to London, and lived in a slum in Drury Lane. Who her father was is still a matter of argument among those interested in these things, as is also the question whether she was legitimate or a love-child. As for the mother, it is as likely as not that she was a prostitute. Nell, however, seems to have been fond of her; anyhow she looked after her even to taking her for a while to live with her. Not for long, however, did Eleanor Gwyn, the elder, remain with her daughter, for she was a person of very unpleasant habits, and drink was to her a necessity. Sir George Etheridge in "The Lady of Pleasure: A Satyr," referred to her:

> "Maid, Punk, and Bawd, full sixty years and more,
> Dy'd drunk with brandy in a common shore."

Mrs. Gwyn died in 1679, being then in her fifty-seventh year, and in Domestic Intelligence for August 5th of that year is the announcement: "We hear that Madam Ellen Gwyn's mother, sitting lately by the waterside at her house by the Neat-Houses, near Chelsea, fell accidentally into the water and was drowned." General opinion inclined to the view that the lady was drunk when she fell into the ditch. The notoriety of Nell Gwyn caused much notice to be taken of her mother's death, and more than one lampoon was written about her. One has the splendid title: "A True Account of the late most doleful and lamentable tragedy of old Maddam Gwinn, mother of Eleanor Gwinn, who was unfortunately drowned in a fishpond at her own mansion-house, near the NeatHouses, with an account how that much to be deplored accident came to pass and what is expected to be the sequel of the same. With an Epitaph, composed against the solemnity of her pompous funeral, and many other circumstances." From this may be quoted the following extracts:

"But oh, the cruel Fate of some sinister Star that ruled her Birth, she there expired, and left the First to be the Executor of her Will to this sad and dismal Tragedy, the which has caused a universal grief among the bucksom *Bona Robas*.[1] So that it is generally believed, that upon so Tragical occasion, the Pallace and Fish-pond will be forfeited to her most vertuous Daughter Maddam Ellen Gwinn, as Lady of the Soil, and chief of all the Bonas-Robas that the Suburban Schools of Venus late have fitted for the Game. And now in Gratitude to this good Matron's Memory, to be imposed upon her Tomb-Stone at the approaching Solemnisation we have composed this Epitaph as followest:

> "Here lies the Victim of a cruel Fate,
> Whom too much Element did Ruinate;
> 'Tis something strange, but yet most wondrous true,
>  That what we live by, should our Lives undo,
> She that so oft had powerful Waters try'd,
> At last with silence, in a Fish-pond dy'd.

---

[1] Bona Robas: an Elizabethan word for a high-class prostitute

> Fate was unjust, for had he prov'd but kind,
> To make it Brandy, he had pleas'd her mind."

Nell gave her mother so magnificent a funeral — the lady was buried in St. Martin's-in-the-Fields — that Rochester wrote in his "Panegyrick on Nelly: "

> "Nor was her Mother's Funeral less her care,
> No cost, no velvet, did the Daughter spare:
> Five gulded 'Scutcheons did the Herse inrich,
> To celebrate this Martyr of the Ditch.
> Burnt Brandy did in flaming Brummers flow,
> Drank at her Funeral, while her well-pleas'd
> Shade Rejoyc'd, ev'n in the sober Fields below,
> At all the drunkenness her Death had made."

Nell had no education whatsoever. If she could read at all, it must have been with the greatest difficulty. Sir Robert Howard, writing to the Duke of Ormond in 1679, when Nell was twenty-eight, says: "She presents you with her real acknowledgments for all your favours, and protests she would write in her own hand, but her wild characters would distract you."

The two following letters written by her, or for her, are not without interest.

"Pray Deare Mr. Hide, forgive me for not writeing to you before now, for the reasone is I have bin sick thre months and sinse I regoverd I had nothing to intertaine you with all, nor have nothing now worth writing, but that I can hold no longer to let you know I never have ben in any companie wethout drinking your health, for I love you with all my soule.

"The pel mel is now to me a dismale place since I have utterly lost Sr. Car Scrope, never to be recoverd agane, for he tould me he could not live alwayes at this rate, and so begune to be a littel uncivil, which I could not suffer from an uglye *baux garscon* [fine young man].

"Mrs. Knight's lady mother dead, and she has. put up a scutchin no beiger then my Lady Grin's scunchis.

"My Lord Rochester is gone in the cuntrei.

"Mr. Savil has got a misfortune, but is upon recovery and is to marry an hairess, who I think wont wont [sic] have an ill time out if he hold up his thumb.

"My Lord of Dorscit apiers worze in thre months, for he drinks aile with Shadwell and Mr. Harris at the Duke's home all day long.

"My Lord Bauclaire is goeing into France.

"We are agoeing to supe with the King at Whitehall and my lady Harvie.

"The King remembers his sarvis to you.

"Now let's talke of state affairs, for we never caried things so cunningly as now, for we don't know whether we shall have peace or war, but I am for war, and for no other reason but that you may come home.

"I have a thousand merry conseets, but I can't make her write me, and therefore you must take the will for the deed. God bye.

"Your most loveing, obedient, faithfull and humbel servant,
                                                    "E. G."

"These for Madam Jennings over against the Tub Tavern in Jermyn ,Street, London.

"WINDSOR, BURFORD HOUSE,
                    "April 14, 1684.

"MADAM,

"I have received y$^r$ Letter, and I desire y$^u$ would speake to my Ladie Williams to send me the Gold Stuffe, & a Note with it, because I must sign it, then she shall have her money y$^e$ next Day of Mr. Trant; pray tell her Ladieship, that I will send her a Note of what Quantity of Things I'le have bought, if her Ladieship will put herselfe to ye Trouble to buy them; when they are bought I will sign a Note for her to be payd.

"Pray Madam, let ye Man goe on with my Sedan and send Potvin and Mr. Coker down to me, for I want them both. The Bill is very dear to boyle the Plate, but necessity hath noe Law. I am afraid Mm you have forgott my Mantle, which you were to line with Muck Colour Sattin, and all my other things, for you send me noe Patterns nor Answer.

"Monsieur Lainey is going away.

"Pray send me word about your son Griffin, for his Majesty is mighty well pleased that he will goe along with my Lord Duke. I am afraid you are so much taken up with your owne House that you forget my Business. My service to dear Lord Kildare, and tell him I love him with all my heart.

"Pray Mᵐ see that Potvin brings now all my Things with him: My Lord Duke's bed, &c., if he hath not made them all up, he may doe that here, for if I doe not get my Things out of his Hands now, I shall not have them until this time twelvemonth. The Duke brought me down with him my Crochet of Diamonds; and I love it the better because he brought it. Mr. Lumley and everie body else will tell you that it'is the finest Thing that ever was seen. Good Mm speake to Mr. Beaver to come' down too, that I may bespeake a Ring for the Duke of Grafton before he goes into France.

"I have continued extreme ill ever since you left me, and I am soe still. I have sent to London for a Dr. I believe I shall die. My service to the Duchess of Norfolk, and tell her, I am as *sick* as her Grace, but do not know what I ayle, although shee does....

"Pray tell Ladie Williams that the King's Mistresses are accounted ill paymasters, but shee shall have her Money the next day after I have the stuffe.

"Here is a sad slaughter at Windsor, the young mens taking yʳ leaves and going to France, and, although they are none of my Lovers, yet I am loath to part with the men.

"Mrs. Jennings, I love with all my Heart and soe good-bye.
                                                          "E. G.

"Let me have an Answer to this Letter."

At the outset it may be said that Nell Gwyn never had a chance to be virtuous—on the other hand, it is probable that she had not the slightest desire to be so. At the age of twelve, even earlier, she was a serving-girl in a brothel, run by the infamous Mother Ross. "I was brought up in a brothel to bring strong waters to the gentlemen," she told Beck Marshall, the actress. It may be taken for granted that it was not long before she was seduced; certainly she was not a virgin when she first appeared on the stage in her fifteenth year. Again to quote Rochester:

> "Then was by Madam Ross expos'd to Town,—
> I mean to those who would give her half-a-crown:
> Next in the Play-house she took her degree,
> As men commence at th' University."

Nell Gwyn was for a while a frequenter of the notorious Lewknor's Lane, on the east side of Drury Lane, opposite Short's Gardens (now named Macklin Street), where, we are told, in that day "young creatures were inveigled into infamy, and sent dressed as orange-girls to sell fruit and attract attention in the adjoining theatres."

It was while selling oranges in the theater that the idea of going on the stage occurred to Nell Gwyn—or it may have been suggested to her by someone who desired her favours, which, indeed, were not difficult to obtain. Charles Hart, the actor, has been credited with introducing her to the boards, and so has John Lacy, the dramatist. It would appear that she was the mistress of both men, whether simultaneously or one after the other is not known. Colley Cibber [2] has it that "Hart introduced Mrs. Gwyn upon the dramatic boards, and has acquired the distinction of being ranked among that lady's first felicitous lovers, by having succeeded to Lacy in the possession of her charms." Nell had been tutored for the stage by these admirers in conjunction, testifying her gratitude to both. However, the point is not material.

---

[2] Colley Cibber (1671-1757) was a British actor-manager, playwright, and Poet Laureate. His acting specialty was broadly comical fop parts. As a tragic actor, he was persistent but much ridiculed, and his plays and poems have not stood the test of time. He was the chief target, the head Dunce, of Alexander Pope's satirical poem *The Dunciad.*

The first mention of her in Pepys's Diary is on October 5, 1667: "And so to the King's House: and there, going in, met with Knipp, and she took us up into the tireing rooms: and to the women's shift, where Nell was dressing herself, and was all unready, and is very pretty, prettier than I thought.

"And so walked all up and down the house above, and then below into the scene-room, and there sat down, and she gave us fruit: and here read the questions to Knipp, while she answered me, through all her part of *Flora's Vagaries* which was acted to-day.

"But Lord! to see how they were both painted would make a man mad and did make me loathe them; and what base company of men among them, and how lewdly they talk! and how poor the men are in clothes, and yet what a shew they make on the stage by candle light, is very observable.

"But to see how Nelly cursed for having so few people in the pit, was very pretty; the other house carrying away all the people at the new play, and is said now-a-days to have generally most company as being better players.

"By and by into the pit, and there saw the play, which is pretty good, but my belly was full of what I had seen in the house, and so, after the play done away home, and there to the writing my letters, and so home to supper and to bed."

From Nell Gwyn's appearance on the stage in 1665, she was a success — "pretty, witty Nell at the King's House," Pepys mentions early in that year. She certainly was never within measurable distance of becoming a great actress; she was a great comedienne, though she was infinitely better in comedy than in tragedy.

In the Epilogue to the tragedy, *The Duke of Lerma*, she had to say:

> "I know you in your hearts
> Hate serious plays — as I hate serious parts."

And it may be taken for granted that she delivered these lines with gusto, as she did also those in the Epilogue to Dryden's *Tyrannic Love*, in which play in 1669 she played Valeria:

"...I die
Out of my calling in a tragedy."

It was her brightness, her merry laugh, her audacity, her pretty self that made her an attraction. Again and again she is mentioned by Pepys. "The women do very well in *The English Monsieur,* but above all little Nelly." "Going out, they called us all in, and brought us to Nelly, a most pretty woman, whotl.cted the great part of Ceolia in *The Humorous Lieutenant* to-day very fine, and did it pretty well: I kissed her and so did my wife; a mighty pretty soul she is." "After dinner with my wife to the King's House to see *The Maiden Queen,* a new play of Dryden's, mightily commended for the regularity of it, and the strain and wit; the truth is, there is a comical part done by Nell, which is Florimel, that I never can hope ever to see the like done by man or woman. The King and the Duke of York were at the play. But so great a performance of a comical part was never, I believe, in the world before as Nell do this both as a mad girl, then most and best of all when she comes in like a young gallant; and hath the motions and carriage of a spark the most that ever I saw any man have. It makes me, I confess, admire her."

Of the numbers or names of most of Nell Gwyn's lovers there is no record. William Oldys mentions a rumour that among them there were the second Duke of Buckingham, then a Gentleman of the Bedchamber, and the Earl of Rochester. Probably Sir George Etheridge and Sir Charles Sedley pursued her. Certainly she was in 1667 the mistress of Charles Sackville, Lord Buckhurst, afterwards sixth Earl of Dorset, who, like the rest, was fascinated by her gay, frolicsome, humorous disposition. He was a patron of letters and himself an author — his song, "To all you ladies now on land" is still well known. He was the friend of Dryden, of Etherege, and of Congreve — the last wrote of him:

"For pointed Satyr I wou'd Buckhurst choose,
The best good man, with the worse natur'd Muse."

Horace Walpole described Lord Buckhurst as "the finest gentleman in the voluptuous Court of Charles II, "and Peter Cunningham has written a happy little character-sketch of him:

"Buckhurst had other qualities to recommend him than his youth (he was thirty at this time), his rank, his good heart, and his good breeding. He had already distinguished himself by his personal intrepidity in the war against the Dutch; had written the best song of its kind in the English language, and some of the severest and most refined satires we possess; was the friend of all the poets of eminence in his time, as he was afterwards the most munificent patron of men of genius that this country has yet seen. The most eminent masters in their several lines asked and abided by his judgment, and afterwards dedicated their works to him in grateful acknowledgment of his taste and favours. Butler owed to him that the Court 'tasted' his 'Hudibras'[3]; Wycherley that the town 'liked' his 'Plain Dealer'[4]; and the Duke of Buckingham deferred to publish his 'Rehearsal'[5] till he was sure, as he expressed it, that my Lord Buckhurst would not 'rehearse' upon him again. Nor was this all. His table was one of the last that gave us an example of the old housekeeping of an English nobleman. A freedom reigned about it which made everyone of the guests think himself at home, and an abundance which showed that the master's hospitality extended to many more than those who had the honour to sit at table with himself. Nor has he been less happy after death. Pope wrote his epitaph, and Prior his panegyric." Lord Buckhurst was passionately in love with Nell Gwyn. So infatuated was he that, to the general regret, he withdrew her from the theatre, so that he could have her all to 'himself. He took her to Epsom, then celebrated for its

---

[3] *Hudibras* was written between 1660 and 1680 and is a satire on the Cromwellians and on the Presbyterian church written by a confirmed Royalist and Anglican. Hudibras, a colonel in the Cromwellian army, is involved in various comic misadventures and is shown to be stupid, greedy and dishonest. The poem is very well written in Chaucerian couplets and was popular for about 150 years, as long as its political attitudes were also popular. (source: www.ExClassics.com)

[4] *The Plain Dealer* is a Restoration comedy by William Wycherley, first performed in 1674, but not published until three years later. The play is based on Molière's *Le Misanthrope*, and is generally considered Wycherley's finest work.

[5] *The Rehearsal* was a satirical play aimed specifically at John Dryden and generally at the sententious and overly ambitious theater of the Restoration tragedy. The play was staged in 1671 and published anonymously in 1672, but it is certainly by George Villiers, 2nd Duke of Buckingham and others. Several people, including Samuel Butler of *Hudibras* fame, have been suggested as collaborators. (source: Wikipedia)

waters, with Sir Charles Sedley, where, according to Pepys, they "keep a merry house."

Then, presently, Charles II came upon the scene, and Nell Gwyn deserted Lord Buckhurst and became his Majesty's mistress. It says much for the cynical humour of the Merry Monarch that some years later he appointed his predecessor in the lady's affections one of the trustees of Burford House, Oxford, which he had settled on her.

The King had, of course, often seen Nell Gwyn before he took her in keeping: he was a frequent visitor to the theatre, and during the Plague, when the theatres were closed, she had acted before him at Whitehall. Etheredge has suggested that she was urged upon him by the Duke of Buckingham, who thought that she might counteract the influence of the Duchess of Cleveland:

> "Dread Sir, quoth B—ham, in Duty bound,
> I come to give your Kingship counsel sound:
> I wonder you should dote so like a Fop,
> On Cleveland—whom her very Footmen g-pe:
> Dost think you don't your Parliament offend
> That all they give you on a Beggar spend;
> Permit me, Sir, to recommend a Whore,
> Kiss her but once, you'll ne'er kiss Cleveland more;
> She'll fit you to a hair, all Wit, all Fire,
> And Impudence to your Heart's desire;
> And more than this, Sir, you'll save Money by her
> She's B[uckhurst]'s Whore at present, but you know
> When Sovereigns want a Whore, that Subjecks must forego."

This may or may not have been the case; but, whether or no, the girl's charm was in itself enough to account for the connection, the date of which is approximately fixed by an entry in Pepys's Diary on January 11, 1668, in which he says that Mrs. Knipp, another actress of the same theatre, told him that, "The King did send several times for Nelly, and she was with him." At first Charles just sent for her when he would; but presently he installed her in an apartment in Lincoln's Inn Fields, where he came to her frequently. He regarded these visits 'as a relaxation, and thoroughly enjoyed them. "She acted all persons in so lively a manner, and was such a constant diversion to the King, that even a new mistress could not drive her, away." Burnet. "But after all, he never treated her with the decencies of a mistress, but rather with the lewdness of a prostitute as she had indeed been to a great many; and therefore she called the King her Charles the Third, since she had been formerly kept by two of that name." The other two, it may be surmised, were Charles Hart and Charles, Lord Buckhurst.

The King, in fact, delighted in Nell Gwyn. He loved her disregard of money—though he gave her plenty; and her lack of respect of rank. Even for Majesty itself she had no reverence. As Etherege wrote of her:

> "When he was dumpish, she would still be jocund,
> And chuck the Royal Chin of C[harles] the Second."

Colley Cibber tells a story about the girl that admirably illustrates her audacious humour. "Boman, then a youth, and famed for his voice, was appointed to sing some part in a concert of music at the private lodgings of Mrs. Gwin, at which were only present the King, the Duke of York, and one or two who were usually admitted upon those detached parties of pleasure. When the performance was ended, the King expressed himself highly pleased, and gave it extraordinary commendations.

"'Then, sir,' said the lady, 'to show you don't speak like a Courtier, I hope you will make the performers a handsome present.'

"The King said he had no money about him, and asked the Duke if he had any.

"To which the Duke replied, 'I believe not above a guinea or two.'

"Upon which the laughing lady, turning to the people about her, and making bold with the King's common expression, cried:

"'Od's fish, what company am I got into?'"

Nell Gwyn continued to act at the King's House, where she was a great favourite with the audiences. Pepys saw her at the end of 1677, when she created Merida in *All Mistaken, or, The Mad Couple*, written by the Hon. James Howard: "To the King's House," he noted, "and there saw *The Mad Couple*, which is but an ordinary play; but only Nell's and Hart's mad parts are most excellently done, but especially hers, which makes it a miracle to me to think how ill she do any serious part, as, the other day, just like a fool or changeling, and in a mad part do beyond imitation almost." This, however, is not the place to trace in detail the actress's theatrical career. It may be mentioned, however, that the production of Dryden's *Conquest of Granada*, in which Nell Gwyn was to play Almahide, had to be postponed, to allow her to give birth on May 8, 1670, to Charles Beauclerk, her elder son by the King. Just about that date Moll Davis, of the Duke's Theatre, was delivered of another royal bastard, presently to be known as Lady Mary Tudor. When *The Conquest of Granada* was produced in the autumn, the author made allusion in the Epilogue to the double postponement:

> "Think him not duller for the year's delay.
> He was prepared, the women were away;
> And men without their parts can hardly play.
> If they through sickness seldom did appear,
> Pity the virgins of each theatre;
> For at both houses 'twas a sickly year!
> And pity us, your servants, to whose cost
> In one such sickness nine whole months were lost."

Shortly after Dryden's play, there was a revival of Beaumont and Fletcher's *A King and No King*, in which Nell Gwyn took part. After that it would appear that she retired from the stage.

Not long after the birth of Charles Beauclerk, the King moved her to a house on the north side of Pall Mall, on the site of which now stands the Army and Navy Club, which has in its possession a Nell Gwyn mirror. In 1671 she took possession of a house on the south side of Pall Mall. This house — Pennant is the authority — "was given by a long lease by Charles the Second to Nell Gwyn, and upon her discovering it to be only a lease under the Crown, she returned him the lease and conveyances, saying that she had always conveyed free under the Crown and always would; and would not, accept it till it was conveyed free to her by an act of Parliament made on and for that purpose. Upon Nelly's death it was sold and has been conveyed free ever since."

The reason for bringing Nell Gwyn from Lincoln's Inn Fields was, obviously, that it was more convenient to the King to have her nearer Whitehall. "I had a fair opportunity of talking to His Majesty in the lobby next the Queen's side, where I presented him some sheets of my History," John Evelyn recorded one day in March, 1671. "I thence walked with him through St. James's Park to the garden, where I both saw and heard a very familiar discourse between him and Mrs. Nellie, as they call an impudent comedian, she looked out of her garden on a terrace at the top of the walk and he standing on the green walk under it. I was heartily sorry at this scene. Thence the King walked to the Duchess of Cleveland, another lady of pleasure, and curse to our nation."

There has been much controversy about the residences of Nell Gwyn. The property now known as No. 53 Wardour Street was settled on her by the King, but she certainly never lived there. It has been said that at one time she had a house in the Pimlico Road, in which neighbourhood her memory is preserved by a Nell Gwynne Tavern and a passage called Nell Gwynne Cottages; but such evidence as this is negligible. That she lived at Chelsea has become so imbued in people's minds that it is impossible to shake the belief. It is generally accepted as a fact that she suggested to the King the idea of Chelsea Hospital for old soldiers, but the official historian of that institution could find no evidence to confirm this. However, unquestionably she had a house at Windsor. The King settled on her Burford House, the site of which is now occupied by the Queen's Mews. The original grant was for life, and afterwards to her only surviving son, then the Earl of Burford (afterwards Duke of St. Albans) and the heirs male of his body; but this was presently amended to include his heirs female, with ultimate remainder to Nell Gwyn in fee.

The world, even the easy-going world of the Restoration period, was scandalised when they heard that Nell Gwyn had been appointed a Lady of the Privy Chamber to the Queen, and very unkind things were said about this matter.

Nell Gwyn, unlike Lady Castlemaine and Louise de Kéroualle, was not grasping in the matter of money. Indeed, money meant nothing to her. When she had some, she spent it. When she had nope, she went cheerily into debt without regard to her resources present or future. The Duke of Buckingham told Bishop Burnet—of all people in the world—that when Nell Gwyn was first brought to the King, she asked for an allowance of only five hundred a year, and that this Charles refused her. It would perhaps have been all the same if he had accepted it. "Gwyn," says Burnet, "the indiscreetest and wildest creature that ever was in a Court, yet continued to the end of the King's life in great favour, and was maintained at a vast expense." The Duke of Buckingham estimated that in the first four years with the King she received about £60,000.

Some idea of the extravagance of Nell Gwyn may be gathered from the following account of a silversmith for ornaments:

### Work done for y^e righte Hon^ble Madame Guinne. John Cooqus, siluersmyth his bill. 1674

| | £ | s. | d |
|---|---|---|---|
| Delivered the head of y^e bedstead weighing 885 onces 12 lb. and I have received 636 onces 15 dweight so that their is over and aboue of me owne silver two hundred and forty eight onces 17 dweight at 7s. lld. par once (y^e silver being a d't worse par ounce according y^e reste) wich comes to... | 98 | 10 | 2 |
| For y^e making of y^e 686 ounces 15 d't at 2s. 11d. par ounce, comes to... | 92 | 17 | 3 |

| | ounces | dweight | | | |
|---|---|---|---|---|---|
| Deliuered y^e kings head weighing | 197 | 5 | | | |
| one figure weighing | 445 | 15 | | | |
| y^e other figure with y^e caracter weighing | 428 | 5 | | | |
| y^e slaues and ye reste belonging unto it | 255 | 0 | | | |
| y^e two Eagles weighing | 169 | 10 | | | |
| one of the crowne[s] weighing | 94 | 5 | | | |
| y^e second crowne weighing | 97 | 10 | | | |
| y^e third crowne weighing | 90 | 2 | | | |
| y^e fowerd crowne weighing | 82 | 0 | | | |
| one of y^e Cupids weighing | 121 | 8 | | | |
| y^e second boye weighing | 101 | 10 | | | |
| y^e third boye weighing | 98 | 15 | | | |
| y^e fowerd boye weighing | 88 | 17 | | | |
| Altogether two thousand two hundred sexty five ounces 2d weight | 906 | 0 | 1 |

| | | | |
|---|---|---|---|
| of sterling silver at 8s. par ounce, | | | 0 |
| Paid of ye Essayes of ye figures and other things into ye tower | 0 | 5 | 0 |
| Paid for iacob haalle [Jacob Hall] dansing upon ye robbe [rope] of Weyer Worck [wicker-work] | 1 | 10 | 0 |
| For ye cleinsing and brunisching a sugar box, a pepper box, a mustard pott and two kruyzes | 0 | 12 | 0 |
| For mending ye greatte siluer andirons | 0 | 10 | 0 |
| Paid to ye cabbenet maker for ye greatte bord for ye head of the bedstead and for ye other bord that comes under it and... boorring the wholles into ye head | 8 | 0 | 0 |
| Paid to Mr. Consar for karving ye said bord | 1 | 0 | 0 |
| For ye bettering ya sodure wich was in the old bedstead | 5 | 3 | 7 |
| Paid to ya smid for ye yorne hoops and for ye 6 yorn baars krampes and nealles | 1 | 5 | 0 |
| Paid for ye wood denpied de staall for one of ya figures | 0 | 4 | 6 |
| Paid ya smith for a hoock to hang up a branche candlestick | 0 | 2 | 0 |
| Paid to ye smith for ya baars kramps and nealles to hold up ye slaues | 0 | 5 | 0 |
| Given to me Journey man by order of Madam Guinne | 1 | 10 | 0 |
| Paid to ye smyth for ye yorn worck to hold up y Eagles and for ye two hoocks to hold the bedstead again the wall | 0 | 3 | 0 |
| Paid for ye pied de stalle of Ebony to hold up the 2 georses | 1 | 10 | 0 |
| For ye mending of ye goold hower glasse | 0 | 2 | 6 |
| Deliuered two siluer bottels weighing 37 onces 17 d't at 8s. paronce, comes to | 15 | 2 | 6 |
| Paid for ye other foot to hold up ye other figure | 0 | 4 | 6 |
| For sodering ye wholles and for repairing mending and cleinsing the two figures of Mr. Traherne his making | 3 | 0 | 0 |
| For ya making of a crowne upon one of ya figures | 1 | 0 | 0 |
| Giuen to my journey man by order of Madame Guinne | 1 | 0 | 0 |
| Delivered a handel of a kneif weighing 11 dweight more then ye old one wich comes with ye making of it to | 0 | 5 | 1 0 |
| For ye cleinsing of eight pictures | 0 | 10 | 0 |
| | £1,135 | 3 | 1 |

[£1,135 represents a sum worth approximately £105,000 (or about $200,000) in 2002 currency.]

Charles II was always at his wits end for money for his mistresses, and often did not know how to satisfy their demands. The Duchess of Cleveland drew part of her income from the Excise; her Grace of Portsmouth from the, Wine Licences; Nell Gwyn was given a grant on the Exchequer:

"Charles the Second, by the grace of God, King of England, Scotland, France and Ireland, Defender of the Faith, &c. To the Commissioners of Our Treasury now being, to the Treasurer, Under Treasurer and Commissioners of Our Treasury for the time being, Greeting. Our will and pleasure is, And Wee doe hereby authorise and require you, out of Our Treasure now or hereafter being or remaineing in the Receipt of Our Exchequer, to pay, or cause to be paid unto Eleanor Gwyn or her Assignes the Annuity or yearly Summe of Five Thousand pounds, dureing Our pleasure, for and towards the Support and maintenance of herselfe and Charles Earl of Burford. To be received by her, the said Eleanor Gwyn quarterly, Att the foure most usuall feats in the yeare by equall porcions. The first payment to begin from the Feast of the Birth of Our Lord God last One Thousand Six hundred Seaventy Eight, and these Our Letters shall be your sufficient Warrant and Discharge in that behalfe. Given under Our Privy Seale at Our Pallace of Westminster the Eleaventh of June in the One and Thirtieth Year of Our Reign.

"Irrotulatur in Officio          "Irrolatur in Officio
Auditoris Receptae              Clerici Pellium
Scaccarii domini Regis          XVIIj$^{vo}$ die Junij,
XVj$^{vo}$ Junij, 1679.             1679."

There are, in the ninth Report of the Historical Manuscripts Commission, entries concerning Secret Service money to April 30, 1675.

"February 4. Paid to Mrs. Helen Gwyn, £1,000.

"March 25. Paid to the Duchess of Portsmouth, £2,000, and to Mrs. Hellen Gwyn, £1,000.

"More ordered to be paid to Mrs. Gwin, £500."

There is, in the same report, a reference to a grant of £16,000 to Nell Gwyn.

This, however, it is certain, is by no means an exhaustive account of the moneys the little lady received. Also, she received for her married sister, Rose Foster, a pension on the Irish Establishment.

Of course, as was only to be expected, Nell Gwyn was utterly incapable of looking after her affairs. Proof of this, if it is wanted, will be found in the correspondence of the Duke of Ormonde, then Lord-Lieutenant of Ireland, some items of which may have to be given. It may be mentioned that Sir Robert Howard was Auditor of the Exchequer, the Earl of Arran Lord Deputy of Ireland, and the Earl of Ossory the eldest son of the Duke of Ormonde.

*Sir Robert Howard to the Duke of Ormonde*
"EXCHEQUER,
July 15, 1679.

"Mrs. Nelly has commanded me to let you know that her agent, Mr. Melish, has not yet completed her pension for the Michaelmas half-year, and also sends her word that he has no hopes when to receive the Lady [Day] half-year last part, for that there is a stop upon it. She begs your Grace's favour in this, and that you would please to command any of your servants to let me know what the condition of it is, and what she may expect, presuming she shall find your kindness enough to assist her in this particular, and has commanded me to assure your Grace that nothing would please her better than to have a share in serving your Grace."

*Sir Robert Howard to the Duke of Ormonde.*
"LONDON,
"November 12, 1679.

"By reason of Mr. Mylius his unjuste ill conduct of Mrs. Gwinn's affairs, I have been necessitated to send one Mr. Alexander Adair, and to contribute a new pension, one Mr. St. Vast, to look after the business, and to call Mr. Mylius to an account, and return such moneys as are due to the Exchequer. Mrs. Gwin has humbly to desire your Grace that if there be any application made to you in her behalf, that you would be pleased to help her by your commands. She presents you with her real acknowledgments for all your favours, and protests she would write in her own hand, but her wild characters would distract you. This, my Lord, was her own natural notion when I showed her your Grace's kind return upon the King's letter, since which I have not heard anything from Mr. Mylius, which gives me some apprehension of him, and caused my sending a messenger on purpose."

*Earl of Ossory to the Duke of Ormonde*
"LONDON,
"December 2, 1679.

"This day I had some discourse with Sir Robert Howard concerning Mrs. Nelly's pretension to some lands and houses pretended to belong to my Lord of Dungannon. I entreated him to write unto you what he thought might be said, as if you were not ready to give a just despatch unto that affair, and more, I undertook that you would give him all the satisfaction you could; which I entreat you to do, because I know the King is set on the thing, intending it as a settlement for my Lord of Burford."

*The Duke of Ormonde to the Earl of Ossory*
"DUBLIN,
"December 24, 1679.

"You may assure Sir Robert Howard that Mrs. Gwin's business concerning Dundalk and Carlingford is done, so far as it depends on me, and beg his pardon for me that I do not at this time give him an account of it myself."

*Ellen Gwyn to the Duke of Ormond*
"September 4, 1682.

"This is to beg a favour of your Grace, which I hope you will stand my friend in. I lately got a friend of mine to advance me on my Irish pension half a year's payment for last Lady Day, which all people have received but me, and I drew bills upon Mr. Lawrence Steele, my agent, for the payment of the money, not thinking but that before long the bills had been paid; but contrary to my expectation I last night received advice from him that the bills are protested, and he cannot receive any money without your Grace's positive order to the Farmers for it.

"Your Grace formerly upon the King's letter, which this enclosed is the copy of, was so much mine and Mrs. Foster's friend as to give necessary orders for our payments notwithstanding the stop. I hope you will oblige me now upon this request, to give your directions to the Farmers, that we may be paid our arrears and what is growing due and you will oblige, etc."

### Ellen Gwyn to the Earl of Arran
"November 2, 1682.

"I hope your Lordship will now oblige me so much as to stand my friend. I have, with much importunity got the Lords of the Treasury to give an order to my Lord Ormond to cause the arrears of my pension stopped in Ireland to be paid what is due to me to last Michaelmas with my sister's Mrs. Foster's and others whom their letter mentions. My agent is Mr. Laurence Steele, to whom I have sent this letter to deliver to your Lordship. Hoping for my sake you will be pleased to give him a speedy despatch in this business, and oblige your, etc."

### Earl of Arran to the Duke of Ormonde
"DUBLIN,

December 5, 1682.

"I have had a letter last post from the Lords of the Treasury by his Majesty's directions ordering me to take off the suspensions of Mrs. Gwyn and some others' pensions, which I shall do."

"I do not hear that Nell's son is to have any honour at all," William Fall wrote to Sir Ralph Verney on August 5, 1675; "but there are to be three dukes, viz., Lord Southampton, Lord Euston, and the Duchess of Portsmouth's son by the King to be Duke of Richmond, Lennox, and Earl of March, by the name of Charles Stuart, etc., these last two had had their patents before this time, had not Lady Cleveland opposed it, for she is resolved that her younger son shall not take the place of the elder, nor Duke of Richmond either." Nell Gwyn, who had her own pride, was furious, and determined that her son should not be slighted in this way. The story goes that when Charles was with her she called the boy to her and called him, "You little bastard." The King was shocked, and asked why she called him that; to which she retorted, "Because I have no better name to give him." The story may or may not be apocryphal; but anyhow, on December 27, 1676, Charles Beauclerk was created Baron Heddington and Earl of Burford, both in the County of Oxford — with special remainder to his younger natural brother James, who, after his brother was raised to the peerage, was known as Lord James Beauclerk. James died at Paris at the age of nine.

The King took a great interest in little Charles, as is shown by the following letter, dated March 1682, from Gay Legge to Lord Preston[6], then Envoy Extraordinary at Paris:

"His Majesty is extremely fond of my Lord Burforde, and seems much concerned in his education, and he being now of an age fit to be bred in the world hath resolved to trust him wholly in your hands; no impertinent body shall be troublesome to you, nor anybody but whom you approve of to wait on him. I am to be your solicitor for providing money and all things necessary for him, and I hope by it to establish your other payments better than otherways we could have compassed. I told his Majesty you would be forced to take a larger house, and your expense must needs be much increased by this; he acknowledged it, and bid me take care that my Lord Burforde should have an appointment ready provided by you in your own house, so that I hope you may compass your own rent free, if your house already will accommodate it, or else that you take a better upon this occasion; masters must be provided for him, the best can be got of all

---

[6] Lord Preston was Charles II's ambassador to Louis XIV and Master of the Wardrobe to James II. He was one of the five peers entrusted with the government of the country when James II fled in 1688. He set out in a fishing boat in the hope of bringing the king back to England in triumph but was apprehended and taken to the Tower of London. Lord Preston was only saved from execution by the pleadings of his youngest daughter.

sorts, but more particularly the King would have him study mathematics, and in that fortification, and that when the King of France moves in any progresses he constantly go with you to view all places in France, etc. My Lord, you see by this I am going to bread a bird to pick out my ownes [sic] eyes, but I owe his Majesty all I have in gratitude, and will by the help of God study all the ways I am able to make him all the return imaginable. Pray fail not to write to the King by the next post."

The Earl of Burford was created Duke of St. Albans in January 1684, and ample provision was made for him by his father. There was the settlement of £5000 a year, chargeable on the Exchequer, he inherited on his mother's death Burford House, and he was given the reversion of the sinecure office of Master Falconer of England and Registrar of the Court of Chancery, both to be hereditary, worth some £1500 a year. Also, Charles arranged for the marriage of his son with Lady Diana de Vere, eldest daughter and virtually sole heiress of Aubrey, twentieth Earl of Oxford of the de Vere line.

Charles was not, of course, faithful to Nell Gwyn, although he was fond of her until the end. Among others there were Louise de Kéroualle and the Duchess Mazarin, as well as numerous passing amours. When the King died on February 6, 1685, he was very sincerely mourned by Nell Gwyn, who really was devoted to him. As Etherege wrote:

> "Nor would his Nelly long be his survivor,
> Alas t who now was good enough to drive her?
> So she gave way to her consuming grief,
> Which brought her past all galley-pot relief.
> Howe'er it were, as the old women say,
> 'Her time was come, and then there's no delay':
> So down the Stygian Lake she dropt."

Tradition has it that the King in his last moments lay upon his brother James the injunction, "Let not poor Nelly starve." James did his best, but the death of Charles II brought down on her all her creditors at once, and she was overwhelmed by her debts. In this awkward predicament she asked for an audience of the new monarch: "Had I suffered for my God as I have done for y^e Brother and y^e I shuld not have neede of y^e kindness or justis to me. I beseech you not to doe Any thing to the setling of my business till I speake w^th you, to apoynt me by Mr. Grahams wher I may speake with you privetly. God make you as happy as my soule prayes you may be."

"Mr. Graham"was, no doubt, the Colonel Graham, one of the Household of James II. The King declined to receive her, but came to the rescue. "The world," Nell Gwyn wrote on another occasion to the King, "is not capable of giving me greater joy and happynes than y^r Ma^ties favour, not as you are King and soo have it in y^r power to doe me good, having never lowed yr brother and y^r self upon that account, but as to y^r persons. Had he lived he tould me before he dyed that the world shuld see by what he did for me that he had both love and value for me and that he did not doe for me, as my mad lady Woster. He was my frind and alowed me to tell him all my grifes and did like a frind advise and tould me who was my frind and who was not. S^r, the honour yr Ma^tie has don me by Mr. Grahams has given me great comfort not by the present you sent me to releeve me out of the last extremity but by the kind expresions hee made me from you of y^r kindness to me, web to me is above al things in this world, having, God knows, never loved y^r brother or y^r selfe interestedly. All you doe for me shall be yours, it being my resolution never to have any interest but y^rs, and as long as I live to serve you and when I dye to dye praying for y^e."The passage beginning, "Had he lived he told me before he dyed," has been interpreted as meaning that Charles had intended to bestow a peerage on Nell Gwyn: it has been said that the title chosen for her was the Countess of Greenwich. That James II did his best for Nell Gwyn may be deduced from some items in the Secret Service account of his reign:

"1685, September. — To Richard Graham, Esq., to be by him paid over to several tradesmen, creditors of Mrs. Ellen Gwynne, in satisfac'on of their debts for which the said Ellen stood outlawed, £729 2s. 3d."

"1685, December. — To Ellinor Gwyn bounty £500."

"To the said Ellinor Gwynne more £500."

"1687, October. — To Sir Stephen Fox, for so much by him paid to Sir Robert Clayton [7] in full of 3,774£, 2s. 6d., for redeeming the mortgage of Bestwoode Park made to Sir John Musters, to settle the same upon Mrs. Ellen Gwynn for life, and after her death upon the Duke of St. Albans and his issue male with the reversion in the crowne ... £1,256 0s. 2d."

Nell Gwyn was taken dangerously ill in March 1687, and in that month Alice Hatton said, "Mrs. Nelly is dying of an apoplexy," and John Verney repeated to Sir Richard Verney, "Mrs. Eleanor Gwin lyes a-dying." Sir Charles Lyttleton wrote on March 29: "Mrs. Nelly has been dying of an apoplexy. She has now come to her sense on one side, for the other is dead of a palsy." She survived until November, when she died in her house in Pall Mall, being then only thirty-six years of age. Four days later she was buried, according to her express desire, in the parish church of St. Martins-in-theFields, the Vicar, Dr. Thomas Tenison (afterwards Archbishop of Canterbury) conducting the service.

Colley Cibber said of her: "If we consider her in all the disadvantages of her rank and education, she does not appear to have had any criminal errors, more remarkable for her sex's frailty, to answer for; and if the same author (Bishop Burnet) in his latter end of that Prince's life, seems to reproach his memory with too kind a concern for her support, we may allow it becomes a bishop to have no eyes or taste for the frivolous charming or playful badinage of a King's mistress. Yet, if the common fame of her may be believed, which, in my memory, was not doubted, she had less to be laid to her charge than any other of those ladies who were in the same state of preferment. She never meddled in matters of serious moment, or was the tool of working politicians; never broke into those amorous infidelities which others, in that grave author, are accused of, but was as visibly

---

[7] Sir Robert Clayton (1629–1707): banker and businessman who was Lord Mayor of London, in 1679, an MP for the City of London, 1678-81, and governor of the Bank of England (1702-05). He was also a supporter of the Whigs and the Exclusionists, and a benefactor of St Thomas' Hospital and Christ's Hospital

distinguished by her particular inclination to the King, as her rivals were by titles and grandeur."

## THE WILL OF NELL GWYN

In the name of God, Amen. I, Ellen Gwynne, of the parish of St. Martins-in-the-Fields, and county of Middlesex, spinster, this 9th day of July, anno Domini 1687, do make this my last will and testament, and do revoke all former wills. First, in hope of a joyful resurrection, I do recommend myself whence I came, my soul into the hands of Almighty God, and my body unto the earth, to be decently buried, at the discretion of my executors, hereinafter named; and as for all such houses, lands, tenements, offices, places, pensions, annuities, and hereditaments whatsoever, in England, Ireland, or elsewhere, wherein I, or my heirs, or any to the use of, or in trust for me, my heirs, hath, have, or may or ought to have, any estate, right, claim, or demand whatsoever, or fee-simple or freehold, I give and devise the same all and wholly to my dear natural son, his Grace, the Duke of St. Albans, and to the heirs of his body; and as for all and all manner of my jewels, plate, household stuff, goods, chattels, credits, and other estate, whatsoever, I give and bequeath the same, and every part and parcel thereof, to my executors hereafter named, in, upon, and by way of trust for my said dear son, his executors, administrators, and assigns, and to and for his and their own sole use and peculiar benefit and advantage, in such manner as is hereafter expressed; and I do hereby constitute the Right Hon. Lawrence, Earl of Rochester, the Right Hon. Thomas, Earl of Pembroke, the Hon. Sir Robert Sawyer, Knight, his Majesty's Attorney-General, and the Hon. Henry Sidney, Esq., to be my executors of this my last will and testament, desiring them to please to accept and undertake the execution thereof in trust as aforementioned; and I do give and bequeath to the several persons in the schedule hereunto annexed the several legacies and sums of money therein expressed or mentioned; and my further will and mind, and anything above notwithstanding is, that if my dear said son happen to depart this natural life without issue then living, or such issue die without issue, then and in such case, all and all manner of my estates above devised to him, and in case my said natural son die before the age of one-and-twenty years, then also all my personal estate devised to my said executors, and the executors or administrators of the survivor of them, or by some of them otherwise lawfully and firmly devised or disposed of, shall remain, go, or be to my said executors, their heirs, executors, and administrators respectively, in: trust of and for answering, paying, and satisfying all and every and all manner of my gifts, legacies, and directions that at any time hereafter, during my life, shall be by me anywise mentioned or given in or by any codicils or schedule to be hereto annexed. And lastly, that my said executors shall have, all and every of them, 100£ a-piece, of lawful money, in consideration of their care and trouble herein, and furthermore, all their several and respective expenses and charges in and about the execution of this my will. In witness of all which, I hereunto set my hand and seal, the day and year first above written.

E.G.

*Signed, sealed, published, and declared in the presence of us, who at the same time subscribe our names, also in her presence.*

LUCY HAMILTON SANDYS,
EDWARD WYBORNE,
JOHN WARNER,
WILLIAM SCARBOROUGH,
JAMES BOOTH.

### FIRST CODICIL

*The last request of Mrs. Ellenr. Gwynn to his Grace the Duke of St. Alban's, made October the 18th, 1687.*

1. I desire I may be buried in the church of St. Martin's-in-the-fields.

2. That Dr. Tenison may preach my funeral sermon.

3. That there may be a decent pulpit-cloth and cushion given to St. Martin's-in-the-fields.

4. That he [the Duke] would give one hundred pounds for the use of the poor of the said St. Martin's-in-the-fields and St. James's, Westminster, to be given into the hands of the said Dr. Tenison, to be

disposed of at his discretion, for taking any poor debtors of the said parish out of prison, and for cloaths this winter, and other necessaries, as he shall find most fit.

5. That for showing my charity to those who differ from me in religion, I desire that fifty pounds may be put into the hands of Dr. Tenison and Mr. Warner, who, taking to them any two persons of the Roman Religion may dispose of it for the use of the poor of that religion inhabiting the parish of St. James's foresaid.

6. That Mrs. Rose Forster may have two hundred pounds given to her, any time within a year after my decease.

7. That Jo, my porter, may have ten pounds given him.

*My request to his Grace is, further –*

8. That my present nurses may have ten pounds each, and mourning, and a year's wages, besides their wages due.

10. That the Lady Fairborne may have fifty pounds given to her to buy a ring.

11. That my kinsman, Mr. Cholmley, may have one hundred pounds given to him, within a year after this date.

12. That His Grace would please to lay out twenty pounds yearly for the releasing of poor debtors out of prison every Christmas-day.

13. That Mr. John Warner may have fifty pounds given him to buy a ring.

14. That the Lady Hollyman may have the pension of ten shillings per week [8] continued to her during the said lady's life.

The following (second) codicil, which escaped the observation of Peter Cunningham, has been discovered by Mr. Gordon Goodwin. It was proved separately, on December 7, 1688, and is registered in the Prerogative Court of Canterbury, 162, Exton:

The second codicil of Mrs. Ellen Gwinn deceased publicly declared by her before divers creditable witnesses after the making of

---

[8] The sum of 10 shillings is equivalent to 63£ or ($120) in 2002 currency.

her last Will and Testament and former Codicil according as it was pronounced in and by the sentence given by the Right Worshipful Sir Richard Raines, Knight, Doctor of Laws, and Master Keeper of Commissary of the Prerogative Court of Canterbury, the nineteenth day of July One Thousand Six Hundred and Eighty Eight in a Cause lately depending before him concerning the proof thereof followeth, viz.:

The said Mrs. Ellen Gwinne did give and bequeath to Mrs. Rose Forster, her sister, the sum of two hundred pounds over and above the sum of two hundred pounds which she gave to her the said Rose in her former Codicil.

To Mr. Forster, husband of the said Rose Forster, a ring of the value of forty pounds or forty pounds to buy him a ring.

To Dr. Harrell [meaning Christianus Harrel, Doctor of Physic, and one of her physicians] twenty pounds.

To Mr. Derrick, nephew of the said Dr. Harrell, ten pounds.

To Dr. Le Febure [meaning Joshua Le Febure, Doctor of Physic, and the other of her physicians] twenty pounds respectively to buy them rings.

To Bridget Long, who had been her servant for divers years, the sum of twenty pounds of lawful money of England yearly during her natural life.

To Mrs. Edling [meaning Anne Edling] a new gown.

And Mr. John Warner, her Chaplain, was present with others at the declaring thereof, and that a little before the declaring of the same she being of perfect mind and memory did order or desire the said Mr. Warner to put into writing what she should then declare. And that the said legacies were wrote and read to the deceased and by her approved as part of her last ,Will and Testament as by the proofs made and sentence given in the said Cause do appear.

# GLOSSARY

**8vo:** Pamphlet. 8vo means the size of a book whose pages are made by folding a sheet of paper three times to form eight leaves. Syn. -- octavo, eightvo

**Bassett:** A game at cards, resembling the modern faro, said to have been invented at Venice.

**Bastinado:** from the word *baston*, which in English becomes baton. A baton is a stick, club, cudgel or truncheon which as 'bastinado' is used to beat of the bottoms of the feet, generally as a form of corporal punishment.

**Caleche:** a two-wheeled horse-drawn vehicle with a driver's seat on the splashboard.

**Chyrugeon:** A Middle-English or Old French word meaning literally "surgeon".

**Confinement:** the state attending and consequent to childbirth

**Corivals:** rivals, literally "co-rivals" [Middle French].

**Conventicling:** the act of meeting for worship not sanctioned by law.

**Dauphin:** the eldest son of a king of France.

**Defalcation:** the act or an instance of embezzling.

**Dowager:** a widow holding property or a title from her deceased husband [Middle French].

**Duenna:** an elderly woman serving as governess and companion to the younger ladies in a Spanish or a Portuguese family.

**Green-bag:** recycling bag for garden waste.

**Hap:** Good luck [Middle English, Old Norse].

**Jade:** a disreputable woman or a flirtatious girl.

**Langour:** listless indolence or inertia.

**Lèse-majesté:** a treasonous crime committed against a sovereign power. [Middle-French]

**Louis [d'Or]:** a French gold coin first struck in 1640 and issued up to the Revolution. Valued at 1£ by Venetian currency trading standards of the day.

**Lying-in**: see Confinement

**Mâitre d'Hôtel:** The head of the catering department (in modern language: Mâitre d')

**Momus:** the Greek god of censure and mockery

**Mumed:** disguised as if by a mask.

*Née:* indicates family of birth (i.e. maiden name)

**Panegyric:** a eulogistic oration or writing

**Parvenue:** a woman who has recently or suddenly risen to an unaccustomed position of wealth or power and has not yet gained the prestige, dignity, or manner associated with it.

**Pasquinade:** a written satire, from Pasquino, a name given to a statue in Rome on which lampoons were posted.

**Patent Letters:** a writing (as from a sovereign) that confers on a designated person a grant in a form open for public inspection.

**Pistole:** French silver coin worth ½ of a Louis d'Or.

**Posset:** a hot drink of sweetened and spiced milk curdled with ale or wine. [Middle-English]

**Rake**: short for rakehell, a dissolute person or libertine (unrestrained by convention or morality).

**Right of the tabouret:** the privilege of sitting on a tabouret in the presence of the sovereign, formerly granted to certain ladies of high rank at the French court.

**Rope-dancer:** an acrobat who performs on a rope stretched at some height above the ground (a tight-rope walker).

**Sack posset:** A name formerly given to various dry Spanish wines. "Sherris sack." –Shakespeare

**Se'n-night:** One week. Among Germanic peoples it was once normal to record the passage of time by the number of nights rather than days. *Sennight* is an abbreviation of the fuller phrase *seven nights,* hence a week.

**Seraglio:** harem, or the palace of a sultan [Italian, Turkish].

**Squibs:** firecrackers.

**Tabouret:** a cylindrical seat or stool without arms or back [see *Right of the Tabouret*]

**Troublous:** troublesome

# BIBLIOGRAPHY

Aubrey, John. *Letters Written by Eminent Persons in the Seventeenth and Eighteenth Centuries; to which are added, Hearne's Journeys to Reading, and to Whaddon Hall, the seat of Brown Willis, and Lives of Eminent Men.* London: Longman, Hurst, Rees, Orme, and Brown, 1813

Baker, C.H. Collins. *Lely & The Stuart Portrait Painters - A Study of English Portraiture Before & After Van Dyck.* Philip Lee Warner, Publisher to the Medici Society, London. 1912.

Burnet, Bishop. *History of My Own Time.* Oxford: Book Description: Oxford Univ Press, 1833.

Carte, Thomas. *An History of the Life of James Duke of Ormonde, from his Birth in 1610, to his Death in 1688. Wherein is contained An Account of the most remarkable Affairs of his Time, and particularly of Ireland, under his Government.* London: J.J. and P. Knapton, 1736

Davis, J.E. & Tighe, R.R. *Annals Of Windsor, Being A History Of The Castle And Town; With Some Account Of Eton And Places Adjacent.* London: Longman, Brown, Green, and Roberts, 1863

Fey, Allan. *Some Beauties of the Seventeenth Century.* London: Methuen & Co., 1906

Hamilton, Count Anthony, translated by Walpole, Horace. *Memoirs Of The Count De Grammont.* London: John Lane, 1928.

Harris, William. An Historical And Critical Account Of The Life And Writings Of James I And Charles I. And of the lives of Oliver Chromwell and Charles II. after the manner of Mr. Bayle. From original writers and State-papers in five volumes. With a life of the author, a general index, &c. London: Rivington et. al., 1814

Jameson, Anna. *The Beauties of the Court of Charles the Second: a Series of Memoirs, Biographical and Critical Illustrating the Diaries of Pepys, Evelyn, Clarendon and Other Contemporary Writers.* Boston: W.D. Ticknor, 1834.

Jesse, John H.. *Memoirs Of The Court Of England During The Reign Of The Stuarts, Including The Protectorate, Vol Three.* London: George Bell, 1900.

Law, Earnest. *The Royal Gallery of Hampton Court Illustrated. Being an historical catalogue of the pictures in the Queen's collection at that palace with descriptive, biographical and critical notes, revised, enlarged and illustrated.* London: George Bell & Sons, 1898.

Philip, Second Earl of Chesterfield. *Letters Of Philip Second Earl Of Chesterfield - To Several Celebrated Individuals Of The Time Of Charles II, James II, William II And Queen Anne With Some Of Their Replies.* London, 1837.

Sergeant, Philip W. *My Lady Castlemaine.* Boston, 1911.

Steinman, George. *Memoirs of Lady Castlemaine.* London, 1871

Williams, H. Noel. *Rival Sultanas: Nell Gwyn, Louise de Keroualle, and Hortense Mancini.* New York: Dodd, Mead & Co, 1915

# INDEX

Printed in the United States
39395LVS00001BA/187-216